Reaching beyond Faith

Reaching beyond Faith

A MODERN MIND READS THE KORAN

IBN FĀRĀBI

iUniverse

REACHING BEYOND FAITH
A MODERN MIND READS THE KORAN

iUniverse books may be ordered through booksellers or by contacting:

iUniverse
1663 Liberty Drive
Bloomington, IN 47403
www.iuniverse.com
1-800-Authors (1-800-288-4677)

ISBN: 978-1-4917-8279-8 (sc)
ISBN: 978-1-4917-8278-1 (hc)
ISBN: 978-1-4917-8280-4 (e)

Library of Congress Control Number: 2015920288

Print information available on the last page.

iUniverse rev. date: 12/29/2015

Contents

Preface

The opening verses of the first substantive *sūra*, or 'chapter', of the Koran are an emphatic declaration on the Book itself:

> This is the Book; there is no doubt in it: A guidance to those who fear God, believe in the unseen, perform prayer, and spend out of what We have provided them, those who believe in what has been sent down to you and what has been sent down before you, and those who believe in the Hereafter.
>
> (2:2–4)

The linchpin of the verses is belief, or faith: belief in the unseen, the Revelation, and the guidance that it provides to those who fear God. This fear is something that, again, is bound up with belief. Faith is central to the Koran. In fact, faith is so essential that the Koran says it provides guidance only to those who already possess the faith, as the above verses suggest. Many other verses in the Holy Book of Islam suggest this as well. Moreover, not only are the contents of the Koran to be believed in, but also the manner of its revelation. The Holy Book was revealed by means of divine inspiration to Muḥammad, the Prophet of Islam, over a period of some twenty-three years. Indeed, it is the divine inspiration, however defined, as well as the book's contents, which makes the Koran divine. More than 1.5 billion people on earth today call themselves Muslim, and a vast majority of them believe in the divine origin of the Koran and the nature of its revelation. In literal Islam, that belief, along with belief in Muḥammad, the purveyor of the divine message, is what makes them Muslim.

In Muslim minds, the divineness of the message of Koran is not only received but also proclaimed. The Koran is required reading for Muslims, as scriptures of other faiths are to their adherents, but it is not to be read like any other book: it is to be recited. In Arabic, *Qur'ān* means 'recitation'. More properly, the Koran is to be chanted. When heard from the mouth of a trained chanter, or *qāri*, the Koran's verses often assume a haunting quality. And the Koran can be chanted only in Arabic, the language in which the Prophet of Islam was inspired. To read or chant the Koran is itself an act of piety. In fact, a large majority of Muslims do not understand the language of the Koran, and yet these Muslims recite it, and listen to it when recited, with pious veneration. The chanting itself is a proclamation of belief in the Divine, and chanting is seen as a way of strengthening that belief.

In the following pages, we will read and explore a substantial number of verses of the Koran from the essentially non-pietistic points of view and in historical, geographic, social, and, above all, human contexts, while recognising the importance that millions of Muslims attach to the purely pietistic value of these verses. The rationale of such an exercise should be rather obvious. Although the state of the human mind that read and tried to understand the Koran some 1,400 years ago can still be evidenced in many parts of the Muslim world, most educated Muslims today would be mortally offended if someone were to tell them that their minds harked back to those ancient times. To them, it is impossible, while reading the Koran, to ignore the epochal strides made in human knowledge and circumstance since Muḥammad was first inspired to say: Read!

The Koran of course had to concern itself with the human as much as with the divine, and as much with the present and the ephemeral as with the eternal. Its messages were meant to change Arab societies of the time and provide detailed guidance regulating private and public conduct. It was meant to touch every aspect of life of individual members of the society. Political implementation of the codes of conduct ordained by God in the Koran was something like the ultimate act of piety; to some, it still is.

That the Koran is primarily concerned with man and his society should be obvious. But the relationship is not simply one in which the divine message is an instrument and the desired change in human society is the result: in fact, the human, as against the divine, pervades the text that delivers the message. The message is conveyed in particular ways that are all too human; it is strewn with human expressions of command, anger, threat, and even frustration, as well as grace. Some of the messages were inspired by personal circumstances of the Prophet of Islam himself; some were changed in response to human concerns. A large amount of human effort went into the collection of the often disparate texts of the message; in the course of which, some of the most mundane of the messages were placed in juxtaposition with the most sublime, in a manner of human bathos. And many of the major events underlying the message were critically influenced by human decisions.

The message was also delivered in particular historical and geographical settings of Arab society. Much of it can be understood only against the background of human knowledge at that time. The major codes of conduct were given in the context of particular incidents or circumstances; often, age-old, pre-Islamic practices were kept alive and given new imprimatur.

The mode of conveyance of the divine message is often all too human. There are a number of dimensions to the human in the Koran: many of the verses make sense only if they are seen as supplications to God, rather than addresses by Him. The opening *sūra* (aptly called *al-Fātiḥa*, or 'opening'), which is recited at every canonical Muslim prayer and which is essentially a human supplication for divine blessing, is an important example. But there are many others. This may not lessen the importance of the divine in these verses to the devout; neither does it lessen the need to go beyond belief and acknowledge the human.

We also see in the Koran divine action, feelings and sentiments that ring truly human. It is, for example, easy to find verses that express not only God's anger, but also His frustrations and exasperations that can be understood only in human terms, or that look very human. There is the human throwing up of hands in verses like: 'How shall God guide those who disbelieved' … (3:86), and 'You think that most of them listen or understand? They are only like cattle' (25:44). Also profoundly human are the numerous examples of divine consolation and expressions of encouragement and support for the Prophet through changing circumstances.

Not to be overlooked are the many verses in the Koran that emphasise acts of human kindness and courtesy to others. That we each should return another individual's address of courtesy by a similar or even greater courtesy is recommended in a remarkable verse. Similarly, giving in charity has been placed among the highest of pieties, and the almoner has been warned against using harsh words to the receiver of the charity. No less remarkable is the high place given to filial piety.

Still on the human in the Koran, the best of man's good life on earth, even more so than his spirituality, is replicated in the afterlife – only it gets better. Descriptions of Heaven have been repeated time and again in the Koran, and they paint a picture of abundance of good things, freely available to the believers: including orchards of luscious fruit, goblets brimming with drinks of the most delightful kind, places of repose by cool streams of pure water, as well as beautiful women companions whom no man or jinn has touched before. We see in the description an idyll of life, not just human in general, but Arab or Middle Eastern in particular. The fruits are dates, pomegranates, and grapes; the water of the rivulets is welcomingly cool; people recline on carpets and under pavilions, and servants cater to their every wish. The human clearly outshines the spiritual.

Many of the actions described in the Koran can be understood only in their historical context. Raiding merchants' caravans as a means of earning a living was, for example, a common practice among Arab tribes. In the Koran, such practice receives divine approval. It is useful to keep this in mind as background for the first battle waged by the Muslims against their brethren and enemy, Quraysh, at Badr, near Medina. Punishments for offence that will be seen as inhuman today are recommended in the Koran. Again, this has to be seen in the context of the time and prevailing tradition, especially the Jewish. The Koran did not call for the abolition of slavery, although in a number of verses it urged humane treatment of slaves. The system was so entrenched in society that even divine intervention to abolish it appeared unavailable, in both the Koran and other contemporaneous scriptures. The system of slavery extended to sexual relationships with those 'whom your right hand possesses', an expression in the Koran for women obtained as war booty or bought outright. In the same vein, the practice of usury, so severely censured in the Koran, could not be turned into a punishable offence.

The geography of Muḥammad's land of birth is no less important than its history. Some of the major prescriptions for piety, such as prayer, fasting, and pilgrimage, would have been quite different, or even impossible, at some other latitudes of the earth's surface. Consider, for example, performing the five daily canonical prayers over the course of a very short day, or fasting in a region where the days are inordinately long or extremely short.

Today, it is impossible to accept literally many of the Koran's descriptions of natural phenomena and biological concepts. These descriptions have to be seen in terms of the background of the stock of human knowledge in Arab societies at the time. While the literalist Muslims, by definition, have little difficulty reconciling the faith-based notions with modern science (often by simply ignoring the latter), liberal Muslims have sometimes been able to confront the issue by arguing that some of the Koranic descriptions have to be seen only in the figurative or allegorical sense. Often, the device employed by liberal Muslims has run into huge difficulties.

The state of human knowledge in those days is amply evident in numerous pronouncements in the Koran itself. This is something that we shall frequently return to in these pages. For the time being, consider verse 73:20 as an example: even the Prophet himself was not blessed with the knowledge that could tell him exactly the length of time of a third or a half of a night, and so forth, as he stood in the middle of the night for his optional prayers for an extended length of time. His knowledge of the physical and biological world left room for much interpretation, as we shall see. In the Islamic tradition, the pre-Islamic era in Arab history is known as *jāhiliyyah*, the Age of Ignorance. In fact, human knowledge did not flower immediately after the advent of Islam; it took a while, and on that score there was little distinction between the early Islamic days and pre-Islamic ones.

It is also largely in the context of the state of human knowledge of the physical environment that man is made to see his role in the affairs of his own life. The Koran sees man's own capacity to improve his condition as strictly limited; the determinants of all that happens are in the hands of God. Thus, the ships that sail are powered by the winds, which in turn obey the command of God; agriculture prospers by means of the rains He sends; the routes followed by the caravans are His creation; and even the garment on man's back is His handiwork. Man's livelihood is, in fact, entirely provided by God, and this has been emphasised repeatedly in the Koran.

The advance in human knowledge that has taken place over the one and a half millennia since the birth of Islam, and its intellectual counterpart in the inexhaustible human urge to reason, inquire, and explore, often lead to agonising conflicts between perceptions based on modern knowledge of the physical world, on the one hand, and pure belief, on the other. The dilemma between reason and belief is a real and most difficult one. But merely shutting our eyes to that reality would not make the dilemma go away.

Many of the directives in the Koran were formulated in response to particular circumstances and incidents. The veil and privacy are notable examples. Even recommendations on etiquette, couched in down-to-earth terms, arose out of such incidents. There are verses in the Koran that were revealed in order to address some personal and household crises for the Prophet, some of them concerning his wives. Divine interventions followed purely human action at remarkable speed.

Even where the verses do not contain specific directives, often they can only be understood in the context of particular circumstances. It would be difficult, for example, to see the meaning of the statement 'And it was not you who threw, but God threw' (8:17), without being told that it was a reference to an action in the Battle of Badr. More importantly, there are also many verses that seemingly convey a general sentiment, principle, or bit of advice, but were not meant to do so; rather, they were intended to deal with specific situations. Thus, a verse like 'Do not lose heart, and do not despair' … (3:139) – a verse which sounds far more profound in Arabic – was revealed in the specific context of the near disaster of the Battle of Uḥud.

The putting together of the Koran in itself required a very considerable amount of human input. This is also an area where more gaps in information exist than convention acknowledges. The history of the compilation of the Koran has generally been limited to the efforts of 'Uthman, the third caliph of Islam, who is credited with having issued the second, and final, official version of the Book which is said to have come down to us through the ages totally unaltered. Far less attention has been given to the fact that individual verses of numerous *sūras* of the Koran were inspired at different historical times, sometimes separated from each other by months and even years. Thus, the compilation of the individual *sūras* of the Koran was in itself a critical process. While divine guidance in the process is taken for granted by all Islamic commentators, it is impossible not to be curious about the role humans played in it.

The state of technology needed to produce a 'book' was rudimentary in the absence of paper, as we know it, or even something close to it; the role of the human it its compilation and preservation was correspondingly large. In many cases, the verses inspired were memorised by the closest followers of Muḥammad and then dispersed among wider circles. Human memory remained a major repository of the verses of the Book. As for its early written versions, a great miscellany of leaves of trees, leather, stone, and animal bones were used as writing materials. All of this made the collection and preservation of the piecemeal narratives of the revelation a truly difficult and precarious human enterprise. Divinity would have instantly done away with such the difficulties, which was obviously not the case.

The above scenario is perhaps not unrelated to the existence of frequent literary juxtaposition of very different themes, sometimes descending from the divine to the mundane, in the collected narrative. We find, for example, a long directive on forbidden food, followed by a proclamation establishing Islam and perfecting it (5:3); a statement on an important spiritual message tagged to the details of what food to eat (5:1); a series of short verses about the Day of Resurrection, followed by a directive to the Prophet not to move his tongue in haste when repeating verses of the Koran that had just been revealed to him (75:1–16); a poetic call for courtesy among members of the community is often abruptly followed by a proclamation of the greatness of God (4:86–87).

There is only one way to understand a book: read it. This may appear too obvious to merit mention. On the other hand, a huge number of people in the Muslim world form opinions on various issues said to have been settled in the Koran, without having first read their sacred text to find out what it says. I have read the Koran, and I am going to read it again, with you, in this work.

The Koran can of course be read, and has been read, while keeping in view the context of the message. 'Contexts of revelation' of various degrees of authenticity are said to exist for many of the verses of the Book, and there are voluminous Koranic exegeses. Yet, to the general Muslim reader of the Koran, exegesis is not of the utmost importance. Verses of the Koran are meant to be read or recited for piety, irrespective of whether the circumstances of their revelation are known. When the context is read at all, this too is done as an act of piety, and the traditional interpretations of the implications or the verse in question almost always prevail. Subjects that are considered 'delicate' are seen as best left alone. Piety trumps inquiry. Outside academia, critical reading of the Koran in order to explore its non-pietistic dimensions, as referred to above, is rarer still among Muslims.

Many years of poring over the verses of the Koran went into the present study. This is no scholarly work, and I do not presume to be a scholar of the Koran. But I do claim to be an informed reader of the Koran, and I have read it in Arabic and in English translation many times and over the course of many years. I have also made a reasonably extensive reading of the traditional commentaries on the Koran. The writing of the present work took me several years, with intermittent breaks.

The roots of the present work run deep. Born into an orthodox Muslim family where the reading of the Koran was an inseparable part of daily life and where a devout father, learned in Arabic, often explained the meaning of its verses to his son, my life began in the supreme certitude of faith. A long period of secular education at home and abroad, and an even longer period of reading and reflection, then began to erode the certainty of the younger days and finally launched me into exploring the Koran beyond the realm of pure faith. There were some strong headwinds, and sirens warned.

This was a period when, in many countries, including mine, literalist Islam was clearly on the ascendant, as it still certainly is. Traditional Islamic education was spreading rapidly; piety, variously defined and not excluding the wearing of the *ḥijab*, was increasingly being emphasised, and the introduction of *shari'a* laws was demanded and in some cases achieved. The process was very largely the result of concerted efforts by a growing number of Islamist leaders claiming to derive legitimacy for their brand of Islam directly from the Koran. Doubt and critical inquiry are of course anathema to their reading of the Holy Book. The goal of righteous living has been unambiguously defined, to the exclusion other possible goals, and the path to it unequivocally laid out. The more recent rise of violent Islamists who not only read the Koran as an act of piety but also, and far more importantly, see in it immutable codes of individual, social, and political conduct, as formulated in the desert of Arabia a millennium and half ago, is one the most remarkable phenomena of our time. It too represents certitude of faith, only of the most aggressive type.

In an age of such burgeoning Islamic fundamentalism and assertive certitude of its protagonists, I especially expect other Muslims, perhaps still the majority, to reach beyond pure faith as they read their Koran. I expect that arguments for more tolerant, vibrant, and pluralist societies in the Islamic world will be strengthened by such effort. I hope they will find the present study a useful framework for their reading. Increasingly, young men and women, some Western educated and, on occasion, even drawn from Western societies, are being attracted to violent Islamism. It is futile to imagine large numbers of devotees of that brand of Islam reading the present work or any of its kind. I still hope that at least some, especially the nascent fundamentalists, might have a look at it. And ponder over it.

To Muslims who read the Koran solely as an act of piety, and particularly those who might consider any other way of reading the Book as impious, I do not address this work. They should rather not go any farther than this preface.

The themes of the present study suggested themselves as I read and re-read the Koran. Some of them have of course been discussed, often ad infinitum, in many forums, but not in the contexts I have chosen for this study. Others are rarely talked about. An alternative set of themes is not difficult to imagine.

Given my emphasis on reading the text of the Koran, I had to rely on translations from the Arabic. I have also read carefully every corresponding verse in the language. I consulted half a dozen translations, including four in English, by well-known authors and commentators (listed in the bibliography at the end of the book), and have often checked the English translations against each other and against translations and commentaries in my native Bengali. The individual verses in the present text are often a synthesis of a number of translated versions, with some of the arcane wordings and formulations of sentences in the original avoided. In each case, its meaning is supported by at least one, often most, of the translations I have consulted. Each verse has been presented in plain prose. This is not to suggest that the meaning of every verse will be plain to all who read it; many of the verses of the Koran are far from easy to understand.

I have only a limited number of books and studies to refer to. The references are given at the foot of the page, following age-old tradition, along with other footnotes.

Following the long-held tradition of work on the subject in the English language, I have used the spelling 'Koran' rather than 'Qur'an' or something similar. Devout Muslim scholars working in English have done the same. I have also used 'God, rather than 'Allah', as well as Muḥammad, without the widely used honorific 'may Allah's blessing be on him' appended in Arabic. Here too I have followed the tradition of works in the English language, and the omission does not mean derogation in any sense. To lessen repetitiveness, I have used interchangeably Muḥammad, the Prophet, the Apostle, and Messenger of God.

Finally, it is painful for me to have to write a book under a pen name, particularly a book that I have laboured many years to complete. The decision was thrust on me by my family and well-wishers, who bear no responsibility whatsoever for the contents of the book. The guise would have been unnecessary in a more tolerant Islamic world. I shall not live to see the time when readers will laugh at the concoction of a name for considerations of a writer's safety. I firmly believe, however, that such a day will come. For now, I can only pride myself on having my name associated with the name of a great writer from the Islamic world, al-Fārābi (*c.* AD 870–950), who lived a long time ago, when unorthodox ideas were allowed to thrive.

Chapter 1
The Koran in Arabic, for the Arabs

That the Koran, revealed among people whose language was Arabic, should have been written in their language is obvious. Indeed, this seems obvious enough not to require any mention. But the Koran itself gives the subject considerable importance and dwells on it in a number of verses. Thus, we read about the 'Perspicuous Book', the Koran:

> We have sent it down, an Arabic Koran, so that you will understand
>
> (12:2)

The book was written in Arabic simply because the people for which its message was meant were Arabs. Any other language would have been irrelevant. Again, we read:

> Thus We have sent it down as a judgement, in Arabic ...
>
> (13:37)

In a passage strongly suggestive of the central connection between the people for whom the divine message was meant, the language of the message, and the messenger, the Koran has this to say:

> And We sent no messenger except with the tongue of his people so that he might make things clear to them ...
>
> (14:4)

The lines above, as well as those at the start of this chapter, were among the many attempts to convince the Arab tribe into which Muḥammad was born that there was nothing unusual about the Prophet Muḥammad being a mortal human who spoke Arabic. The Jews had their own Moses who spoke their language. But the verses also throw up a rather obvious question: if a people or a nation, as defined by its language, is given divine messages only in its own language, was Islam not meant for non-Arabs too? While the Koran has emerged as the sacred book of Muslims, Arab and non-Arab, it does not confront the issue. The book was addressed to Arab polytheists, Arab Christians, and Arab Jews; the rest of humanity remained beyond the pale. The later imperial expansion of Islam outside Arabia has no sanction in the Koran itself.

The following verse, in fact, narrows even further the circle of Muḥammad's audience:

> And thus We have sent down by revelation to you a Koran in Arabic so that you may warn the Mother of Cities, and those who dwell around her, of the Day of Assembly of which there is no doubt …
>
> (42:7)

The next verse follows up on the theme and stresses the separate entity of the people for whom the Koran was meant:

> And if God had so willed, He could have made them one nation …
>
> (42:8)

But He did not so will, and there was a great diversity of peoples around the world at that time, among them the Arabs. The Mother of Cities is of course Mecca, and the divine message, embodied in the Koran, is meant for the inhabitants of the city and its surrounds, and is naturally given in Arabic. The verse thus seems to limit the number of inhabitants of the Arabian peninsula at whom the Koran was aimed.

That limit is implicit in another important verse from a different *sūra*. It is repeated later, in Chapter 8, in a different context, but it is well worth taking up here:

> And complete the *Ḥajj* and the *'Umra* for God. But if you are prevented, send whatever offering you may find, and do not shave your heads until the offering reaches its place of sacrifice …
>
> (2:196)

In Islam, it is obligatory on the part of the *ḥajj* pilgrim to offer an animal for sacrifice within the precincts of the pilgrimage. The last part of the verse implies only a short distance between the location of the person offering the sacrifice and the precincts of the *ḥajj* pilgrimage. Given the mode of transport in those days, the distance would have had to be short enough for the news of the sacrifice to reach the person offering it, within the prescribed period of the pilgrimage. This should exclude much of the Arabian peninsula itself and, by definition, non-Arabic speakers beyond it.

The theme of the Arabic Koran is repeated many times:

> Thus We have sent it down, an Arabic Koran …
>
> (20:113)

Elsewhere, the angel Gabriel comes with the inspiration so that the Prophet may admonish the unbelievers:

> Truly this is a revelation from the Lord of the worlds.
>
> (26:192)

And the admonition is in:

> Clear Arabic tongue
>
> (26:195)

Some commentators have insisted that this verse, in effect, suggests that the Koran is the one, and only the one, that is written in the Arabic language.[1] While the Bible is the Bible in whatever language it is written

[1] Maulana Muhiuddin Khan, *Qur'ānul Karim, Bengali Translation and Brief Commentary* (originally *Tāfsir M'āriful Qur'ān* by Hazrat Maulana Mufti Muḥammad Shafi) (Medina, Saudi Arabia: King Fahd Qur'ān Printing Project, H 1413, 1992/93) (hereafter Qur'ān/Muhiuddin).

in, this cannot be said of the Koran. The Koran does not rise to the level of divinity except in Arabic; it cannot be recited in any other language, although it can be read in other languages. The recitation from the Koran that is an integral part of the canonical daily prayer obligation of all Muslims can be made only in Arabic.

By the same token, the question of God revealing the Koran in Arabic to non-Arabs does not arise:

> If We had sent it down to a non- Arab,
>
> (26:198)

> And he then had recited it to them, they would not have believed in it.
>
> (26:199)

The refrain of Koran in Arabic is repeated twice in a single *sūra*:

> A Book whose verses have been laid out in detail, a Koran in Arabic for people of understanding.
>
> (41:3)

And:

> If We had revealed the Koran in a non-Arabic language they would then said: Why have not its verses been explained ? What, a Koran not in Arabic and (its bearer) an Arab!
>
> (41:44)

Chapter 2

And So It Is Written: Revelation and Compilation of the Koran

In the Islamic tradition, the Koran was revealed to Muḥammad over a period of some twenty-three years. Yet the Koran itself, which has a great deal to say on what the Book is about, has only a few verses suggesting the mode of the revelation. There are, however, a number of *ḥadiths,* or traditions and sayings of the Prophet, and other sources that describe the mode.

There are few landmarks in the history of inception and propagation of Islam that are better known among Muslims than the occasion of the first revelation. The chapters of the Book are not ordered chronologically, and the first verse revealed is not the first verse of the book. In fact, it is among the very last.

The tradition has it that the first revelation, or inspiration, came to the Prophet in a cave, called Hira, near Mecca. According to a *ḥadith*[2] the first revelation came to the Prophet 'in the form of true dreams in his sleep', wherein the angel Gabriel came to him and asked him to read. After repeated protestations by the distressed Prophet that he could not read, the angel said:

> Recite in the name of your Lord, who has created (all that exists).Has created man from a clot of congealed blood. Read! And your Lord is the Most Bountiful, who has

[2] al-Bukhāri, *Sahih Al-Bukhāri* (Arabic-English), vol. 6, tr. Dr Muḥammad Muhsin Khan (Riyadh, Saudi Arabia: Darussalam, 1997), 401 (hereafter al-Bukhāri). Al-Bukhāri is one of the six collections of *ḥadiths* traditionally said to be the most reliable.

> taught (the writing) by the pen. Has taught man what he did not know.
>
> (96:1–5)

These lines, verses 1 through 5 of *Sūra* 96 (*Iqraa*), are, in the majority view, the earliest verses revealed and recorded in the Koran. Note, in particular, that the words of the verses were spoken by the angel Gabriel, while the strictest Islamic tradition holds that every word in the Koran is the word of God. As we shall see throughout our discussion, the Koran is full of instances where it requires a huge leap of faith to attribute the words spoken *directly* by God.

A modern reader might wonder at the abruptness of the angelic command to Muḥammad. There was no introduction and no salutation. We would have expected that the angel would introduce himself and state the purpose of his visit. Gabriel did not even reveal to the unsuspecting Muḥammad at the first encounter that he had been chosen to be the Messenger of God. We would also be perplexed by the seeming abruptness of the end of the first message, at least until we were told about normal breaks in divine revelations that mark quite a few of the verses of the Koran. No less bewildering is the mention, at that very first encounter, of the clot of blood as the beginning of human life, and the swift transition to the pen.

We get a slightly different version of the incident of the first revelation in Ibn Ishaq.[3] Here, Gabriel came to the Prophet while he was sleeping, bearing a coverlet of brocade with some writings on it. Gabriel said to the Prophet: Read. The most important aspect of the revelation is the dream in the Prophet's sleep, something that tradition appears to gloss over. This aspect of the scenario is the same in both versions.

The experience of the first inspiration was immensely unsettling to Muḥammad. At first, he thought that he might have been possessed. The possibility so distressed him that he considered throwing himself from the top of the mountain, whereupon, as narrated by Ibn Ishaq, Gabriel came into his presence again, his feet, according to Muḥammad, astride the horizon, and told him: 'O Muḥammad! Thou art the apostle of God

---

[3] Ibn Ishaq, *The Life of Muḥammad,* tr. A. Guillaume (Karachi, Pakistan: Oxford University Press, 1995), 106 (hereafter Ibn Ishaq).

and I am Gabriel'. A modern reader would perhaps have expected that these words of Gabriel were a more appropriate introduction to the first revelation than the abrupt command to read.

It is easy to appreciate why the two encounters with Gabriel, however interpreted, overwhelmed Muḥammad, who came home trembling, approaching Khadījah, his wife, and pleading: *Zammalūni! Zammalūni!* 'Cover me! Cover me!'.[4] Whereupon Khadījah had the shivering Muḥammad wrapped in blankets. He then told her what had happened. Khadījah appeared to feel in her heart that these were prophetic matters and took him to see Waraqah b. Nawfal, a cousin of hers, a venerable old Christian and who was well versed in scriptures. (In some versions of the story, Khadījah went by herself.) After hearing the story, Waraqah was said to have been ecstatic and told Khadījah it was indeed Gabriel who had visited Muḥammad. In effect, he said that Muḥammad was the new prophet of the community, and Waraqah had been expecting the Prophet's arrival.

The above account of the first revelation is the most widely known, and the most widely accepted, in the Islamic tradition. There are, however, other accounts of Muḥammad's encounter with Gabriel and the verse or *sūra* to have been inspired first. Though less well known, they greatly undermine the neatness of the generally accepted version of events.

One version of the story of the first revelation, or inspiration, has it that as Muḥammad came out of Hira at the end of one of his long periods of contemplation, he heard a voice calling him.[5] He looked right, looked left, looked in front, but saw nothing. And then he looked up and saw Gabriel. In a further variant of the story, Muḥammad was walking in the street when he heard a voice, and as he looked up, he saw Gabriel sitting in a chair straddling the heavens and the earth. There was no message from the archangel, but the vision overwhelmed Muḥammad. He hurried home and said to Khadījah: '*Zammalūni! Zammalūni!*' Khadījah had him wrapped in blankets, and thereupon God revealed *Sūra* 74 (*Muddaththir*), which begins with:

---

[4] *Zammalūni* is the Arabic used in Al-Bukhāri, rather than *zammilūni,* which is used in some of the other versions.

[5] I have based this and the following two paragraphs on al-Suyūṭī, *Al-Itqān fi-'Ulum al Qur'ān, The Perfect Guide to the Sciences of the Qur'ān* (Reading, UK: Garnet Publishing, 2011), 41–44 (hereafter al-Suyūṭī); and al-Bukhāri, vol. 6, 401–402.

O thou shrouded in mantle! Rise and warn!!

(74:1–2)

One view is that 74:1–2 were the first verses revealed, not the verses of *Sūra* 96 (*Iqraa*), given above. Verse 74:1 in Arabic is *ya aiyuha al-muddaththir,* where *muddaththir* has the same meaning as *muzzammil* ('wrapped up', whence *zammalūni*). This seems to add a superficial attraction to the idea of the *sūra* being the first to be revealed. Nevertheless, this appears to be a minority opinion among exegetes. On the other hand, if *zammalūni* is the clue to verse 74:1–2, being the first verses to be revealed, there is the eponymous *Sūra Muzzammil* (*Sūra* 73), which would then have a better claim to be the first. No such claim has been made for the *sūra,* however.

There is a third body of opinion which holds that *Sūra al-Fātiḥa* was the first to be inspired (revealed). Coming at the beginning of the Koran, *al-Fātiḥa,* or 'opening', looks at first blush to be eminently suitable as the first group of verses to be revealed. But the Koran is not chronologically laid out, and those who hold that view are only a small minority of *ḥadith* narrators and commentators. But then, at what stage of the compilation of the Koran was *al-Fātiḥa* added to it? There is little information about that important question.

For a modern reader of the Koran trying to understand the Holy Book of Islam systematically, these are important questions. There can be only one way in which the first revelation reached Muḥammad. There can also be only one verse which is the first to have been revealed. The diversity of views on these matters, recorded by Muslim exegetes themselves, challenges the neatness of what to the true believers is a divine, and therefore a faultless, narrative.

Over the next twenty-three years, inspiration would come to Muḥammad, and verses of the Koran would accumulate. There are more than 6,300 verses in the Koran, broken into 114 *sūras,* of which 86 are said to be mainly Meccan – that is revealed before Muḥammad's *hijrah,* or 'migration', to Medina – whilst 28, among them some of the longest, are Medinan.

There are a number of *ḥadiths* describing the mode of these revelations. According to a *ḥadith* in *Sahih Al-Bukhāri,* for example,[6] the

[6] al-Bukhāri, vol. 1, 46.

Prophet, having been asked by a companion how the divine revelation came to him, said it sometimes sounded like a ringing of a bell. This form of revelation was said to be the hardest of all, and then this state passed after he had grasped the revelation. He also said sometimes the angel Gabriel came in the form of a man and talked to him, and he grasped the message brought.

The angel Gabriel is considered to have been the intermediary between God and Muḥammad. It is he who brought in the entire Koran, piece by piece, and made the Prophet recite it. There are, however, a number of *ḥadiths* which suggest that some of the *sūras,* and at least in one case part of a *sūra,* were accompanied from Heaven by a host of other angels. Their number was astoundingly large but varied from *sūra* to *sūra.* Thus, *Sūra* 6 (*An'ām*), was said to have been accompanied to earth by seventy thousand angels.[7] It is said that the host of angels accompanying the *sūra* filled the horizon, and the earth trembled and reverberated with the praise of God. According to some *ḥadiths,* the number for *al-Fătiḥa,* for example, was eighty thousand, and each of the verses of *Baqara* was accompanied by eighty thousand angels as well. According to one *ḥadith,* a particularly important verse, *ayat al-Kūrsi,* of the latter *sūra* was escorted by thirty thousand angels. A modern mind will find it hard to envisage the precise form and nature of these modes of conveyance of the *sūras* of the Koran, as well as the reasons for their selection. It is difficult to envisage a *sūra,* disembodied or embodied, being 'carried', especially when the action is not presented as allegory. It is also hard to conceive of part of a *sūra* (for example, *ayat al-Kūrsi*) being borne separately from the main body of the *sūra* itself (*Baqara*). Equally important, we would also like to know how these scenes of revelation conform to the *ḥadith* above, where the Prophet hears bells tingle, or someone in human form talks to him. It is difficult to envisage the two forms of divine communication of verses to be true at the same time, without any further intermediation between the two.

In the Koran itself, the revelation comes to the heart of Muḥammad, a mode that is far more profound, far easier to comprehend, and that leaves open the possibility that while the inspiration was divine, the speech was that of the Prophet, the human being. Thus:

---

[7] al-Suyūtī, 83.

> And truly this is a Revelation from the Lord of the Worlds, brought down by the Faithful Spirit, to your heart so that you may admonish.
>
> (26:192–194)

The 'Faithful Spirit' here is Gabriel, who comes down with the revelation.

Muḥammad's grasping and reciting whatever was said or read to him is graphically alluded to in the following verses of the Koran, rare ones of their kind in the Book:

> Move not your tongue with it to hasten it.
>
> (75:16)

'It' is the Koran just revealed. This is followed by assurances:

> It is for Us to collect it and to promulgate it.
>
> (75:17)

> So when We recite it, follow its recitation.
>
> (75:18)

> Then it is for Us to explain it.
>
> (75:19)

It is necessary to point out here a question of major importance that will be taken up in greater detail later (in Chapter 4): juxtaposition of disparate themes. Verses 75:16–17 are wedged in a *sūra* concerning resurrection. That event, according to the Koran, will follow destructions of enormous magnitude. The verse preceding 'Move not your tongue with it to hasten it' (75:16) concerns judgement of man for his doings in life; it has nothing to do with the collection and promulgation of the divine words. Verse 75:20 reverts to resurrection just as abruptly.

Note that God himself has the responsibility to collect the pieces of the Koran, which come to earth over a long period of twenty-three years. However, the collection has to be manifested physically, and undertaken by human hand. As we will see, the actual collection was far less smooth than verse 75:17 would have us believe.

Of very similar import are the following verses that contain an important caveat:

> We shall make you recite (the revelation) so that you will not forget –
>
> (87:6)

> Except what God wills …
>
> (87:7)

Note, first, that the two very short verses are akin to verses 75:16–19, above, in an altogether different *sūra*. They are also preceded by totally unconnected verses on God's creation, and followed by other unconnected themes.

Traditional exegesis explains that when Gabriel came with verses of the Koran, Muḥammad grew anxious lest, first, there should be any difference between what he heard and what he recited for memorisation or a later transcription, and, second, he should forget some parts of what had just been revealed to him. He would thus recite the revelation with great urgency, moving his tongue rapidly.[8]

The two verses above make a single sentence. This suggests that God will make sure that no portion of the message is erased from the memory of Muḥammad, except those which it is His will to erase. While some exegetes have chosen to gloss over a difficulty here, others have laboured to find a rationale. To a modern mind, the question is likely to arise: why would omniscient God need to correct Himself by erasing a message he had inspired earlier? Exegeses in the translations of the Koran that I have used skirt around that critical question.

Muḥammad's anxious efforts could have been made unnecessary if, by some divine will, the Koran had been sent down in one go, all collected and ready to be read. Indeed, the Meccan polytheists demanded to know why God did not do just that.

The Koran itself says:

[8] Qur'ān/Muhiuddin.

> The unbelievers say, 'Why has not the Koran been sent to him (Muhammad) as one single collected volume?' …
>
> (25:32)

The question should be seen as coming naturally enough from people presented with something which the Prophet claimed was divine. Surely God had the power to send the complete book to mankind, ready to be read. The answer is given in the second part of the verse above, now addressed to Muḥammad, an answer that acknowledges the inability of a mortal, even if he is a prophet, to comprehend and assimilate the revelation in its entirety all at once:

> … (It is revealed to you as We have) so that We can strengthen your heart, and recited it (to you) slowly and distinctly.
>
> (25:32)

Beyond that divine explanation, nevertheless, there was the important practical matter of the compilation of the Koran.

According to tradition, the Koran came in instalments of different sizes, and there were lapses of time of various lengths between inspirations. Tradition also says that the inspired verses were written down by scribes from among the companions of Muḥammad. It seems impossible that the scribes were on hand to write down the verses on all occasions of their inspiration, since these inspirations came under very different circumstances, some of which might not have been propitious for instant inscription. For example, Muḥammad could be sitting among his companions, or he could be walking, be on camelback, be on the battlefield, or even be in his bedchamber when an inspiration came. In many such cases, it is difficult to envisage scribes at the ready to take down the verses inspired. In one case, verses (on the *ḥijab*)[9] were said to have been inspired while Muḥammad, having waited impatiently for his guests to depart from the feast he had arranged on the occasion of one of his marriages, finally entered the bridal chamber. In some such circumstances, the verses inspired required instant memorisation, until

[9] See Chapter 14.

such time as they could be transcribed at the first opportunity, and it was inevitable that there would be time lags of various lengths in between inspiration and inscription. This in turn presupposed extraordinary power of memorisation on the part of Muḥammad.

Memorisation was, in fact, a critical part of the process. Once a batch of verses was revealed to Muḥammad, he was required to commit it to memory, even in the rarest of situations when a scribe was ready to write it down. No revelation came directly to the scribe in, say, the form of a dictation while the Prophet was still having the inspiration. Only the Prophet could receive it, commit it to memory, and then dictate it to the scribe.

The great diversity of the occasions of inspiration must have made the inscription of the verses of the Koran a very arduous and risky enterprise. The tradition has been rather sparse on a subject of such critical importance. The *Sahih Al-Bukhāri,* for example, has only six *ḥadiths* related to collection of the Koran, compared with twenty-nine on the ritual of bathing. While there are a large number of *ḥadiths* relating to the occasion of the revelation of the *sūras* and verses, there are only a very few from which the process of inscription of the revelation can be gleaned. Among the latter is a *ḥadith* in *Sahih Al-Bukhāri* reporting that when a particular verse (4:95) was revealed to Muḥammad, he said someone: 'Call Zaid for me and let him bring the board, the inkpot and the scapula bone … '[10] The tradition has few other instances of this kind. The *ḥadith* literature and history have practically nothing to offer on the critical matter of how, in what circumstances, and on which kind of materials individual *sūras* and verses were inscribed for the first time, or who the scribe might have been. For the Meccan *sūras* and verses, there is a further area of uncertainty. Since the number of companions of Muḥammad in Mecca was very small, and they were mostly illiterate, the question arises: who inscribed the majority of the *sūras* of the Koran?

Paper, as we know it, was still absent from Arabia, though parchment and scrolls are mentioned in the Koran, in verses 6:7 and 52:3, for example:

---

[10] al-Bukhāri, vol. 6, 427. The Zaid in question is Zaid b. Thābit, a close scribe of the Prophet.

the former perhaps means 'papyrus', and the latter, 'parchment'.[11] It was one and a half centuries after the death of Muḥammad that paper appeared on the scene, in the wake of Arab conquests in central Asia, which also yielded the knowledge of papermaking to the conquerors. Tradition has it that the verses of the Koran were written down on tree leaves, pieces of animal hide or skin, chips of stone, animal bones (as in the above *ḥadith*), and in some cases, parchment. It is difficult to think of an agglomeration of hundreds, even thousands, of such heterogeneous materials as these forming the 'book' that was the Koran. There must have been a very considerable amount of work involved in transcribing the verses into tolerably homogeneous 'pages' or 'leaves' (*suhuf*) that could be collected to constitute a book. Islamic tradition tells us precious little about that critical work.

Some of the *sūras* of the Koran were said to have been revealed as a whole. Perhaps most of the shorter *sūras* were so revealed. The tradition has it that some of the longer *sūras* were also revealed whole. Examples cited[12] of the longest *sūras* revealed whole are 37 (*Sāffāt,* 182 verses), 6 (*An'ām,* 165 verses), and 77 (*Mursalāt,* 50 verses). Did Muḥammad commit the *sūras* to memory the instant they were revealed? An ordinary mortal would need many days to memorise each *sūra* of such length. For comparison, a modern-day *ḥafiz* (literally 'memoriser') of the Koran, who commits the entire Koran to memory, usually takes several years of single-minded effort to memorise the Holy Book. Muḥammad was of course no ordinary mortal. Still, the feat needed to memorise such long *sūras,* and to retain them long enough for them to be written down, must seem truly extraordinary. The process of writing down the inspirations must have been long and arduous, given the kind of writing materials and the nature of calligraphy involved. Not the least important was the utter care with which each word was required to have been written. A verse like 75:17, above, assures Muḥammad of divine collection of the Koran; and

---

[11] Johannes Pedersen, *The Arabic Book,* tr. Geoffrey French (Princeton: Princeton University Press, 1984), 55. Pedersen translates *raq* in 52:3 as 'parchment' and *qirtas* in 6:7 as 'papyrus'. A Yusuf Ali, *The Holy Qur'ān: Text, Translation and Commentary* (Brentwood, MD: Amana Corp., 1983) (hereafter Qur'ān/Yusuf Ali). Qur'ān/Yusuf Ali translates *raq* in 52:3 as 'scroll' and *qirtas* in 6:7 as 'parchment'.

[12] al-Suyūtī, 81.

yet, the work that still needed to be done by the human hand in order to accomplish the inscription remained shrouded in mystery.

Poets, unconstrained by the need to memorise what others want them to, can write, or dictate, long verses inspired by events or recollections. Muḥammad, the Koran takes pains to point out, was no poet, and he was subject to such constraints, even when it came to matters divine. The Koran itself acknowledges that human limitation, as in verse 25:32, above.

Again, there is no tradition saying which kind of materials individual whole *sūras* were written on. For the shorter *sūras,* or the *sūras* that were revealed in small parcels, the task of writing them down was easier, though their collection into what could be considered the single entity of a *sūra* was not; neither was their preservation. For long *sūras,* the problem must have been far greater. What did a long *sūra,* such as *Sūra* 2 (*Baqara*) look like? Was it available in its entirety on parchment or on a scroll? Or was it recorded partly, say, on a scapula bone, partly on leaves, and partly on animal hides, or on any other material? Again, the *ḥadith* literature has hundreds of traditions concerning minor rituals and etiquettes, but none on this. Yet such questions are of critical importance to the next step in the process of compilation of the Koran: the collection of the *sūras* into a book.

Memorisation played a critical part in the process, particularly in a society where the vast majority could not read or write. Muslims memorised pieces of the Koran, as whole *sūras* or in part. Unless Muḥammad himself taught them, which appears implausible, most of them learned verses of the Koran second-hand from those of their brethren who could read, or from those who had memorised them. The memory of each individual person was one important niche for the verses of the Koran.

We can thus envisage the Koran at the time of Muḥammad's death as pieces of various lengths, written on slabs of stone, dried animal skins, date-palm leaves, and scapula bones of camels. All these pieces were in a great variety of shapes and sizes, some unwieldy, some brittle, all difficult to store. Copies of each piece must have been made on correspondingly heterogeneous materials. These were hardly ideal materials to write on, and the quality of substances used for ink must also have been extremely poor. There is also no evidence that, once written on, these pieces of materials were kept in safe custody at a central place, and it is likely that they were fairly widely scattered among the population and had a rather precarious existence. And perhaps there were verses passing from lips to lips, including those for which a written version was unavailable, as the *ḥadith* below suggests. That would complete the heterogeneity of the state of the verses and *sūras* of the Koran.

Transcription of the text of the whole of the Koran was not done during the lifetime of the Prophet. According to one *ḥadith* in *Sahih Al-Bukhāri,*[13] there was no compilation of the Koran during his lifetime. It also describes what is generally considered to the first important step in the collection of the Koran. We note in particular that the materials from which the Koran was compiled, as mentioned in the *ḥadith,* do not include parchment, much less paper.

In the Islamic tradition, the historical background for the first compilation of the Koran was the death in battle of a large number of the *Qurrā,* men who knew the Koran by heart and were public readers of the book. The ranks of the *Qurrā* were being depleted, threatening the most used source of the Koran. The need for preservation of the Koran must have been keenly felt. According to the above *ḥadith,* Abū Bakr [14] sent for the above-mentioned Zaid and ordered him to go about compiling the Koran. After an initial reluctance engendered by the enormity of the task, Zaid agreed. As he himself put it, he started 'looking for the Koran' and collecting it from inscriptions on palm-leaf stalks and stones, and also from men who knew it by heart. According to the *ḥadith,* Zaid duly completed the compilation, and the completed version remained with Abū Bakr till his death. It was then passed on to 'Umar, the second caliph. On the latter's death, the manuscript came into the possession of Ḥafsah, his daughter and Muḥammad's wife.

The above story, well accepted in the Muslim world, deserves a critical look. As we have seen above, the extremely heterogeneous array of materials used to inscribe the individual verses of the Koran – of which there were to be over 6,300 – and the collection and collation of individual 'scripts', which were perhaps widely dispersed around the land, must have resulted in a very lengthy compilation process. In other words, it must have taken Zaid a very long time to compile the Koran into a single manuscript. How long did it take him? There is no information on this,

[13] al-Bukhāri, vol. 6, 424.

[14] The first caliph of Islam.

either in this *ḥadith* or in others, and traditional Islam has glossed over this important aspect of the compilation of the Koran, perhaps in the belief that the awkward questions which must have had arisen were sorted out by divine intervention.

Furthermore, it is unclear what type of writing material was used for the purpose. It could have been parchment, but there is no evidence that it was. An intriguing question also arises here. Why did Abū Bakr and 'Umar, the first and the second caliphs, not circulate the text compiled by Zaid, rather than leave it with Ḥafsah? And then why leave it in the private custody of Ḥafsah at all, rather than in the custody of the caliphs as heads of the community?

According to tradition, the next landmark in the compilation of the Koran came during the caliphate of 'Uthmān. Various versions of the Koran were said to exist at the time, and the caliph directed a group of the Prophet's companions with intimate knowledge of the Book, including the aforementioned Zaid, to make a definitive and final compilation. According to tradition, the caliph had a number of copies of the final version of the Koran made, and then he ordered that all other extant copies be destroyed. It is still not clear from the *ḥadith* what material the complete copy of the Koran was written on.[15] A *ḥadith*, in *Sahih Al Bukhāri,*[16] tells us that 'Uthman ordered Zaid and three other scribes to make a final and authoritative copy of the Koran, the reason being that there were many copies in circulation, all of which differed. The scribes were to base their work on the version then in the possession of Ḥafsah. A number of copies of the 'final' version were made, and 'Uthman had a copy sent to each provincial governor as the authoritative version of the Koran, and, as stated, he then ordered that all other versions be burnt, whether versions of the complete Koran or fragments of it.

Perhaps the enterprise was not as smooth as the above story appears to imply. One version of the story of collection of the Koran suggests that 'Uthman summoned twelve men of Quraysh and the Anṣar for the work and that there were lengthy deliberation and disputations over verses

[15] The scholar Pedersen writes, 'We may hazard a guess that the oldest compete Qur'ān was written on one of the two materials [parchment or papyrus], probably parchment.' (Pendersen, 55.)

[16] al-Bukhāri, vol. 6, 425.

missing from the codices they had been working on.[17] In this version, the codices were made available to them from a chest kept in the house of 'Umar, a piece of information not available in the *ḥadith* above. 'Uthman's emphasis, rightly, was to have only one *mashaf* (meaning, 'codex'). How the differences were smoothed out is not made clear. Nor is it clear how long the work took, given the short tenure of the caliphate of 'Uthman.

It is impossible not to recognise that a very large number of individual human decisions, made under different circumstances and over many years, must have gone into the compilation of the Koran. Tradition provides no clue as to the absence of divine intervention to see that the Koran was compiled, in perfect order, during the lifetime of the Prophet. Whatever the reason, the lack of any divine intervention to give the Koran its final shape as a book during the lifetime of Muḥammad hugely enhances the role of humans in the enterprise after his death.

That role looms especially large in the compilation of the individual *sūras* of the Koran. There are numerous *sūras* in the Koran where individual verses were said to have been inspired at different points in time. This is true not only of the longest verses but, remarkably, of some quite short verses as well. Some *sūras* contain verses from both Meccan and Medinan periods, which were many years apart. Putting together verses inspired at different times and in different places so as to form a particular chapter of the Koran must have taken very considerable human effort and ingenuity, though history, and even the *ḥadith* literature, does not record it. It is important to take a look at a few instances where *sūras* contain verses from different points in time. The list below is meant only to illustrate and does not claim to be exhaustive.

The first five verses of *Sūra* 96 (*Iqraa*), given earlier in this chapter, are recognised by a majority of exegetes in the Islamic tradition as the very first verses of the Koran. There was then a long break in inspiration, traditionally called *fātrā*, lasting many months. There were several other breaks of this kind during the prophetic life of Muḥammad. A verse in *Sūra* 93 (*Dhuḥā*), for example, is said to allude to such breaks:

> Your Lord has not abandoned you, nor is He displeased.
> (93:3)

[17] al-Suyūtī, 142–43.

The above refers to one such period of absence of inspiration that caused the Prophet great frustration. This verse comes as a consolation and reassurance.

Fātrā is a difficult concept, given that the inspirations were a one-way flow from the Divine to a mortal. God, by definition perfect and prescient, of course cannot be seen as being incapable of sending revelations at regular intervals. In fact, it is even more difficult to see Him reveal the first few verses of a *sūra,* the very first ones for that matter, and then wait for days or months to reveal the rest, as in the case of *Sūra* 96. To a modern reader of the Koran, a rough parallel to a *fātrā,* in human terms, would be writer's block, which has plagued authors through the ages.

To go back to the narrative of *Sūra* 96, the next verses we read in that *sūra* are not the next verses obtained by inspiration in chronological order of the revelation of the Koran. While exegetes appear to agree that the interruption, *fātrā,* came after verses 1 through 5 of *Sūra* 96, there are differences regarding which verses followed next in the chronology of revelation. The group of verses that followed in chronological order belongs to an altogether different *sūra.* But which *sūra*? That *sūra* could be 68 (*Qalam*), according to some commentators,[18] or 74 (*Muddaththir*) according to others.[19] Verses 6 through 19 of *Sūra* 96 were added later, after an interval that probably lasted many months and during which other verses, meant for other *sūras* – 68 or 74 – were inspired. Islamic commentators of the Koran do not seem to find any oddity in the procedure of inspiration, but in the practical matter of compilation of the *sūras,* this surely is highly unusual. If the compiler is the omniscient God, to attribute such a method of communication with His creation is to question His omniscience. Why would God start to reveal a series of verses, interrupt Himself and then start on some other series? This seems strange for an all-knowing and all-seeing God, unless His decision to start on the first series was wrong in the first place. But this cannot be since, of course, God cannot commit a mistake. This makes it necessary to look for explanations of the *fātrā* elsewhere.

Sūra 5 (*Māida*) is reported to be late Medinan, containing some of the latest revelations in the Koran. With 120 verses, this is a long *sūra.* The long verse 5:3 starts with the theme of forbidden and permissible food:

---

[18] Qur'ān/Yusuf Ali.

[19] Qur'ān/Muhiuddin.

> Forbidden to you are carrion, blood, the flesh of swine, and what has been slaughtered invoking a name other than God's …
>
> (5:3)

The verse then goes on to describe forbidden food in further detail. In the midst of this rather mundane matter comes a sentence that would be considered profound:

> … Today I have perfected your religion for you, completed for you My favour and bestowed on you Islam as your religion.
>
> (5:3)

The sharp contrast of themes in the same verse is in itself important to note, and we shall take it up later (in Chapter 4). Equally important in the present context is the fact that the proclamation: 'Today I have perfected … ' is said to be the very last verse to be inspired in chronological order, having been revealed to Muḥammad during his last pilgrimage to Mecca in AH 10.[20] Therefore, it must have been added to *Sūra* 5 later on.

The inclusion of the sentence in 5:3 should also be viewed against the background of another *sūra* of the Koran. The very last complete *sūra* in the Koran is said to be 110 (*Naṣr*),[21] which seals the victory of Islam over the pagans, symbolised by the conquest of Mecca:

> When God's help and victory come, and you see men entering His religion in throngs, proclaim the praise of God and ask for His forgiveness. Surely He is most forgiving.
>
> (110:1–3)

It too was probably inspired during Muḥammad's last pilgrimage to Mecca, or soon afterwards. It is intriguing, therefore, that the sentence in

[20] *Hijrah* is the year that begins the Islamic calendar, marking the migration of the Prophet from Mecca to Medina in 622 of the Christian calendar. It is often denoted by the abbreviation AH (Anno Hegirae).
[21] Qur'ān/Yusuf Ali.

verse 5:3 – 'Today I have perfected your religion' – presumed to be the last sentence to be inspired, is close to the spirit of the last *sūra* (110) but is not contained in it, and, instead, is found in an earlier *sūra*, in an altogether different context. In his exegesis Yusuf Ali points this out, but he does not see any need to explain the uncommon placement of the sentence.

As can be expected, there is considerable difference of opinion over the last *sūra* to be revealed, as well as over the last verse.[22] Some are of the opinion that the last *sūra* to be revealed was 9 (*Barāat*) and the last verse to be revealed was verse 176 of *Sūra* 4 (*Nisa*): 'They ask you for a legal decision' ... (about inheritance). Others take verse 281 of *Sūra* 2 (*Baqara*): 'And fear the Day you shall be brought back to God' ... as the last verse. In any case, the last verse revealed is not part of the last *sūra* revealed, which once again suggests that some verses have been shuffled to their final place.

These illustrations bring to light another important issue. In cases where verses from different points in time are seen to be present in a single *sūra*, it is unclear whether the whole *sūra* was compiled only after all the verses that finally went into it had been collected, or whether the *sūra* sans the later verses was already in use (in recitation and prayer). For example, was *Sūra* 5 in use before the addition of verse 5:3? If it was, a further question arises: how could a divine authority allow use of a *sūra* which was by definition imperfect?

To return to the illustration, *Sūra* 9 (*Barāat*) is said to have been inspired in Medina over a number of months in AH 9, which makes it one of the very late Medinan *sūras*. In the matter of compilation, this *sūra* is unique in that it is said to have been originally intended – it is not clear by whom – to be part of *Sūra* 8 (*Anfāl*), but it was finally treated as a separate *sūra*. Yet this is the only *sūra* in the Koran to which the usual *Bismillah* [23]is not prefixed. Its status as a separate *sūra* thus remains undefined. On the other hand, *Anfāl* was an early Medinan *sūra*, whereas *Barāat* is a very late Medinan *sūra*. Therefore, it is not clear why the two were even considered to be part of the same *sūra*.

[22] al-Suyūṭī, 49.

[23] More fully, *Bismillahir Raḥmanir Raḥim* ('In the Name of God, Most Gracious, Most Merciful'), is the invocation that the *sūras* of the Koran begin with (all except one, *Sūra* 9). Muslims begin most of their work – from recitation of the Koran, to eating – with a *Bismillah*.

There is a miscellany of exegetic explanations for the absence of *Bismillah* at the beginning of *Sūra* 9 (*Barāat*). They are wholly inadequate. It is said, for example, that the Prophet indicated its place in the order of the chapters as coming after *Sūra* 8 (*Anfāl*), but he did not leave any instruction about the introductory *Bismillah* for it. The 'Uthmanic Koran 'therefore' – so the explanation goes – was without the *Bismillah*. This of course does not explain why the Prophet did not have the *Bismillah* written on the *sūra* in the first place. It has also been suggested that if the two *sūras* were meant to be a single *sūra*, to place a *Bismillah* in the middle of it would have been highly inappropriate. There is an additional suggestion that the *Bismillah*, which bears an intrinsic sense of peace and security, would not have been appropriate when placed before a *sūra* with a main theme of denunciation of the unbelievers and abrogation of treaties with them. Thus, it appears that the exegetes have been struggling to explain away something which, to a modern reader of the Koran, is a critical question in the collection and compilation of the Holy Book of Islam.[24]

Apparently, divine guidance in the matter was not available, and the decision to treat *Anfāl* and *Barāat* as separate *sūras* was a purely human one. And if the absence of *Bismillah* was accidental, it could hardly be divine.

Sūra 16 (*Nahl*) is a Meccan *sūra* consisting of 128 verses. According to some commentators, the last three verses (16:126–128) were inspired in Medina after the Battle of Uḥud.[25] These verses concern the reaction of the Prophet to the mutilation of bodies of many of the Muslims slain by the enemy during that battle; thus, they cannot be Meccan verses. According to some commentators, verse 16:110 and some of the verses that follow it were also revealed in Medina.[26]

Sūra 17 (*Bani Isrāil*) was inspired in the late Meccan period. This verse starts with a reference to the *mi'rāj*, the Prophet's ascension to

---

[24] Islamic Foundation Bangladesh, *Al-Qur'ānul Karim* (in Bengali), (Dhaka, Bangladesh: Islamic Foundation, 2005) (hereafter Qur'ān/Islamic Foundation).
Marmaduke Pickthall, *The Meaning of the Glorious Koran: An Explanatory Translation* (New York and Toronto: Everyman's Library/Alfred A. Knopf, 1992) (hereafter Koran/Pickthall).
I have scoured exegeses of various lengths in Qur'ān/Muhiuddin, Qur'ān/Islamic Foundation, Qur'ān/Yusuf Ali, and Koran/Pickthall for these explanations.

[25] Qur'ān/Muhiuddin.

[26] Qur'ān/Yusuf Ali.

Heaven, which, according to tradition, happened in Mecca. There is a single verse (17:81) in the *sūra* which was inspired after the conquest of Mecca, or more than a decade after the other verses had been revealed. The verse in question reads:

> And say, 'The truth has come and falsehood has vanished;
> for falsehood is certain to vanish.'
>
> (17:81)

According to some commentators, these words were uttered by Muḥammad as he entered the holy precincts in Mecca and raised his cane at each of the idols assembled there, whereupon the idols collapsed one by one. This fixes the time of the verse's revelation.

Sūra 22 (*Ḥajj*) is commonly held to have been inspired in Medina. But some commentators[27] hold that some of its verses may have been revealed in Mecca, which puts some chronological distance between verses in the same *sūra*. Others point to verses 22:39–41 where Muslims are given permission to fight. But commentators differ on whether this inspiration was given shortly before the migration of the Prophet to Medina or soon afterwards.

Sūra 25 (*Furqān*) is said by some commentators to be an entirely Meccan *sūra*. Some have suggested that it was 'mainly' an early Meccan *sūra,* and some are of the opinion that it is mainly Medinan. That some verses of the same *sūra* were inspired at different times seems not to be of any consequence to these commentators.

Sūra 33 (*Aḥzāb*) has as its background a great diversity of subjects, ranging from war to household matters concerning the Prophet, and its verses were revealed over a number of years, probably between AH 5 and AH 7. A major theme of the *sūra* is the Battle of the Trench which took place in AH 5. A number of verses concern the Prophet's marriage to Zaynab, wife of his adopted son, which took place sometime after the battle. Some of the verses are said to have been inspired after the expedition to Khaybar a few years later.

Sūra 45 (*Jāthiya*) is Meccan. Some commentators [28] think that it

[27] Ibid.

[28] Qur'ān/Muhiuddin.

contains a single verse – 45:14 – which was inspired in Medina, though the reason for thinking that this verse is Medinan is not made clear. This *sūra* contains thirty-eight verses. Tweaking a single Medinan verse from among such a number must have been an exegetic feat.

Sūra 48 (*Fāt-ḥ*) is said to be have been revealed while the Prophet and his companions were on their way back from Hudaybiyah to Medina.[29] This places the *sūra* as inspired in AH 6. However, verses 48:11–15 concern desert Arabs who did not join the Prophet on his trip to Mecca, which led to the Treaty of Hudaybiyah, but who were eager to sign up when it came to joining an expedition that promised booty. This is a reference to the Khaybar campaign which was waged in AH 7.

Sūra 55 (*Raḥman*) is said by many commentators to be simply Meccan, while others consider it to be early Meccan. Still others think that it was revealed in Medina. Some commentators suggest that, while some of the verses may have been revealed in Medina, a greater number were revealed in Mecca.

According to some commentators, *Sūra* 56 (*Wāqi'a*) is Medinan. Others consider it Meccan. Still others consider it an early Meccan *sūra*, 'with the possible exception of one or two verses'[30]

Sūra 73 (*Muzzammil*) is by consensus early Meccan. But verse 73:20 contains a reference to those who fight in the cause of God: (God knows that there are) 'yet others fighting in God's Cause.' The question of waging wars, or *jihad*, for the sake of Islam began to occupy the Prophet only after his migration to Medina. One explanation is that this verse was inspired in Medina long after other verses of the *sūra* had been inspired,[31] and the verses were put together even later. Note in particular that 73:20 is a long verse, considerably longer than an average verse of the Koran. The part of it that has to do with *jihad* consists only of the six words quoted above. Their addition to the verse long after the other verses had been in existence is truly extraordinary.

Sūra 107 (*Ma'un*) has only seven verses and is an early Meccan *sūra*. Although it is a short *sūra*, about half of it is said to have been of a later period[32].

---

[29] See Chapter 5.

[30] Qur'ān/Yusuf Ali.

[31] Ibid.

[32] Ibid.

There is a long list of verses inspired at different points in time and yet put in the same *sūra*. There are, on the other hand, verses related to the same incident, or closely related incidents, at a certain point in time, which are scattered over a number of *sūras*. Consider the following verses:

> *Sūra A'rāf*
> If a counsel from Satan entices you, seek refuge with God ...
>
> (7:200)
>
> *Sūra Hājj*
> We sent not an apostle or prophet before you, but that when he framed a fancy, Satan cast his interpolation into it; but God annulled what Satan threw in ...
>
> (22:52)
>
> *Sūra Bani Isrā'il*
> They nearly swayed you from what We revealed to you, that you might forge something different (from what we revealed); and then they would have taken you as their friend.
>
> (17:73)
>
> And had We not given you strength, you would have inclined towards them a little.
>
> (17:74)
>
> *Sūra Najm*
> Have you seen Lāt and 'Uzzā.[33]
>
> (53:19)

[33] This is a literal translation, following Qur'ān/Yusuf Ali. A. J. Arberry, *The Koran Interpreted* (New York: Simon & Schuster, 1996) (hereafter Koran/Arberry) and Maulana Muḥammad Ali, *The Holy Qur'ān with English Translation and Commentary* (Ohio: Ahmadiyya Anjuman Isha'at Islam Lahore Inc., 2002) (hereafter Qur'ān/Muḥammad Ali) translate this as 'have you considered ...'. Koran/Pickthall's rendition is: 'Have you yet thought upon.' These are more apt translations, which also better fit the context, as explained below. Qur'ān/Muhiuddin is also in the same vein.

> And Manāt, another, the third (goddess)?
>
> (53:20)

A reading of the individual verses above as a matter of pure piety alone is unlikely to yield a clue to their meaning. We need to go far beyond piety. The vital connection between the verses above, coming from four different *sūras*, is an incident that traditional Islamic commentators deny ever took place, but for which evidence in Islamic literature exists. It is said that Satan instigated the Prophet to insert, after verse 53:20, the words 'These are the high-flying cranes; verily their intercession is accepted with approval.' This was a significant concession to idolatry, which was anathema to the religion that Muḥammad had begun to preach. That these words have come down in history as the Satanic Verses attests to its putative author, but pious Muslims might also see in the appellation evidence of satanic mischief. To most traditional Islamic commentators, the incident is offensive enough to not even merit a direct mention.[34] On the other hand, the possibility of Satan meddling with Muḥammad's mind is acknowledged in the Koran itself. Verse 7:200, above, is an example. And we see it also in the following verse:

> ... If Satan ever makes you forget, do not, after you have remembered, sit in the company of wrong-doers.
>
> (6:68)

The historian al-Tabarī is the main source for the incident and the verse, 'These are the high-flying cranes ...,' quoted above. This is from his monumental work on the history of the time.[35] We also cannot fail to notice that a verse such as 22:52 or 17:73 must have as its background some incident of considerable importance to the Koran. Al-Tabarī also reports that soon after the insertion of the Satanic Verses, the archangel

[34] Qur'ān/Muhiuddin, in its commentary on 22:52, says only that in the *ḥadith* literature an incident has been described that has come to be known as the *gharaniq* story. It points out that most *ḥadith* commentators consider the incident to be baseless. The *gharaniq* are the high-flying cranes.

[35] al-Tabarī, *The History of al-Tabarī*, vol. 6 (Albany, NY: The State University of New York Press, 1989), 108 (hereafter al-Tabarī).

Gabriel arrived with a new revelation that nullified them. The new verse, now 53:23, says:

> These are only names you yourself have named, you and your fathers, God has sent down no authority to them ...
> (53:23)

'These' of course refers to the goddesses mentioned in the verses above, and 'you' to the pagans.

It is not Satan alone who was involved here. Critically, as in other areas of the Koran, so were humans. While traditional Islamic commentators deny the incident ever happened, they do not deny the history of attempts by the pagans of Mecca to entice Muḥammad away from his mission, and to have him say a good word or two for their gods. The Meccans were as zealously attached to their gods as the Prophet was to his God, and there were attempts by the pagan citizenry to get the Prophet to change his mind. While discussing *Sūra* 109 (*Kāfirūn*), one commentator reports that a number of major pagan personalities of Mecca approached the Prophet with a proposal which would have him worship their god and them worship his god on alternate years.[36] While the Prophet ultimately stuck to his guns, we can see the vulnerability of the human mind here, something that even prophets are not immune to.

To return to the compilation of the Koran, rearranging a text already revealed can hardly be called an intervention of the Divine, which is by definition infallible and omniscient – a definition that the Koran holds to be the essence of faith. Other forms of amendment to the text cannot be called an intervention of the Divine either. It is therefore interesting to look at some of the instances where amendments have been made, and have been seen as such in mainstream exegeses, and where the opinion of mortals led to certain revelations or to changes in verses already revealed.

In regard to the hour before dawn, when eating and drinking must stop and fasting must begin, during Ramadan, verse 2:187 (*Baqara*) says, 'And eat and drink, until the white thread of dawn appears to you distinct from its black thread; ... ' In the original verse, the words 'of dawn'

[36] Qur'ān/Muhiuddin.

were absent. Some of the Prophet's companions used to tie their legs, alternately, with black and white threads. They would keep eating till the white thread was distinguishable from the black thread. God then revealed the words 'of dawn', meaning, poetically, the transition from night to day.[37] The editorial nature of the correction is hard to overlook.

Given the absence of the clock, the amount of ingenuity that these companions showed may seem comic but is not to be belittled. This was arguably one way of trying to figure out the time to stop eating. A clarification was nevertheless necessary; but to attribute it to the Divine is to rid it of its omniscient nature.

Of course, the absence of the requisite knowledge was not limited to ordinary people; in fact, it extended to the Prophet himself, who, the Koran stresses, was but a human being. The Book recognises this. Thus, as we have seen before, in verse 73:20 (*Muzzammil*) God tells the Prophet, while asking him to pray at night for 'two-thirds of the night, or half the night, or a third of the night,' that He knows that the Prophet was unable to keep track of time.

Next, we have a major instance of divine revelation seemingly coming at the behest of a mortal. 'Umar, one of the closest companions of the Prophet, and the second caliph of Islam, is reported to have said, 'I agree with Allah in three things.' The three things are the following: First, his 'intervention' is said to have resulted in an addition to verse 2:125; specifically, the sentence 'And take the Station of Abraham as a place of prayer.' The emendation was done after 'Umar had urged the Prophet to give the place the special honour it deserved.[38] Second, it was 'Umar's insistence that led to the revelation of verses about the veil in *Sūra* 33. Third, it was his unhappiness over the conjugal behaviour of some of the wives of the Prophet that led to the revelation of a verse in *Sūra* 66 threatening theses wives with dire consequences unless they behaved themselves. [39]

Here is an extraordinary story of a mortal, who was not a prophet, who was a lesser person than the Messenger of God, but who said he

---

[37] al-Bukhāri, vol. 6, 44; Al-Suyuti, 71.

[38] After the emendation, the verse became: 'And remember We made the House a place of assembly and safety for men; and take the Station of Abraham as a place of prayer'.... The 'House' is the House of God, or the Ka'ba, which Abraham is said to have built.

[39] al-Bukhāri, vol. 6, 29–30; Al-Suyūṭi,71. For the verse in question, see Chapter 14.

had 'Allah's agreement', (or, 'My Lord agreed with me'), and whose intervention called forth revelations of specific and important verses of the Koran. This is as close as we can get to suggesting that the Divine needed human prompting.

The above verses are not the only ones that 'fulfilled the wish' of Umar. Here is a piece of information from al-Suyūti.[40] A Jew reportedly taunted 'Umar, saying that Gabriel, whom the Prophet claimed as his friend, was an enemy of the Jews. 'Umar then retorted by saying, 'Whoever is an enemy to God, His angels and His Messengers, to Gabriel and Michael – God is an enemy to the unbelievers'. Whereupon God is said to have revealed verses 2:97–98, with identical wordings.

In *Sūra* 56 (*Wāq'ia*) the Koran says, in verses 13 and 14, that in the Garden of Paradise there will be 'Many from among the ancients,' 'And a few from those of later times.'[41] It is said that this was taken to mean a larger number of people from before the time of the Prophet, and only a few from among his contemporaries. When the verses were inspired, they are said to have caused considerable grief to the companions of the Prophet, who apparently expected that the followers of the Prophet would be a large majority of the inhabitants of Heaven. Two later verses of the same *sūra* were therefore sent down to mollify the companions. The verses, 39 and 40, now said, respectively, that there will be 'Many from among the ancients' 'And many from later times.'[42] Again, it is truly extraordinary to be told that divine revelation was changed at the behest of humans. Note also that the earlier pair of verses, now invalid, remains intact in the *sūra*, along with the latter pair, separated by a few dozen verses.

A *ḥadith* in *Sahih Al-Bukhāri* relates how a revelation was changed no sooner than it was made.[43] The necessity for the change is well understood and was humane, but it is at odds with the idea of the omniscience of God, and it therefore underlines the role of thinking humans. In one instance, the Prophet was dictating to Zaid b Thābith what would be verse 4:95: 'Not equal are those among the believers who sit at home … and those who fight in the cause of God' … A blind man, by the name of Ibn Umm

---

[40] al-Suyūṭī, 72.

[41] See Chapter 11.

[42] Qur'ān/Muhiuddin.

[43] al-Bukhāri, vol. 6, 97–98.

Makhtum, came along as the Prophet was dictating and protested that of course he would fight but for his disability. So, according to Zaid b Thābith, the following caveat was introduced after 'sit at home': 'except those who are disabled (by injury or are blind or lame)'.[44]

And there were verses in the Koran that no longer appear in it. According to *Sahih Al-Bukhāri,* there was this Koranic verse: 'Inform our people that we have met our Lord. He is pleased with us and He has made us pleased.' The words in quotes are those of a group of martyrs who had been sent by the Prophet to proselytise to a tribe. The verse was later abrogated and does not appear in the Koran, unlike other abrogated verses that continue to be part of the text.[45]

There are a number of verses in the Koran that are said to have been abrogated, or made *mānsukh,* and replaced by a new verse, termed *nāsikh*[46]. The concept of abrogation, like *fātrā,* is a difficult and puzzling one for the modern reader of the Koran. Verse 2:106 (*Baqara*) is the primary pronouncement on the subject.

> For whatever verse We abrogate or cause to be forgotten,
> We bring a better one or something like it ...
>
> (2:106)

A certain amount of queasiness about abrogation prevails among translators and exegetes of the Koran. There are those who de-emphasise the subject. Still, there is reason to be wary of the idea of abrogation. Those who see nothing wrong with abrogation argue that a new verse was introduced to take account of changing circumstances. This, however, is not always the case. There are a number of verses on inheritance and maintenance for widows, principally in *Sūras* 2 (*Baqara*) and 4 (*Nisāa*), that are said have been abrogated by other verses, and these changes were not on account of changing circumstances. Neither, for example, are the changes made in verses in *Sūra Wāq'ia,* above. Some exegetes argue, however, that some of the verses apparently abrogated are not abrogated at all. This of course would make verse 2:106 meaningless.

---

[44] The verse now read: 'Not equal are those among the believers who sit at home and receive no injury, and those who fight ...'

[45] al-Bukhāri, vol. 4, 54.

[46] *Mansukh*: 'abrogated'; *nasikh*: 'that which abrogates'.

The crux of the problem with the idea of abrogation is of course that it conflicts with the idea of the omniscience of God. God's words are supposed to reflect that omniscience. Abrogation tends to go against it.

Finally, *Ibn-e-Majah,* one of the six major collections of *ḥadiths* that are considered in the Islamic tradition to be beyond reproach, contains a *ḥadith*[47] that has a profound bearing on the compilation of the Koran. It quotes no less an authority than 'A'ishah, the favourite wife of the Prophet, that there was indeed a verse on the stoning to death for fornication. The verse was supposedly written on a piece of 'paper'. It was a day when everybody was busy with the burial of the Prophet, and a goat found its way into 'A'ishah's quarters and ate the paper.

If the incident is true, a verse of the Koran must be presumed to have been misplaced and does not appear in the book. It is also at variance with a verse we read earlier, where God is says in regard to the collection of the Koran that it was for Him to collect and promulgate it (75:17).

---

[47] Ibn-e Maja, *Sunan Ibn-e-Majah,* vol. 3, tr. Muḥammad Tufail Ansari, 3rd edn (New Delhi, India: Kitab Bhavan, 2005) 167–168.

Chapter 3
Speech of God

In traditional Islam, the Koran is simply the word of God. The Koran is recited as the word of the Almighty Allah. The devout Muslim would read a particular piece of the Holy Book, no matter what its theme is, and would consider the reading itself an act of piety, just as a Christian would when reading the Bible. But the Koranic text of what is perceived as God's words is not simply a unidirectional speech addressed by God to His creation. The text is an amalgam of different forms of speech that makes it unlike any other text. God might, for example, speak in the first person singular or, more often, in first person plural. Or, He might speak in the third person singular. In many cases, God Himself is being addressed; evidently, in those cases, the text is an address by somebody other than God. In many instances, the speech of God is a monologue; in many cases, a directive; in still others, a dialogue, such as His exchange with Iblis (Satan). In numerous instances, He is praising Himself. Very often His speech expresses human anger and even frustration. The verses that follow illustrate the variety of God's speech in the Koran. As in other chapters of this work, the illustrations are not exhaustive.

In numerous places in the Koran God speaks of Himself in the third person; often He addresses Muḥammad and the faithful in the first person; sometimes He speaks in the first and third person in the same verse. A few examples should suffice.

Thus, in the first person (beautiful in the Arabic):

> And when My servants ask you about Me, I am near. I listen to the prayer of the caller who calls. Let them also

> listen to my call and believe in Me so that they may be on the right path
>
> (2:186)

And, in the third person, is the evocative:

> He is the creator of the heavens and the earth: when He decrees a thing He says "be" and it is.
>
> (2:117)

And:

> That then is God, your Lord! There is no god but he … So worship Him; He has guardianship over everything.
>
> (6:102)

Here, in an extraordinary presentation, again in the third person, is God quoting Himself:

> And God says: 'Take not two gods.' He is only one God; so fear Me alone.
>
> (16:51)

The following verse begins with God in the third person, quickly reverts to first person plural, and then comes back to the third person, all in the same sentence:

> And God took a covenant from the Children of Israel, and We raised from among them twelve chieftains. And God said: 'I am with you' …
>
> (5:12)

A major, and popular, verse, given below, begins with God in the third person and quickly switches to the speech of a supplicant, starting with 'Our Lord'. The difficulty present here is reflected in one translator's insertion of the word 'pray' before 'Our Lord'; this insertion is absent in the Arabic. Other translations that I have seen do not bother about the sudden change of person and apparently see no difficulty here:

> On no soul does God place a burden greater than it can bear. It gets what it earns and on it returns what it deserves. Our Lord! take us not to task if we forget or are in error …
>
> (2:286)

In numerous verses, God, speaking in the third person, is seen to bless or glorify himself:

> Glory to Him who took His Servant for a night journey from the Holy Mosque to the Farther Mosque, whose precincts We blessed, so that We might show him some of Our signs: He is the one who hears and sees.
>
> (17:1)

Once again, note that in a remarkable medley of various forms of speech, God, in 17:1, above, starts speaking in the third person: 'Glory to Him who took His servant … '. The narrative then switches in the same verse to first person plural: 'whose precincts We blessed … '. It changes once again to third person: 'He is the One Who hears and sees … '.

Whether spoken in the first or third person, the text has often been taken to be the speech of God, even when He is glorifying Himself. In many cases, however, it is impossible not to see the text as the spoken words of someone other than Him. The following verse, for example, must be seen as the speech of Muḥammad:

> Clear proofs have come to you from your Lord. Anyone who sees clearly, it is to his own gain; and anyone who is blind it is to his own loss. I am not here to watch over you.
>
> (6:104)

These clearly are Muḥammad's words, as evident from 'I am not here to watch over you.' The implication of this has not eluded translator Yusuf

Ali, who has imagined the word 'Say' at the beginning of the verse. He further put the verse in quotation marks, so as to make the entire verse look like the words of God, pure and simple. Other translators have refused to go for such a dissimulation.

In verse 21:112, not reproduced here, Yusuf Ali again uses 'Say', instead of 'He said', at the beginning, making the entire verse the speech of God. This is quite arbitrary. Other translators correctly translate the Arabic *Qāla* at the beginning of the verse as 'He said'. The 'he' here refers to the Prophet, which makes the verse *his* speech, not God's.

The following verses, among many more, are unequivocally the words of Muḥammad, not God:

> And whatever you may differ on, the decision is God's: in Him I put my trust and to Him I return.
>
> (42:10)

And:

> Hasten then to God: I am a clear warner from Him to you.
>
> (51:50)

Both God and Muḥammad are speaking in the following verse:

> (I am commanded) to recite the Koran and if one accepts the guidance he does it for his own soul and if one goes astray, say: "I am but a warner."
>
> (27:92)

'I am commanded' has been taken from the preceding verse. When we put it together with the first part of this verse, we have 'I am commanded … for his own soul'; these are the Prophet's words. The part of this verse that says, 'and if one goes astray, say "I am but a warner"', can only be God's words.

Sometimes, even where God is unambiguously addressing Muḥammad, the address itself can be considerably puzzling.

Here, for example, is God asking the Prophet to:

> Say: 'O my servants who believe! Fear your Lord. Good is the reward for those who do good in this world' ...
>
> (39:10)

Throughout the Koran, humans are referred to as servants of God. Nowhere does the Prophet address the believers as his servants. And yet here is God asking his Prophet to address those who believe as 'My servants'. It appears that traditional translators do not see any oddity here; nor do they offer any explanation. [48] To a modern reader wishing to understand the Koran, it is nevertheless a highly perplexing speech.

This is repeated in another verse in the same *sūra*:

> Say: 'O my Servants who have been prodigal regarding their souls! despair not of the mercy of God: surely God forgives all sins' ...
>
> (39:53)

Similarly puzzling is the following verse:

> Do they take intercessors besides God? Say: 'What, even if they have no power whatever and no understanding?'
>
> (39:43)

'They' in the second line apparently refers to the idols the pagans worshipped. The difficulty arises with the word 'intercessor'. In all the translations I have gone through, this is the English word used to translate the Arabic word *shāfāā'*. It is to God that intercessions are supposed to be made; for example, by the Prophet, on behalf of the sinners. Here, God himself is presented as an intercessor, a word that presupposes someone to whom intercession is to be made. The very definition of God should make this impossible.

The difficulty reappears in the verse that follows (39:44). In his translation, Yusuf Ali seems to recognise the difficulty here and

[48] Three of the English translations I have consulted use 'servants'; one English translation uses 'bondmen'. Bengali translations use very similar expressions.

parenthetically adds 'the right to grant' before the word 'intercession'. But the addition is uncalled for, and others translators do not use it.

Here is Arberry:

> Say: 'To God belongs intercession altogether' ...

Pickthall's translation is:

> Say: 'Unto God belongeth all intercession' ...

None of the other translations I have looked into use the convenient 'the right to grant'.

The question of whose speech, precisely, a particular verse is, becomes acute where God is seen to swear by His own name. There are numerous verses of this genre in the Koran. The following is an example:[49]

> But no! I swear by the Lord of the Easts and Wests – that surely We are able to bring in their place others better than them; and We shall not be overcome.
>
> (70:40–41)

It is difficult to see God swearing by His own name. The difficulty is compounded by God swearing by the Lord of the East and the West.

In the following verse, God is speaking to Muḥammad and swearing 'by thy Lord', as He promises to gather the wrongdoers together:

> So, by thy Lord, We shall certainly gather them together.
>
> (19:68)

In the Koranic text, read as the word of God, God adulates Himself and proclaims His power, glory, and greatness in numerous instances. The following verse, in the absence of quotation marks in the original, clearly contains the direct words of God:

---

[49] Koran/Arberry. Both Koran/Pickthall and Qur'ān/Muhiuddin use 'I swear' at the beginning of the verse. Yusuf Ali uses 'I do call to witness'.

> O people! Serve your Lord, who created you and those who came before you, so that you may learn righteousness.
> (2:21)

There is a breath-taking array of such verses. The following is a small selection:

> God! There is no god but He; He will surely gather you together On the Day of Judgment, about which there is no doubt …
> (4:87)

> Praise be to God, who created the heavens and the earth, and made the darkness and the light …
> (6:1)

> Your Lord is God, who created the heaven and the earth … Blessed be God, the Lord of the Worlds!
> (7:54)

> The seven heavens and the earth, and all those there, declare His glory:There is not a thing that does not celebrate His praise …
> (17:44)

> So glory to Him in whose hands is the dominion of all things …
> (36:83)

> The heavens are almost rent asunder from above them And the angels celebrate the praises of their Lord, …
> (42:5)

The following verse is noteworthy in its sweeping adulation of God, which, in the Arabic, rises to a crescendo absent in the translation:

> He is God, besides Him there is no other god; the Sovereign; the Holy; the fountain of Peace; the Guardian; the Preserver of Safety, the Mighty, the irresistible, the Supreme: glory to God! …
>
> (59:23)

Metaphorical hyperbole reaches new heights in the following verse:

> Say: 'If the ocean were ink for the words of my Lord, sooner would the ocean be exhausted than would the words of my Lord, even if we added another ocean, like it as aid.'
>
> (18:109)

The list of verses where God praises or adulates Himself can easily be lengthened. One final example should be sufficient here. Muslims are required to begin their ritual prayer with recitation of the first *sūra* of the Koran, the *al-Fātiḥa*. Read as a servant's prayer to God, it makes eminent and straightforward sense:

> Praise be to God, the lord of all Being;[50] Most Gracious, Most Merciful; Master of the Day of Judgment. Thee do we worship, and thy help do we seek; guide us on the right path; the path of those on whom thou hast bestowed thy favours, not those upon whom wrath has been brought down and those who go astray.
>
> (1:1–7)

Read as the words of God, all these verses land us in an enigma of God praising Himself. It is far easier for us to see the verses as Muḥammad's words.

Reading these verses of adulation as coming directly from God might have struck even the earliest followers of the Prophet as something curious. There is at least one *ḥadith* that might be seen as a partial response. The

[50] Some translators have used 'the worlds' or 'all creatures' instead. 'The worlds' implies the existence of worlds other than the earth. There was no concept of worlds beyond the earth in the seventh century.

ḥadith reports the Prophet as having said, rather cryptically, 'And there is none who likes to be praised more than Allah.'[51]

Still, the phenomenon will strike modern readers as highly unusual. The traditional response, on occasions when such matters come up for discussion at all, is that God wishes His servants to say these words of adulation. This of course brings these words more in line with the servant-master relationship between humans and God. This also makes them words of humans.

There are, however, a large number of verses in the Koran that can only be the direct speech of a master; and yet, they are utterly human in tone and timbre. These verses express feelings that are all too human: anger, hate, resignation, and even frustration and vindictiveness. These are sentiments we would not associate with one who is omnipotent, omniscient, and infinite. The verses that follow illustrate this.

For the unbelievers who keep refusing to turn to God's path:

> God has set a seal in their hearts and on their hearing, and on their eyes is a covering; and a severe penalty awaits them.
>
> (2:7)

The imagery of an angry and vindictive master is plainly in evidence here. Instead of guiding the recalcitrant human, God sets a seal on his heart and hearing. He goes further:

> In their hearts is a sickness; and God has increased their sickness ...
>
> (2:10)

In the same *sūra,* He uses a poetic parable to even greater effect:

> Their parable is that of a man who lighted a fire; when it lit all around him, God took away their light and left them in total darkness so they could not see.
>
> (2:17)

---

[51] al-Bukhāri, vol. 9, 301.

The imagery of a forlorn man fighting darkness in a desolate cave by making a fire, which God then snatches away, is truly amazing but hardly edifying. The verse is then followed by this burst of frustration on God's part:

> Deaf, dumb, and blind: so they will not return.
>
> (2:18)

There is curse:

> Those who disbelief, and die in a state of disbelief – on them is the curse of God, the angels, and all mankind;
>
> (2:161)

There is resignation:

> How shall God guide those who disbelieved after they believed and bore witness that the Messenger was true and clear signs came to them? God guides not a people unjust.
>
> (3:86)

There is vengeance:

> Say: 'He has power to send punishments on you, from above you and from below, and throw you in confusion, and to make some of you taste the violence (of one sect) against another.'
>
> (6:65)

Natural calamities were seen as evidence of God's vengeance and anger, perhaps in all societies, including pagan Arab, and the above verse makes good use of the fear associated with these disasters. Man-made calamities were hardly less prevalent. Intertribal strife and bloodshed were permanent features of Arab societies at the advent of Islam, and a constant source of human misery. The above verse sees this as one more instrument available to God for the purpose of wreaking vengeance on disobedient peoples.

The following verses stand out as vents for God's anger and frustration:

> Surely the worst of beasts in the sight of God are the deaf and the dumb, those who do not understand.
>
> (8:22)

> You think that most of them listen or understand? They are only like cattle. Nay, they are further astray from the path.
>
> (25:44)

God subdues by terror:

> ... We do not send Signs, except to frighten. [52]
>
> (17:59)

> ... We put terror into them, but it only increases their disobedience!
>
> (17:60)

God jeers in human fashion. Here He is, addressing communities facing God's punishment and consequently fleeing their homes:

> Do not run! Return to the good things in life you had and to your dwellings; ...
>
> (21:13)

The following verse is akin to the childhood threat of the loss of a beloved toy. This should be familiar to any of us recollecting the imminent loss of a precious toy to a benefactor:

> Shall We then take away the Message from you, because you Are a prodigal people?
>
> (43:5)

[52] Some translations have instead used 'by way of terror' or 'warning' here.

Here is promise of punishment to unbelievers, where the Prophet is seen as being unable to turn them to the right path by himself:

> So leave Me alone with them who reject the message: We shall little by little get hold of them that they would not perceive of it.
>
> (68:44)

In these verses, Almighty God is clearly challenging tiny mortals, in the mode of one mortal challenging another:

> And they plotted, God too plotted. And God is the best of plotters.
>
> (3:54)

> Those before them plotted, but all plots are God's.
>
> (13:42)

> As for them, they are scheming, and I am scheming.
>
> (86:15–16)

And there is even despair on the part of God:

> Alas for (my) servants! Never does an apostle come to them but they mock him.
>
> (36:30)

The 'Alas' in the English translation used here does not equal the sense of despair in the critical Arabic words *ya hāsrat*. The Arabic *hāsrat* conveys a sigh of anguish coming from the human breast.

While the above verses ring with human sentiments in their various manifestations, and thus appear strange coming from the Almighty, to the modern mind, the ones that follow are truly difficult to reconcile with godliness. Modern sensibility would recoil from this description of punishment to be meted out to the sinner on the Day of Judgement:

> Nor has he any food except foul pus, that none but the sinners eat.[53]
>
> (69:36–37)

In the following verses, the wrath of God is wholly undiscriminating. It is so frightening that innocent children get hoary-headed in terror, mothers forget to nurse their babies, and pregnant women, sinners or not, suffer miscarriages:

> How then shall you, if you disbelieve, guard yourself on the day that will make children hoary-headed?
>
> (73:17)

> … every mother giving suck will forget her suckling, and every pregnant one will lay down her burden …
>
> (22:2)

There are other graphic depictions of the humiliation of man. Humans are, after all, God's own creation. In some of the verses, the sinners are likened to cattle, yoked and dragged.

In a well-known and oft-recited *sūra* of the Koran, the following verse stands out:

> We have placed fetters round their necks reaching up to their chins, so that their heads are forced up …
>
> (36:8)

Ironically, this *sūra* is traditionally among those read aloud at the bedside of the sick, and also as part of the rituals following death. This *sūra* begins with verses on the Koran as a divine revelation from God, and Muḥammad's mission (verses 2 through 6). The above verse quickly follows the opening verses (2 through 6). I have often wondered about this. Could this humiliating depiction of man be a source of strength for the sick or salvation for the dead? People recite it without knowing

---

[53] Yusuf Ali translates the punishment as 'consumption of corruption from the washing of wounds'.

its meaning; they sweep it along in the chant, without realising the incongruity of it in relation to the occasion. I have asked people well versed in the Koran about this, as it is extremely odd to me. I never received a satisfactory answer.

There is inevitability about such retributions. The following verse is among God's words on this:

> … And the world of thy Lord shall be fulfilled: I shall fill hell with jinns and men all together.
>
> (11:119)

Among the largest categories of God's speech are the verses of the Koran addressed to Muḥammad the Prophet. To Muslims, it should be emphasised, Muḥammad is the most ideal among human beings, and far above normal human faults and foibles. As we read the Koran we shall have occasion to see him in the light of that high ideal. The verses that follow often show him as a human in dire need of warning and comfort. Some of them are words of consolation. Some are guides to his conduct, the tones of which vary according to the circumstances in which Muḥammad found himself. It is easy to find in these verses a sense of resignation, realism, indignation, and/or frustration on the part of God Himself, which we have seen earlier. But it is also easy to find in them reflections of the state of mind of a man who is also a prophet. Gabriel's message would not seem connected to such reflection.

The following is a selective reading of these verses, starting with the first substantive *sūra*. The importance of these passages calls for a fairly extensive reading.

Here is the first such verse:

> As for the unbelievers, it is the same to them whether you warn them or do not warn them; they will not believe.
>
> (2:6)

Such pessimism in a Medinan *sūra* looks unusual because, by that time, many years had passed since Muḥammad first started to propagate Islam, and some success had been achieved.

And yet, here again, we read:

So if they believe as you believe, they are indeed on the right path; but if they turn back, they are clearly in schism; God will suffice you against them …

(2:137)

You are not responsible for guiding them; but God sets on the right path whomsoever He wishes …

(2:272)

It is not for you to decide whether He turns towards them again or chastises them …

(3:128)

And your people reject this, and this is the Truth. Say: I am not a guardian over you.

(6:66)

If God had wished, they would not have associated others with Him: But We have not made you their keeper. You are not their guardian.

(6:107)

Let not what they say grieve you …

(10:65)

If it had been your Lord's will, all of those on earth would have believed. Would you then compel mankind into believe?

(10:99)

Most of mankind will not be believers, however eagerly you might wish it.

(12:103)

And be patient for thy patience is from God; nor grieve over them. And do not distress yourself over their plots.

(16:127)

> ... We have not sent you to be a dispenser of their affairs for them.
>
> (17:54)

> ... The Messenger's duty is only to preach the clear Message.
>
> (24:54)

> And those who take as protectors others besides Him, God watches over them; and you not a guardian over them.
>
> (42:6)

> We know what they say; and you not one to compel them. So admonish with the Qur'an those who fear my warning.
>
> (50:45)

> And bear with them over what they say and part with them in dignity.
>
> (73:10)

> Thou art not charged to oversee them.
>
> (88:22)

The above verses are parts of *sūras* with diverse themes, of which comforting the Prophet is one. There are *sūras* which are devoted in their entirety to comforting him. *Sūra* 93 (*Dhuḥā*) is said to have been inspired in the very early days of the Prophet when, after the first revelations, no further revelations were coming to him. The intermission, or *fātrā,* was agonising to Muḥammad. He wondered if God had abandoned him. And then, one day, inevitably, came the assurance (in the eleven verses of *Sūra Dhuha,* not reproduced here) that his Lord had not abandoned him, and neither was He displeased. *Sūra* 94 (*Inshirāh*) was another personal morale booster, ending in the oft-quoted assurance that for every difficulty there is relief. Both verses can easily be envisaged as reflections of Muḥammad's all-too-human self-doubt, followed by self-assurance.

Also personal is the background of the next *sūra.* Muḥammad had no male child. Khadījah bore him two sons who died in their infancy. In a society where having male progeny was a matter of prestige and pride, as well of necessity, this provided the Prophet's Meccan detractors one more opportunity to ridicule him. In *Sūra* 108 (*Kauthar*) God assures him abundance of other things far better, and denounces his enemies. Would not Muḥammad the man occasionally console himself as well as denounce his detractors?

Some of the verses comforting and counselling the Prophet have sometimes been taken to imply liberalism and tolerance in Islam. Verses such as 2:272, 3:128, 6:66, 6:107, 10:99, 17:54, and/or 73:10, and verses saying to the Prophet that he is no disposer of affairs of man, or that his duty is only to preach and nothing more, all seem to fall in this category. This is, however, an entirely unwarranted interpretation of such verses, which were inspired in particular circumstances; in addition, it is easy to find many verses in the Koran which dispense very different ideas. In practice, the Prophet was certainly a 'disposer' of others' affairs, and he certainly did more than preach.

It is of course people in general to whom most of the words of God are considered to have been addressed, often directly, and sometimes through the medium of the Prophet. Sometimes the people – *nāās*, in Arabic – are directly addressed; often the message is clearly meant for them, even where they are not so addressed. The messages themselves come in a wide variety of themes. They come in often bewildering ways. And they came to mankind from the heart of a man passing through changing circumstances and perceptions.

Chapter 4
Juxtaposition of Disparate Themes

The Koran calls itself an easily understandable book. It repeats this refrain in numerous verses:

> ... These are verses of the Qur-ān, – a manifest Book
>
> (27:1)

> (This is) a Book the verses of which have been explained in detail ...
>
> (41:3)

And God swears:

> By the Book that makes things clear,
>
> (43:2)

Yet, to an inquiring reader, the text of the Koran is often far from easy to understand. It is unlike any other book, lay or divine. Many, if not most, of the verses need an exegetic elaboration, and sometimes the explanation provided by the exegetes remains inadequate or unconvincing. Conflicting exegeses abound, and this does not help.

One of the major sources of the difficulty is the juxtaposition of ideas and imperatives that can often be puzzling. A modern reader will often find an absence of the logical sequence normally required of every book, and this pertains to the arguments, directives, and even plain narratives of the Koran.

This chapter highlights some of the areas where such juxtaposition is particularly hard to understand. It also brings into focus, once again, the critical role played by humans in the compilation of the Koran and the shaping of it into a book to be read and understood.

Verse 2:189 begins with the theme of the new moon:

> They ask you about the new moons. Say 'They set the time for people and for the Pilgrimage ...'
>
> (2:189)

There follows immediately, in the same verse, a totally new theme of the proper manner of entering a house:

> It is no piety to enter your houses from the back: it is piety to fear God. So you enter houses through proper doors, and fear God – that you may prosper.
>
> (2:189)

We would look in vain for a connection between the two parts of the same verse. The verse is then followed by one concerning *jihad*:

> Fight in the cause of God those who fight you, but do not transgress limits; For God does not like transgressors.
>
> (2:190)

Consider, once again, verse 5:3, which we read earlier. We read the first half of the long verse dealing with forbidden food, which includes carrion, blood, flesh of swine, and flesh of animals which have been slaughtered after invoking a name which is not God's. This long list of forbidden food is immediately followed by the following, in an unbroken narrative:

> ... This day those who disbelieve have despaired of your religion. Do not fear them; fear Me. This day I have perfected for you your religion, completed my favour to you and bestowed on you Islam as your religion.
>
> (5:3)

Chronologically, this part of the verse is said to have been inspired as the last piece of revelation,[54] and as such, it has a profundity that sits oddly at the end of the veritably mundane list of forbidden food. The incongruity increases as the matter of forbidden food is taken up and elaborated upon again, immediately afterwards, also in the same verse:

> But if one is compelled by hunger, with no wish to transgress, God is surely Forgiving, Merciful.
>
> (5:3)

The rise from the mundane to the sublime, followed by a descent to the mundane again, *in the same verse* is truly remarkable. None of the exegeses I have read of these verses mention these juxtapositions, much less discuss them. One exegesis, for example, goes into great detail (a few pages in length) on the matter of the items of forbidden food, and then goes on to discuss 'This day I have perfected for you your religion … ', with no explanation of the apparent oddity of the transition.[55] The oddity was perhaps not lost on at least one translator, who introduced a break in the narrative after the list of forbidden food, and another break after the sentence on God choosing Islam as the believers' religion.[56] This is of course quite arbitrary, and the commentator does not offer an explanation for it.

Verse 6:118 again concerns food, this time permitted items:

> So eat of that on which God's name has been pronounced …
>
> (6:118)

Note, however, that this follows a rather long narrative (verses 6:111–117) on the disobedience of men, their impiety, and a call to follow God's path. Verse 6:117 proclaims: 'Surely your Lord knows best who strays from his Path … ' The 'So' at the beginning of verse 6:118, above, even appears to suggest a link between the verse and the themes of the preceding verses, where no link appears to exist. The bathos of the descent from the discussion on piety to that on permitted food is hard to escape,

[54] See Chapter 2.
[55] Qur'ān/Muhiuddin.
[56] Qur'ān/Yusuf Ali.

unless of course God's 'path' is no more divine that the eating of *ḥalal* meat, an interpretation that traditionalist Muslims themselves will find impossible to accept.

Or consider the following verse:

> To God belongs the most beautiful names: so call Him by them and shun those who blaspheme His names …
>
> (7:180)

This is, however, wedged between verses that have no apparent relationship with the beautiful names of God. Verse 7:179 proclaims: 'Many are the jinns and men We have made for hell' … ; while verse 7:181 could not be more different in its message: 'And of those We have created a community who direct others with truth, and do justice therewith.'

Jihad is the single theme of the following verse:

> O you who believe! Fight the unbelievers who are near you, and let them find firmness in you: and know that God is with the god fearing.
>
> (9:123)

Yet the very next verse has no relationship with *jihad*, and is, instead, devoted to faith and the Koran:

> And whenever a sūra is revealed some of them say: 'Which of you has it strengthened in faith?' But indeed those who believe, their faith is increased. And they rejoice.
>
> (9:124)

Verse 13:11 begins thus:

> For him there are angels before him and behind him, guarding him by the command of God …
>
> (13:11)

This is immediately followed, in the same verse, by:

> Surely God never changes the condition of a people, until they change what is in themselves,
>
> (13:11)

The above verse is a practical advice of great value to any community or nation, but it has no apparent connection to the preceding sentence in the very same verse.

A cluster of verses, beginning with 17:31, enjoins men not to kill their children, commit adultery, take a life except for just cause, grab the property of orphans, or walk the earth with insolence. These verses also require men to give full weight and measure in trade. The last of these verses reads:

> These are of the wisdom which thy Lord has revealed to you: associate not another god with God, or you will be cast into hell, reproached and cast away.[57]
>
> (17:39)

This is then followed by an entirely unconnected verse:

> Has then your[58]Lord favoured you with sons and taken for Himself daughters from among the angels? Surely, this is a monstrous thing you say!
>
> (17:40)

Verses 17:61–65 are a narration of Satan's intransigence and insolence, and provide an exchange between God and Satan.

The verse following them is on an entirely different plane:

> Your Lord is He who speeds the ship for you on the sea, in order that you may seek of His bounty. He is unto you most Merciful.
>
> (17:66)

---

[57] Here, it is extraordinary that the Prophet himself is warned that he would be thrown into hell if he took another object of worship, along with God. This is unambiguously addressed to him, in the singular.

[58] This is addressed to the pagans.

Verses 27:83–85 are narratives on the Day of Judgement. These verses are followed by the words below, in 27:86:

> Do not they see that We made the Night for them to rest in and the day to see. Surely there is sign in this for those who believe.
>
> (27:86)

It is difficult to see a connection between this verse and the verses describing the Day of Judgement. After the apparently abrupt break, the next verse, 27:87, returns to the theme of the Day of Judgement, when the trumpet will be blown.

The following verse is a narrative on Moses:

> And indeed We gave Moses the Book: but disputes arose in it. Had it not been for a decision given beforehand by your Lord, the differences would have been resolved between them.
>
> (41:45)

There is then this abrupt shift of theme in the next verse:

> Whoever does good, it is for his own soul; and whoever does evil, It is to his own loss. And your Lord is never unjust to His servants.
>
> (41:46)

The theme is not developed, however, and in the subsequent verse, we find yet another group of very different themes:

> It is He who has the knowledge of the Hour. No fruit emerges from its sheath without His knowledge, nor any female conceives and brings forth.
>
> (41:47)

Verse 42:48 is one of many verses in the Koran where the Prophet is consoled and comforted by God: he was not to grieve; his duty was only to convey the message.

The next verse concerns a very different subject:

> To God belongs the kingdom of the heaven and the earth: He creates what He pleases. He grants whomsoever He pleases females and to whomsoever He pleases males.
>
> (42:49)

Here is a narrative on bestowing some women with children and keeping other women barren, all by the will of God:

> Or He grants them both male and females, and He leaves barren whom He will: Surely He is all-knowing and all-powerful.
>
> (42:50)

A modern reader would wonder why the omnipotent and yet merciful God would indulge in what appears to be totally capricious. And if there were any plans of His concerning childbearing females, we must wonder what it was, especially in the cases of mothers who bore evil sons throughout history, whose barbarism inflicted huge suffering on mankind.

To turn once again to the juxtaposition of verses, the next verse goes on to a theme that could not be more different:

> It is not up to any man that God should speak to him except by inspiration, or from behind a veil, or by sending a Messenger to reveal by His permission what He pleases …
>
> (42:51)

Verses 46:29–32 are a narrative on a company of jinns listening to the Koran, accepting Islam, and warning their companions of the grave error of not accepting the Prophet's invitation to God. These verses appear to have no connection, however, with either the verse that precedes them or the verse that follows.

Thus, Verse 46:28 reads:

> Why then no help came from those they took for god besides God – those they worshipped in order to be drawn closer to God? No, they failed them. And this was their lie and this was what they invented.
>
> (46:28)

Verse 46:33, on the other hand, says:

> Do not they see that God, who created the heavens and the earth, and is never tired with their creation, is able to give life to the dead? Verily, He is the possessor of power over everything.
>
> (46:33)

Verse 61:4 proclaims God's love for those who wage *jihad*:

> Surely God loves those who fight in His way in ranks, as if they were a solid wall.
>
> (61:4)

This comes after a verse which is unconnected to it. The very next verse concerns a theme that also has nothing to do with *jihad*:

> And when Moses said to his people : 'Why do you malign me' …
>
> (61:5)

The narrative in the next verse then moves to Jesus, son of Mary.

A notable example of descent from the sublime to the mundane is verse 57:25. The first part of the verse says:

> Certainly We sent our apostles with clear proofs and sent down with them the Book and the Balance so that men might uphold justice …
>
> (57:25)

But then, in the next sentence, there is a sharp turn away from the divine to the mere base metal, iron:

> ... And We sent down Iron, in which is lies great strength and benefit for mankind.
>
> (57:25)

Verse 66:8 is a warning to all believers:

> O you who believe! Turn to God with sincere repentance: It may be your Lord will remove from you ills and admit you to the Gardens in which revers flow ...
>
> (66:8)

This is followed by an entirely unrelated exhortation to the Prophet:

> O Prophet! Strive hard against the unbelievers and the Hypocrites, and be firm against them. Their abode is hell ...
>
> (66:9)

Verses 75:16–17 stand out as an illustration of incongruous juxtaposition. The preceding long series of short verses, 75:1–15, assert the inevitability of resurrection after death and decry man's refusal to see that inevitability.

And then comes this stunning turn of narrative, a verse we have read before:

> Move not your tongue with it to hasten it. It is for us to collect it And promulgate it
>
> (75:16–17)

There are many *sūras* in the Koran, especially the longer ones (but not limited to them), that have no central or unifying theme. The narratives in these verses seem to flit from one disparate topic to another, sometimes shifting back and forth between them. Among the *sūras* answering to this description, *Sūra* 33 (*Aḥzāb*) stands out. A major aspect of the background of this *sūra* is the Battle of the Trench and the vanquishing of the tribe of Banu Qurayzah. But there are other equally significant events that this *sūra* alludes to. The interweaving of narratives concerning very different events makes this *sūra* one of the most difficult to understand without a very large measure of exegetical help. This is well worth illustrating for a meaningful reading of the Koran. (We shall return to this *sūra* later, in Chapter 14).

Modern readers will be puzzled by verse 64:11. It begins with:

> No calamity befalls, except by the leave of God:
>
> (64:11)

What follows immediately appears totally unconnected:

> And if one believes in God, his heart is guided by Him.
> For God knows all things.[59]
>
> (64:11)

Among the many Koranic descents from the sublime to the mundane is the following verse:

> O you who believe! Fulfil your obligations. Lawful to you are all four-footed animals, with the exceptions recited to you: But games are not permitted to be hunted while you are in the Sacred Precincts ...
>
> (5:1)

The above lines make a single verse in the Arabic. The critical word here is 'obligations' – *ūqūd,* in Arabic – which has also been translated as 'bond' or 'agreement'. One commentator goes into a long discourse on the

[59] Available exegeses fail to connect the two parts of the verse. Qur'ān/Yusuf Ali, for example, offers this unconvincing interpretation: 'What we consider calamities may be blessing in disguise. Pain in the body is often a signal of something wrong, which we can cure by remedial measures. So in the moral and spiritual world, we should in all circumstances hold firmly to the faith that nothing happens without God's knowledge and leave; and therefore there must be some justice and wisdom according to His great universal plan'...

inclusive nature of the word, beginning with 'the divine obligations that arise from our spiritual nature.'[60] This would make the word *ūqūd* truly sublime. Its spiritual connotation, combined with its inclusive nature, make it a weighty word indeed. Yet the very next sentence goes on to describe the kinds of animals that are permissible as food, to the exclusion of other kinds of obligations, such as the spiritual. The incongruity could not have escaped translator Yusuf Ali, who splits the verse into two stanzas and thus attempts to put some distance between the mundanely detailed second stanza and the spiritually comprehensive first. This, however, does not dispel the difficulty of the juxtaposition of the two stanzas. Other translators do not make the distinction.[61] A more traditional exegete has shorn the weighty word in question of any sublime meaning, and has seen no difficulty in defining it in the mundane terms of the four-footed animals deemed *ḥalal*.[62]

Jihad and martyrdom have a prominent place in *Sūra* 22 (*Ḥajj*). Verses 22:58–60 assure those who die in the cause of God that He will 'admit them to a place with which they will be well pleased.'

In continuation of the theme of fighting, 22:60 states:

> … And one who retaliated to no greater extent than the injury he received and was then oppressed, God will help him …
>
> (22:60)

The theme of this verse is at serious odds with the preceding idea, in 22:59, of God admitting martyrs to a place they would be pleased with. More importantly, it is impossible to understand why the next verse, 22:61, is placed where it is:

> That is because God causes night to enter into day and day into night and verily God hears and sees.
>
> (22:61)

There are numerous examples in the Koran where the sequence in the narrative is difficult to understand. We have discussed only a handful

[60] Qur'ān/Yusuf Ali.

[61] Qur'ān/Muhiuddin and Koran/Pickthall, for example.

[62] Qur'ān/Muhiuddin.

of the most important cases of disparate juxtapositions of ideas. Islamic tradition considers the Koran to be entirely the creation of the Divine. To attribute the apparent incongruities to the Divine is therefore unthinkable. This inevitably takes us back to the critical subject of the compilation of the Koran we discussed earlier. While a purely devotional reading of the Book can gloss over the problem, it becomes too important to ignore once we step beyond pure belief. A critical reader would attribute the incongruities largely to the human process of the assembly of the Koran, which necessitated contending with strips of verses inspired at different points of time and originally written on a huge assortment of materials, of every shape and size, over many years.

Chapter 5

Expeditions, Battles, and Booty

There are many verses of the Koran that must be read in the context of the many battles fought and expeditions embarked on during the lifetime of the Prophet of Islam. These verses are scattered over many *sūras* of the Book, and it is often necessary to go into history in order to link a verse to a particular event. Many readers of the Koran tend to view the battles and expeditions as one glorious sweep of divine action. The reality was far more complex. A close reading of the verses in this area and their historical background reveals the complexities. It also shines light on the life of Muḥammad – the prophet, the leader, and the man.

In the early history of Islam, in common with human history over the millennia, many battles were fought and many sieges were laid, with all the brutalities that such actions entail. Some of the battles were mere skirmishes, while others were major undertakings, the results of which would determine the future of the new faith. Some of the expeditions were similarly very small affairs, often ending in no fighting. In the Islamic tradition, expeditions waged and battles fought, big or small, have often been treated under the generic name of *ghazwa,* variously meaning 'a military expedition' or 'a holy war'. *Sahih Al-Bukhāri* treats battles, expeditions, and sieges all together in its book of *Al Maghazi,* meaning 'holy battles and deeds of the *ghazi,* or holy warriors'.[63] Somewhat oddly, at least for modern readers, it also includes a number of assassinations, presumably because these were actions to further the cause of Islam. There are only a few verses in the Koran where battles and expeditions are explicitly named. Yet these events form the background of numerous

[63] al-Bukhāri, vol. 5, 176.

verses in the Holy Book. And a long *sūra* bears the title 'Spoils of War', or 'Booty' (*Anfāl*). There are many narratives in the Koran which are impossible to understand without knowledge of battles fought and expeditions launched. Many of the directives of the Book derive from circumstances of war against the infidels.

Raiding trade caravans, circumstances permitting, was a common practice among pagan Arabs. Remarkably, such raids were among the pre-Islamic practices retained by the followers of the new religion. Economic necessity and tradition trumped moral questions of the propriety of plunder. From their refuge in Medina, the Muslims made sorties, or expeditions, of this nature, primarily against caravans of Quraysh, Muḥammad's estranged tribe. Muḥammad himself led some of these expeditions. Some of the early expeditions had the main objective of intercepting the caravans of Quraysh[64] The importance of war booty comes alive in a *ḥadith* in *Sahih Al-Bukhāri,* in which the Prophet says, 'My livelihood is under the shade of my spear.'[65]

The division of booty obtained from these raids was naturally a matter of some importance. The chain of expeditions that started soon after Muḥammad's migration to Medina began as raid for booty. Apart from *Sūra Anfāl,* verses in several other *sūras* of the Koran also make pronouncements on booty. The following verse, for example, not only makes booty permissible but also presents it as a gift of God:

> God has promised you many gains that you will acquire and He has hasten them for you and held back men's hands from you …
>
> (48:20)

The word 'gains', above, has been used by several translators and clearly means 'booty'; other translators are more straightforward, simply using 'booty'.[66]

Among the early raids that brought up the question of the division

[64] al-Tabarī, vol. 7, 15.

[65] al-Bukhāri, vol. 4, 108. The translator of the volume found it necessary to explain that 'under the shade of my spear' meant 'from war booty'.

[66] Koran/Pickthall and Qur'ān/Muhiuddin. The translation of *Anfal* as 'Voluntary Gifts' in Qur'ān/Muhammad Ali was not meant to be ironic.

of the booty among the participating Muslims, and for which historical records exist, was the one at a place called Nakhlah. A fifth of the booty from the Nakhlah expedition was earmarked for the Prophet, and the rest for the participants.[67] The earmarking of a large part of the booty – a fourth – for the tribal chief was a pre-Islamic tradition.

Since the amount of booty at the Battle of Badr was certainly far greater than in earlier Muslim expeditions, its division was probably a matter of more than usual contention. This is reflected in *Sūra Anfāl,* which begins with the emphatic statement:

> They ask you about spoils of war. Say: 'Spoils are for God and the Apostle; so fear God, and keep straight the relations between yourselves, and obey God and His Apostle, if you are believers.'
>
> (8:1)

This is followed by verses 8:2–6, which leave no doubt in the minds of the believers that this dispensation of God must be obeyed.

The Koran set rules of division of the booty in the same *sūra,* after the Battle of Badr:

> And know that of whatever booty that you acquire, a fifth is assigned to God and to the Apostle, and to near relatives, orphans, the needy, and the wayfarer, ...
>
> (8:41)

A final verse on booty in *Sūra Anfāl* calls on the believers who had just won the battle to enjoy what they had just gained from it:

> So enjoy whatever booty you have acquired, lawful and good; but fear God; for God is All-forgiving, All-Merciful.
>
> (8:69)

Since the pre-Islamic Arab practice was for the chief of the tribe to receive a fourth of the spoils of war, the above must be considered an

[67] al-Tabarī, vol. 7, 20.

improvement, especially in consideration of the mention of its use for charity. The attraction of booty could often verge on the purely venal, as the following example shows. As the Prophet led his companions on the pilgrimage to Mecca that resulted in the Treaty of Hudaybiyah,[68] he asked some of the desert tribes to accompany him. The tribes vacillated and ultimately stayed put. The Koran castigates the desert Arabs for this. Shortly afterwards, the Prophet led an expedition to Khaybar. This time, the desert Arabs who had declined to join the Prophet on his pilgrimage were rather keen to join, allured by the prospect of rich booty. Those who participated in the pilgrimage and other expeditions naturally resented the participation of the desert Arabs in the Khaybar expedition, since it would have reduced the loyal participants' share of the spoils of war. But God relented and promised them 'goodly reward' if they showed obedience now:

> Say to the desert Arabs who lagged behind: "You will be called upon to fight against a people of great prowess till they submit. Then if you obey, God will give you goodly reward.
>
> (48:16)

Battles were of course not fought for spoils alone, even though the spoils almost always remained an important adjunct. Three of the most discussed battles fought by the Prophet were important for the very survival of the new faith. They inspired many of the verses of the Koran that pronounce in detail the conduct of wars, the rewards of martyrdom, and the punishment for those fighting against the true religion.

The expedition to Nakhlah is of considerable importance not only because the booty it generated gave rise to the question of the division of spoils of war, but also, and perhaps more importantly, because it formed the background of one of the first pronouncements in the Koran on the conduct of war. In the month of Rajab of the second year of the *hijrah* (AH 2), the Prophet sent a group of about ten men to Nakhlah, somewhere between Mecca and Al-Tai'f, to gather information on Quraysh. They were under no orders to fight. They did, however, encounter a small

[68] Described later in this chapter.

Quraysh caravan. The two antagonists were in all probability equally scared of each other, limiting the possibility of a fight. Furthermore, it was the month of Rajab, one of the four sacred months in which fighting was prohibited by Arab tradition (the three other months being Muharram, Zul-qa'd, and Zul-ḥajj). Nevertheless, the Muslim raiders did attack the caravan – albeit after some hesitation – killing one of its members and capturing two of them.

When the news of the fighting reached the Prophet, he expressed his displeasure. He did not permit the raiding party to fight; their mission was only to gather information. That the Muslims fought during a sacred month was a disgrace in the eyes of their enemies. Soon, however, a Koranic revelation came to their rescue:

> They ask you about fighting in the Prohibited Month. Say: 'Fighting in it is heinous offence. But more heinous in the sight of God is to hinder men from the path of God, to deny Him and the Sacred Mosque, and turning people out of it. And persecution is graver than slaughter' ...
> (2:217)

This in effect rationalised the killing and the taking captive of the two Quraysh, by referring to injustices to Muslims, even ones in which the individuals killed and captured here did not necessarily have a role. History is replete with instances of innocent individuals punished for collective offence, and this was perhaps no exception, apart from the fact that it now received divine imprimatur. The captives were finally released to Quraysh on payment of ransom, another of the old Arab traditions that the Muslims continued to follow religiously. The killing and taking of captives at Nakhlah served as the precursor to the first major battle the Muslims fought against the polytheists, the Battle of Badr, fought in the second year of the *hijrah*.

Although the Battle of Badr has been glorified in Islamic tradition as the first battle of the Muslims against the infidels, who were routed by a numerically weak enemy, its origin is quite mundane. The battle has also been seen as one where the Muslims fought a defensive engagement against the polytheist Quraysh, who came all the way from Mecca with the express objective of annihilating the Muslims and putting an end to the new faith. The historical circumstances leading to armed conflict are more complex.

A caravan of Quraysh led by Abū Sufyān, the Meccan chief and a cousin of Muḥammad, was returning from Syria, laden with merchandise. The story has often been told. Here is one commentator's spin on the story: 'The design of the Meccans was to gather all the resources they could, and overwhelming force, to crush and annihilate Muḥammad and his party. To this end, Abū Sufyan was leading a rich-laden caravan from Syria to Mecca.'[69] The commentator thus considers a normal trade mission on the part of a trading community as preparation for war. This appears far-fetched, and historians do not seem to agree with his version of the story. He imputes a direct motivation for which there could not be any proof. The well-known trade route between Mecca and Syria lay close to Medina. According to some accounts, when Muḥammad heard that the caravan of Quraysh was in the vicinity, he said to the Muslims, 'This is the caravan of Quraysh, containing their wealth; so go out against it, and it is to be hoped that God will give it to you as booty.'[70] The response of his followers was mixed. 'The people answered his summons, some eagerly, others reluctantly because they had not thought that the Apostle would go to war.'[71] The primary objective of the expedition was to attack the caravan, and there was probably little active opposition to it. While the Meccans were preparing to come to the assistance of their caravan, the Prophet was proceeding to Badr on the Syria-Mecca trade route, where he hoped to waylay Abū Sufyān.[72]

When it became apparent that this would lead to full-fledged fighting, the Prophet asked his followers for their advice. The leading followers from among the Muhājirūn,[73] including Abū Bakr and 'Umar, readily and forcefully agreed to fight. The Prophet was initially less sure about the willingness of the Anṣar to fight. According to Ibn Ishaq, he was afraid

[69] Qur'ān/Yusuf Ali, n. 352 to verse 3:13.

[70] al-Tabarī, vol. 7, 35.

[71] Ibn Ishaq, 289.

[72] Martin Lings, *Muḥammad: His Life Based on the Earliest Sources* (London: George Allen & Unwin, 1983), 140.

[73] The Muhājirūn are the followers of Muḥammad who migrated from Mecca to Medina. The Anṣar (literally 'helpers') are Muḥammad's Muslim allies in Medina.

that the Anṣar would not feel obliged to help him unless he was attacked by an enemy in their own territory of Medina.[74] But they too agreed to follow him to the battle, having been roused by Sa'd b. Mu'ād, one of the most devoted followers of Muḥammad from among the Anṣar.

The Battle of Badr is an important background to *Sūra Anfāl*. Behind the divine words, again, lay many human doubts, decisions, and actions that were far removed from divine ones. And this is quite beside the unholy nature of a war for booty. As the Prophet was leading his men, for example, he came to a village between two mountains. On being told the names of the mountains, which indeed had rather unsavoury names, he saw in them bad omen and avoided proceeding between them. This story portrays Muḥammad as a deeply superstitious man. The seeking of the advice of his followers in the decision to fight, mentioned above, plainly suggests the importance the Prophet attached to human motivations. The Prophet was also fully receptive to human suggestions about battle strategies and was not relying on inspiration alone. Thus, the critical decision to stop up the wells within reach of the Quraysh caravan in order to deprive them of water was done on the advice of men from the tribe of Banu Salama.[75] Expressing doubts about the viability of the Prophet's initial choice of place for positioning of his fighters, a man from the tribe reportedly said to him, 'O Messenger of God, do you consider that this is the position in which God has placed you, and that it is not for us to move it forward or back, or do you consider that it is a matter of judgement, tactics and stratagem.' The Prophet replied, 'Certainly not; it is a matter of judgement, tactics and stratagem.'[76] Depriving the enemy access to water might seem a less-than-noble action, but it worked. And it was a purely human battle strategy.

In the Koran and in early historical literature of Islam, such 'judgment, tactics and stratagem' have often been termed acts of God. Even individual acts of killing of the unbelievers have been so described. In almost all cases, the events can be explained and understood primarily in human terms.

The news of the impending Muslim attack on the caravan soon

---

[74] Ibn Ishaq, 294

[75] Ibid. 296.

[76] al-Tabarī, vol. 7, 47.

reached Abū Sufyān, who took alarm and sent a messenger to Mecca, calling on Quraysh to come post-haste in defence of their property. Meanwhile, having sensed the presence of the Muslims from Medina, Abū Sufyān left the vicinity of Badr and made for the sea coast. This put the caravan out of immediate reach of the Muslims. Quraysh, already angered by the Nakhlah incident, were spurred into action by the new menace to their livelihood and prosperity. In the battle that followed, the Muslims were outnumbered by the Meccan forces, 3 to 1. The size of the Muslim forces is said to have been only about three hundred, while Quraysh mustered a thousand men.

There are reasons for supposing that many Quraysh were primarily interested in preventing their caravan from falling into the hands of the Muslims, not in fighting them, even though there were elements who did want to fight. Thus, after he managed to lead the caravan to safety, Abū Sufyān suggested to his compatriots from Mecca that since they had come to defend the caravan which was now safe, they should go back home. That counsel of the most prominent chief of Quraysh does seem to suggest prevarication. A number of people, belonging to one confederate clan, did go back.[77] There were also expressions of sentiment against fighting and killing people who, after all, belonged to the same tribe, as the Prophet and his Meccan companions of course did. All of this tends to suggest that, despite their numerical superiority, Quraysh did not appear as the monolith of a determined enemy. The disadvantageous terrain that they stood on at Badr, the lack of drinking water (largely thanks to the Muslim strategy of stopping up of the wells within reach of their enemy), and the long trek from Mecca must also have taken their toll on the Quraysh ability to fight. The Muslims, on the other hand, stood solidly with the Prophet, who had made a solemn promise of Paradise to each and every one killed on that day. In other words, each Muslim fought to either win or die a martyr.

Inspired after the event,[78] many of the verses of *Sūra Anfāl* reflect on various aspects of the Battle of Badr. They range from commentaries on the decisions and actions of the Prophet and his followers, to the ways in

---

[77] al-Tabarī, vol. 7, 46.

[78] Ibid. vol. 7, 80, informs: 'When the events of Badr were over, God revealed *al-Anfal* (*Sūra* 8) in its entirety.'

which God guided and helped the believers, to sharing of the booty and taking of prisoners of war, to urging the believers to wage *jihad*.

Muḥammad's primary objective was the caravan of Quraysh, not war. Armed conflict became inevitable only after Quraysh marched to defend their caravan. Verse 8:7 puts this somewhat differently:

> And when God promised you that one of the two parties would be yours, you wished for the one unarmed. But God desired to establish the truth by His words and to cut off the roots of the unbelievers.
>
> (8:7)

Capture of the caravan without the need to fight was of course the preferred alternative, which the verse alludes to. The inevitability of war, once the decision was taken to attack the caravan, is presented here as divine intervention that led the Prophet to choose war which 'cut off the roots of the unbelievers.'

Some of the actions of the Prophet and his followers were similarly seen in retrospect as divine intervention, as in the following verse:

> You did not slay them; it was God who did. And it was not you who threw, but God threw.
>
> (8:17)

The sentence 'And it was not you who threw, but God threw' is poetic in Arabic. (It must be read in Arabic to appreciate the poetry: *Wā māā rāmayta ez rāmaita wā lakinna Allāhā rāmāā.*) This verse is a reference to the story of the Prophet throwing a handful of dust at the enemy in the thick of the battle, presumably causing confusion among them.

In this *sūra*, God's intervention also takes the form of angels helping the Muslims against the infidels:

> When you sought the assistance of your Lord, He answered you: "I will assist you with a thousand angels, coming one after another."
>
> (8:9)

In a different *sūra*, the number of angels involved is said to be three thousand.[79]In a narrative believed to be about the Battle of Uḥud, which soon followed Badr, God reminds Muḥammad about what happened at Badr:

> And God certainly helped you at Badr, when you were weak …
>
> (3:123)

And:

> (Remember) When you said to the Faithful: 'Does is not suffice you that your Lord should help you with three thousand angels sent down?'
>
> (3:124)

And (in a narrative continuing into the next verse), the number of celestial fighters rises to five thousand:

> Yes, if you remain patient and god fearing even if the foe should rush headlong towards you, your Lord would help you with five thousand angels creating havoc.'
>
> (3:125)

Divine intervention in the shape of a thousand angels during the Battle of Badr has been much cited in traditional Islamic literature, in awe and even in pride. A moment's thinking should, however, raise an awkward and non-frivolous question: why should it take a thousand angels to help defeat a mere thousand infidels? Angels, it should be noted, are depicted in Islam and other monotheistic religions as prodigiously powerful beings. If it had been God's wish to deploy angels to assist the Muslims in battle, surely He – Himself all-powerful – could make do with far fewer angels than the number of the enemy, mere mortals.

The Koran describes other instances of divine intervention during the

[79] The discrepancy in the number of angels reported at Badr is evident. One exegesis I have seen (Qur'ān/Muhiuddin) gives barely credible explanation of the discrepancy. Yusuf Ali is silent about the matter.

Battle of Badr, much of which came in subtler ways. Verse 3:13 describes how the enemy 'saw with their eyes twice their (the Muslims') numbers'. In other words, the unbelievers' perception of their own relative numerical strength was seriously downgraded by divine intervention. A variation of the theme, more explicitly made, is in *Sūra Anfāl,* where God exhorts the Prophet:

> O Prophet! Rouse the believers to the fight. If there are twenty of you, all steadfast, they will defeat two hundred; if a hundred, they will defeat a thousand unbelievers ...
>
> (8:65)

A firm belief in such Muslims' superiority in battle against infidels would influence Islamic thinking for centuries to come.

There are naturally a number of verses in *Sūra Anfāl* on *jihad,* or 'fighting the unbelievers'. Even though many of the verses of the *sūra* have a direct bearing on the Battle of Badr, the implications of some of the verses on fighting can easily be, and have indeed been, generalised. (We shall return to verses of this nature in the separate chapter focused on jihad, Chapter 7).

About fifty men of Quraysh were slain in the Battle of Badr. Some accounts put the dead on the Muslim side at eight.[80] The Koran does not talk about the treatment of the dead, but *ḥadiths* relating to the battle do describe it. According to *Sahih al-Bukhāri,*[81] the Prophet ordered that the corpses of twenty-four Quraysh be thrown into one of the dirty wells of Badr. The Prophet then visited the well and called out the names of those killed 'to reprimand them and slight them and take revenge over them and caused them to feel remorseful and regretful.' There is no mention of how the other dead were treated.

The taking of prisoners has been a part of warfare ever since mankind learned to fight. The Battle of Badr was no exception. As the Muslims routed the infidels, they also took prisoners. And, like other belligerents of the time, they held some prisoners for ransom and put others to the sword.

---

[80] Ibn Ishaq, 337 - 38.

[81] al-Bukhāri, vol. 5, 188–89.

According to Ibn Ishaq, forty-three Quraysh were taken prisoner. Other accounts put the number at seventy.[82] Al-Tabari narrates how, after the victory, the Prophet started on his way back to Medina with the booty and the prisoners. History records that two of the captives were killed on orders from the Prophet, for no apparent reason. In a poignant story, one of the prisoners about to be killed asked the Prophet who would look after his children. The Prophet is reported to have replied, 'Hellfire.' But other captives were treated kindly, with the Prophet having told his companions, 'Look after the captives well.'[83] Some among the Anṣar are reported to have given their ration of bread to the captives in their custody, while the Anṣar themselves ate a humbler diet of dates.

The question of taking prisoners for ransom came early on. In fact, as the battle was still being fought, S'ad b. Mu'ādh, standing beside the Prophet and guarding him, was angered by the sight of Muslims sparing the lives of the infidels and taking them as prisoners for ransom instead. In the end, many of the captives were set free on payment of ransom; in some cases, handsome ones. But was it the right thing to do? Among the most prominent companions of the Prophet, Abū Bakr was in favour of releasing the prisoners for ransom, while 'Umar would have them all killed. The verse inspired in this context was close to the position of S'ad and 'Umar. It is remarkable how human sentiments expressed during an event were reflected *ex post* in the narrative. The verse inspired is clearly a reprimand for Muḥammad. It could just as easily be the result of a severe inner conflict of the man.

> It does not befit a Prophet that he should take prisoners of war until he has triumphed in the land. You look for the temporal goods; but God desires the Hereafter; And God is Mighty,Wise.
>
> (8:67)

In the event it was left to humans to make a decision, prisoners of war were freed on payment of ransom. This was primarily for the practical reasons of worldly gain for the impoverished Muslims. Humanitarian

---

[82] al-Tabarī, vol. 7, 65.

[83] Ibid. vol. 7, 67.

reasons played a part, especially when it came to the choice of either killing or ransoming Abbas, an uncle of the Prophet, who always had a soft corner for him. As could be expected, the strong words of the above verse were soon softened by what appears as a mere rebuke in a verse that followed immediately:

> Were it not for a previous prescription from God, a severe chastisement would have befallen you, for what you took.
> (8:68)

In human terms, it sounds like rationalisation, which becomes clearer in the very next verse, 8:69, quoted earlier: 'So enjoy whatever booty you have acquired, lawful and good' ...

Some exegetes have carried much further the story of ransoming prisoners taken at Badr. In the Battle of Uḥud, which soon followed Badr, seventy Muslims were killed. This is said to have been the toll that God exacted as punishment for the release of seventy prisoners of war at Badr.[84] Such a reading of God's will, however, runs counter to His imprimatur in 8:69, which we read above. Seen as punishment, the responsibility for this rested with those companions of the Prophet who advised releasing prisoners for ransom rather than killing them. It is not known whether the seventy killed included all those who called for release of prisoners for ransom. Apparently, this was not the case. Abū Bakr, for example, was not harmed at Uḥud. Plus, the Muslim community as a whole still paid the price, if punishment was indeed what it was.

These are all considered to be acts of divine will. However, the events can be seen equally well in lay terms as consequences of purely human decisions juxtaposed on the vagaries of wars. Given that there are differences of opinion about the number of Muslims killed, the lay explanation at least does not have the task of squaring the figure of the dead at Uḥud with that of the captives set free for ransom at Badr.

A number of small expeditions were launched by the Muslims between the battles of Badr and Uḥud. It suffices here to mention the expedition to al-Qaradah, a watering place in Najd. The Meccans were so afraid of the

---

[84] Ibid. vol. 7, 81. Similar is the view in Qur'ān/Muhiuddin.

Muslims in Medina after Badr that they began to avoid the trade route to Syria, taking the route to Iraq instead. A Muslim expedition dispatched by the Prophet spotted a Meccan caravan of merchants at al-Qaradah. Abū Sufyān, the Prophet's old nemesis, was among the merchants in the caravan. The caravan was captured, and the booty was brought back to Medina.

Far more important were three other events: two assassinations and the expulsion of the tribe of Banu Qaynuqa.

Ka'b b. al-Ashraf, a Jewish poet, wrote poems bewailing those of Quraysh who were killed at Badr. He was obviously not well disposed towards the Prophet. He is also said to have written a poem of an amatory nature about the wife of Abbas, the Prophet's uncle. According to *Sahih Al-Bukhāri,*[85] the Messenger of God said, 'Who will kill Ka'b b. al-Ashraf who has hurt Allah and His Messenger?' Whereupon Muḥammad b. Maslama, a companion of the Prophet, offered to kill Ka'b. The plot to kill him did involve some deceit, and the Prophet permitted him to use it. B. Maslama, accompanied by a few others, went to the house of Ka'b, brought him out under a ruse, and killed him.

Soon after, Abū Rafi, also a Jew, was assassinated. The reason for his killing was said to be that he used to take Ka'b b. al-Ashraf's side in the latter's inveighing of the Prophet.[86] Other accounts put it down to reports that he was inciting the Jews of Khaybar against the Prophet. Many of the Jews of Medina had been banished to that area, and Abū Rafi lived in a well-fortified house there. The Prophet sent a band of Muslims, headed by 'Abd Allah b. 'Atik, who did the killing by stealthily securing entrance into the fortress-like house. *Sahih Al-Bukhāri* describes the killing in gory detail.[87] After accomplishing the mission, b. 'Atik announced to his companions, in a manner reminiscent of many instances where human action was imputed to God, that Allah had killed Abū Rafi, and then he proceeded to report the accomplishment to the Prophet.

The tribe of Banu Qaynuqa was perhaps the first among the Jewish tribes who were expelled by Muḥammad from their settlements around Medina. The outcome of the Battle of Badr had probably convinced

---

[85] al-Bukhāri, vol. 5, 221–22. Note that written words were said to have 'hurt' Allah and His Prophet.

[86] al-Tabarī, vol. 7, 99.

[87] al-Bukhāri, vol. 5, 223–25.

Muḥammad that the Jews of Medina would now tilt towards accepting Islam. He was disappointed. The three prominent Jewish tribes of Medina – Banu Qaynuqa, Banu al-Nadir, and Banu Qurayzah – remained stubbornly opposed to the new faith propagated by Muḥammad, even though there were contacts between Jewish leaders and the Prophet, and, more importantly, between the rabbis and the Prophet.

The antagonism of the Banu Qaynuqa, a Jewish tribe comprised mostly of goldsmiths, came into the open when one day, soon after Badr, the Prophet went to their marketplace and called upon them to embrace Islam, duly reminding them of what happened to the polytheists at Badr. The Jews were clearly angered by the allusion to the defeat of a band of enemies of Islam, and retorted that they, unlike Quraysh, were the real fighters and that Muḥammad should not treat them lightly. In the end, however, the tribe took fright and withdrew to their fortress. The Prophet had in the meantime received an inspiration that was singularly appropriate to the situation:

> And if you fear treachery from any people, throw back (their treaty) to them, so as to be even with them: for God does not love the treacherous.
>
> (8:58)

There apparently was no actual act of treachery; the fear of it was considered sufficient *casus belli*. The Prophet reportedly said to the archangel Gabriel, who had just brought the revelation, that he feared Banu Qaynuqa.[88] There was no fighting, but the Muslims besieged the fortress which soon fell to them. As punishment for a potential act of treachery on its part, the tribe was banished. Their property was confiscated and distributed as booty among the Muslims.

The Battle of Uḥud, fought in AH 3, resulted directly from the humiliating defeat of Quraysh at Badr the year before. Some three thousand Quraysh men, accompanied by a number of women to uplift their spirits, gathered at Uḥud, a short distance to the north of Medina. As at Badr, Muḥammad sought the advice of his followers on the strategy of the battle. Some

---

[88] al-Tabarī, vol. 7, 86.

suggested that the Muslims should stay in the city, barricading themselves, while others urged him to lead them out to the battlefield. The latter group won the argument, even if there were second thoughts. As at Badr, human decisions were crucial to the outcome, as were human follies and greed. Unlike in the Battle of Badr, however, the Koran records no instance of divine help given to the Muslims during the Battle of Uḥud. Although the Koran is silent here, *Sahih al-Bukhāri* says that the Messenger of Allah was 'accompanied by two men fighting on his behalf. They were dressed in white and were fighting with extreme bravery ... ' It is said that they were the angels Gabriel and Michael.[89] On this evidence, divine intervention was extremely limited. An interesting lay hypothesis thus presents itself: the Koran attributed the clear human victory at Badr to divine succour, but only *after* the event; the less glorious outcome at Uḥud was not something that could be attributed to divine intervention, and so the Book remained properly silent in the matter. On the other hand, the two angels could be presumed have been enough to destroy the enemy. But exegetic zeal based on dubious facts glosses over such consideration.

The Battle of Uḥud was a near disaster for the Muslims. Their initial success was followed by a serious setback, when those placed in defensive positions, with orders not to budge, reportedly left their posts in pursuit of booty, making it possible for the Meccan cavalry to break through Muslim defences and wreak havoc. Muḥammad himself was wounded and had to be helped to safety. The threat to the life of the Prophet was serious enough for him to cry out for help: 'Who will sell his life for us?',[90] which was a very human reaction, though not a very laudable one. He was also wearing two coats of mail, instead of the normal single coat, making it difficult for his companions to move him to safety. The story is also at odds with the *ḥadith* cited above, which describes two powerful angels fighting alongside the Muslims. Why did Gabriel and Michael not come to the aid of Muḥammad?

The Muslims rallied later in the battle, after suffering heavy losses of life, and the Meccans failed to turn their early successes into victory. In a sharp reversal of numbers, sixty-five Muslims were killed at Uḥud, as compared

---

[89] al-Bukhāri, vol. 5, 235.

[90] Ibn Ishaq, 380.

to twenty-two polytheists, according to Ibn Ishaq.[91] As we have seen above, according to some exegetes, the number of Muslim martyrs at Uḥud was said to be the same as that of the Meccan enemies ransomed at Badr.

The brutality of war seems to have changed little with time. Uḥud had its own tale of brutality. Ḥamzah, the brave fighter uncle of Muḥammad, was killed by an Abyssinian mercenary. His javelin pierced the lower part of Ḥamzah's body and came out between his legs. This was a particularly ghastly scene, as was the ritual chewing of the dead man's liver by Hind, Abū Sufyān's wife, to fulfil a vow. A number of the Muslim dead were mutilated in the battle by Quraysh. The mutilation of Ḥamzah's body so angered Muḥammad that he vowed to mutilate thirty Quraysh in future battle. He later relented.

Most of the allusions to Uḥud in the Koran are to be found in *Sūra* 3 (*Āl-i-ʿImrān*). Ibn Ishaq mentions some sixty verses in the *sūra* that concern Uḥud, even though Uḥud is not mentioned even once, and many of the verses can fit into other contexts as well. Other exegetes mention a similar number of verses. The relevant verses actually start on a note of reflection on the battle. Thus, we read:

> And when you went forth from your family at dawn to assign the believers their posts for the battle: God is Hearing and Knowing.
>
> (3:121)

At the outset, some people of questionable allegiance, the so-called Hypocrites,[92] deserted. There were differences of opinion about what to do in the situation. In an altogether different *sūra*, the Koran says:

> Why should you be split into two parties over the Hypocrites when God has turned them back for what

[91] Ibid. 403. This is at variance with the number of Muslims killed given in other sources. (See above.)

[92] The term *Hypocrites* has been used in the Koran principally to refer to groups of people of Medina who initially professed solidarity with the Muslims but then resented the latter's ascendency. They were not a monolithic group and could be found among diverse tribes. In the Islamic tradition, Abdullah b. Ubayy, chief of a clan belonging to the tribe of al-Aws, was the archetype of the Hypocrites.

> they had done? Do you wish to guide whom God leaves in error?[93]
>
> (4:88)

To return to *Āl-i-'Imrān,* the Muslim's tribulations at Uḥud hang heavy in many of these verses. There is a wistful allusion to the victory at Badr:

> And God helped you at Badr, when you were puny.
>
> (3:123)

God's help to the Muslims in the Battle of Badr, in the shape of three thousand angels, is also remembered, in 3:124.That no such help came at Uḥud made the recollection especially wistful and, once again, human.

The following verses are also said to have been inspired in the context of the Battle of Uḥud:

> Do not lose heart, and do not despair, for you must gain the upper hand if you are believers.
>
> (3:139)

> If a wound has afflicted you, a similar wound has afflicted the others …
>
> (3:140)

> Do you think you will enter Heaven until God has known who strove hard and who were steadfast?
>
> (3:142)

Since God is omniscient and does not need to test human beings to find out their feelings, these verses sound much like a human mind reflecting on that difficult day and attempting to find solace in God.

The incident of Muḥammad being wounded and presumed dead is

---

[93] Qur'ān/Yusuf Ali, among other sources, places this in the context of the Battle of Uḥud. As is often the case, it is not clear why this particular verse is in *Sūra Nisāa* while the rest are elsewhere.

alluded to in the following verse, even if it contrasts with his urgent cry for help reported above:

> Muhammad is but a Messenger: many were the Messengers who passed away before him. If then he dies or is killed, will you turn on your heels? And one who turns on his heels, he will not harm God in the least ...
>
> (3:144)

Muslims should not lose heart in any circumstances:

> And how many a Prophet fought, and with him fought many godly men. They never lost heart on account of what befell them in God's way. They neither weakened nor humbled themselves. And God loves the steadfast.
>
> (3:146)

The near defeat of the Muslim army is here ascribed to human greed and lack of discipline:

> And God certainly fulfilled His promise to you when you with His leave were about to annihilate the enemy, – until you lost heart and fell to disputing about the order and disobeyed after He had brought you in sight of what (the booty) you loved. There are some among you who desire this world and those who desire the Hereafter. Then He turned you away from them, so as to test you ...
>
> (3:152)

The next verse of the *sūra* has a similar import:

> You were climbing the high ground, without heeding any one, and the Apostle behind was calling you. So God gave you grief on grief that you might not grieve over what escaped you or over what befell you ...
>
> (3:153)

Note that here God Himself gave the Muslims 'grief on grief', while human greed and fickleness were sufficient to explain the debacle suffered by them. But there is also forgiveness, not least of all because, Satan, God's old nemesis, is mixed up in it. It is he who caused humans to fail:

> Those of you who turned back on the day the two armies met, it was Satan who caused them to slip for whatever they had done. And God certainly has pardoned them. Surely God is Forgiving, Forbearing.
>
> (3:155)

Once again, human fault was enough to explain the near defeat, without the aid of Satan. Further, was it God who caused one grief after another, as in 3:153, or was it Satan that caused the Muslims to fail, as in 3:155? The diametrically opposed explanations, in two verses in such close proximity, are too evident to ignore.

Nevertheless, in the end, we have God addressing Muḥammad thus:

> Not for you, (but for God), is the concern: whether He turns in mercy to them or punish them. Surely they are indeed wrong-doers
>
> (3:128)

Quraysh and their allies finally despaired of victory and left the battlefield of Uḥud. In a shrewd move, Muḥammad sent a band of Muslims who fought at Uḥud in pursuit of the enemy. It was not a hot pursuit – the Muslims were hardly up to it so soon after a devastating battle – but it was meant to demonstrate to the enemy that Muḥammad's army remained a strong force not significantly weakened by the casualties suffered.[94]

The following verse was perhaps inspired in the aftermath of Uḥud.[95] It is extraordinary in its tenderness, as well as its tact in dealing with human beings whose allegiance Muḥammad could not always take for granted:

---

[94] al-Tabarī, vol. 7, 139.

[95] Qur'ān/Muhiuddin, exegesis of *Sūra* 3 (*Āl-i-'Imran*).

> It was by some mercy of God that you were gentle to them. Had you been hard-hearted, they would have broken away from you. So pardon them and ask forgiveness for them, and consult them in the matter. But when you have taken a decision, put your trust God. Surely God loves those who put their trust in Him.
>
> (3:159)

No such tenderness was reserved for everybody. Soon after Uḥud, Muḥammad expelled the Jewish tribe of Banu al-Nadir from the vicinity of Medina. The event was of considerable significance. As described by Ibn Ishaq and the *ḥadith* literature, the immediate and ostensible reason for the expulsion was an alleged attempt to kill Muḥammad by dropping a stone on him while he was visiting the tribe. The story of the plot can be viewed with a great deal of scepticism,[96] and it is quite possible that it was used as an excuse to act against the tribe, thereby ridding them as a potential threat. The location of the tribe was probably also considered as strategic, and getting the Jews out of the way may have been one of Muḥammad's predetermined objectives.

The *sūra* concerning Banu Nadir's expulsion is *Sūra* 59 (*Ḥashr*). It says only that the Jews were punished for resisting God, but it does not mention any plot:

> That is because they opposed God and His Apostle: and if any one opposed God, verily God is severe in retribution.
>
> (59:4)

---

[96] Not long after Uḥud, Muḥammad was visiting the tribe, seeking help to raise the blood money he was bound by custom to offer in a killing of two men by an associate of his. The tribe leaders readily agreed to help in raising the money. No sooner had the deal been done than they hatched a plot to kill Muḥammad by dropping a stone on him from the wall of a house. Muḥammad, accompanied by some of his associates, was resting by the wall of a house which the plotters selected for the purpose. The speed needed to put their plan into action, the too-convenient coincidence of a suitable house beside which Muḥammad was said to be resting, and the presence of his associates, who included such stalwarts as Abū Bakr, 'Umar, and 'Ali, throw doubt on the story. There could be hardly any doubt that the tribe wished to kill the Prophet, if they could. But the veracity of the story is not beyond doubt.

This is perhaps as clear a verse as any in the Koran suggesting that opposing or resisting God can be enough to warrant punishment. There is no mention of treachery or plot.

In the face of attack by the Muslims, the Jews withdrew to their fortress. In one of his first acts to punish the tribe, Muḥammad ordered its date-palm orchards to be cut down and burnt. The date palm occupied such an important place in Arab societies that this was considered a drastic step, and it is easy to imagine that questions were asked about its propriety. The following verse, addressed to the Muslims, justifies the destruction of the orchards:

> Whatever palm-tree you cut down, or left standing on its roots, that was by leave of God, and in order that He might abase the transgressors.
>
> (59:5)

A modern reader would almost certainly be puzzled by the presentation of the act of cutting down the palm trees as a way of 'abasing' or humiliating the tribe. The falling back on divine imprimatur of course takes the matter out of human culpability.

Sūra Ḥashr is a remarkable chapter of the Koran in that its sole theme is Muḥammad's expulsion of Banu al-Nadir. There is no other *sūra* of this length which deals with a single theme. The *sūra* views the banishment of the tribe thus:

> And had it not been that God had decreed for them the exile, He would certainly have chastised them in this world. And in the Hereafter, there is the punishment of Fire for them.
>
> (59:3)

In other words, in banishing the tribe Muḥammad actually did the tribe a favour, since the alternative was death. Banishment was not enough for the Jews, however, for in the afterlife, hellfire awaited them.

The Jews were allowed to escape with their lives. They were allowed to take with them as much of their property as they could carry. It is said that they tore their homes down to the plinths, partly to salvage the structures they could carry, and also to deprive their enemies of the property. The Koran describes the scene:

... they thought that their fortress would defend them against God!

> But God came to them from quarters not expected by them, and cast terror into their hearts. So they demolished their houses with their own hands and the hands of the believers ...
>
> (59:2)

The portion of the verse about the act of destroying by the hands of the believers is probably meant to show that the believers also did the good deed of destruction, while the responsibility for it lay with the unbelievers themselves.

The tribe could not have carried all their possessions – hence the destruction mentioned above – and so substantial booty fell to the Muslims. The Koran proclaims on its division:

> Whatever God has bestowed on His Apostle from the people of the townships, belongs to God, to His Apostle and to kindred and orphans, the needy and the wayfarer, so that it is not taken by the rich among you.
>
> (59:7)

To a modern lay mind, it is remarkable that a *sūra* concerned essentially with conflict – including the expulsion of a people and the destruction of their orchards and their homes, and the division of the spoils following that conflict – would end abruptly with two long verses of cascading glorification of God, rendered in fine lyrics that are lost in translation. Only one such verse is reproduced here:

> He is God beside whom there is no god: He is the Sovereign, the Holy, the Author of Peace, the Provider of Security, the Guardian, the Mighty, the Supreme. Glory to God! ...
>
> (59:23)

Banu al-Nadir was deported and scattered. Some of its members went to Khaybar, a short distance to the north of Medina. Some went as far as Syria.

Shortly thereafter, several chiefs of the exiled Jews in Khaybar, and a few others, visited Mecca in secret to build an alliance with Quraysh against the Muslims. They found Quraysh only too willing to join hands with the Jews to fight Muḥammad one more time. A confederacy was put together in which, besides Quraysh and tribes and clans closely allied to it, there were the tribes of Ghatafan, Banu Asad, Banu Sulaym, and a number of others. The combined strength of these armies was probably about ten thousand. A part of these forces took up position to the north or north-east of Medina, while others stationed themselves to the south-east. The confederacy against the Muslims constitutes a major theme of the eponymous *Sūra* 33, *Aḥzāb.*

The news of a new threat from his enemies reached Muḥammad well in time to allow him to make defensive preparations. Here, an ingenious plan put forward by Salman Farsi, a former slave living in the Jewish tribe of Banu Qurayzah and a recent convert to Islam, proved potent to the outcome of the conflict, and perhaps changed the course of the history of Islam. He suggested that a trench be dug around Medina to keep the enemy out and the inhabitants of the city in. The idea, he told Muḥammad, was not a novelty in his native Persia, where trenches were a fairly common device of defence, though it certainly was novel to the Arabs. Muḥammad eagerly accepted the idea, and a trench was hurriedly dug around much of the city. A great deal of communal hard work, in which the Prophet himself fully participated, went into the making of the trench. The few areas of the defences of the city where the trench could not be extended were manned by strong contingents of Muslim fighters. The total Muslim strength was probably in the order of three thousand.

The Muslims, Anṣar and Muhajirun alike, were united under Muḥammad. Yet there were doubters in Medina. *Sūra Aḥzāb* recounts it thus:

> And when a party among them Said: 'O people of Yathrib! You are not able to stand this (onslaught), so go back!' And a party among them sought permission of the

> Prophet saying, 'Our houses are unprotected,' though they were not unprotected. They only wanted to run away
>
> (33:13)

The believers, on the other hand, had to be roused, and roused in these terms:

> Say: Running away will be no good to you, if you are fleeing from death or slaughter; and (even if you escape) the enjoyment allowed to you will be brief.
>
> (33:16)

There is also praise for the true believers:

> And when the believers saw the Confederate forces, they said: 'This is what God and His Apostle had promised us, and God and His Apostle told us the truth.' And it only added to their faith and their submission.
>
> (33:22)

The armies of Quraysh and its allies in the confederacy had never seen anything like a trench and must have felt totally at a loss. There was a siege but little fighting. The few rather half-hearted sallies on the part of the enemy to cross the trench were fairly easily foiled by the Muslims. A serious wounding of a close associate of the Prophet, would, however, soon prove to be of tragic consequences.

While human ingenuity was crucial to the outcome of the siege, hardly less important were human manoeuvres that included deceit and fully exploited self-interest, suspicion, and fear. To start with, the Jewish emissaries from Khaybar had already promised the tribe of Ghatafan half the Khaybar harvest of dates if it participated in a war against Muḥammad.[97] In the course of the siege, Muḥammad made a similar proposal to Ghatafan, offering a third of the date harvest of Medina if they agreed not to fight him. Nothing came of the latter manoeuvre, and no agreement was signed, primarily because the hardliners among

[97] Martin Lings, 215.

Muḥammad's followers were against such an agreement with a polytheist tribe.[98] This suggests, once again, the extent to which the Apostle of God was swayed by human counsel, especially when he felt there was no divine guidance to fall back on. In the present case there was none.

Perhaps more important were the intrigues behind the scene. Banu Qurayzah inhabited an area that was strategically important as an access to the city. It was also said to have been bound by a treaty of friendship with Muḥammad, although the nature of this treaty is not very clear. The Jewish allies of Quraysh therefore set about to get the tribe on their side or, failing that, to at least neutralise it. It was the diplomatic skill and tenacity of Ḥuyay, chief of Banu al Nadir, that ultimately led Banu Qurayza to renounce its treaty with Muḥammad.[99] But he was yet to reckon with Muḥammad's ability to outmanoeuvre him.

Muḥammad secretly sent a man named Nu'aym b. Mās'ud, a relatively new convert to Islam, to Banu Qurayzah to try to turn it against Quraysh and its allies. Nu'aym's conversion to Islam was still unknown to his tribe, a fact that was a considerable advantage to him in his mission. As al-Tabarī reports, the Messenger of God told him: 'You are only one man among us. Make them abandon [each other], if you can, so that they leave us; for war is deception.'[100] *Sahih Al-Bukhāri* also reports, without the context, that the Prophet said simply, 'War is deceit.'[101] The Prophet thus clearly instructed Nu'aym to make use of deception to achieve his objective. Nu'aym duly made a secret journey to Banu Qurayzah and succeeded in convincing the leaders of the Jewish tribe that Quraysh and its allies could not possibly be their friends, and that the interest of the tribe was better served by distancing itself from the enemies of the Muslims. He then went over to Quraysh and told them that Banu Qurayza had been regretting their renunciation of the treaty with Muḥammad and therefore could not be trusted. He then told them something that must have sounded particularly ominous to Quraysh. He swore that Banu Qurayzah had told Muḥammad something to this effect: 'We regret what we have done. Will you be satisfied with us if we take nobles from the tribes of Quraysh and Ghatafan and give them to you, so that you can behead them?' So if the

---

[98] al-Tabarī, vol. 8, 17–18.

[99] Martin Lings, 221.

[100] al-Tabarī, vol. 8, 23.

[101] al-Bukhāri, vol. 4, 165.

Jews asked for hostages from Quraysh (in return of pledge of alliance), Nu'aym told Quraysh leaders that not a single man should be sent to them. That would be like sending him to their deaths. Nu'aym then went to the Ghatafan and repeated the same canard. When the leaders of Quraysh and Ghatafan sent word to Banu Qurayzah, repeating their pledge of friendship and asking for their cooperation in their fight against the Muslims, the latter duly asked for hostages. This of course confirmed their worst suspicions, so skilfully planted in them by Nu'aym. The deceit worked, and Quraysh and their allies were forced to abandon any hope of cooperation from Banu Qurayzah.[102] That deception, despair at their inability to cross the trenches, and some particularly inclement weather all combined to finally persuade Quraysh and their allies to lift the siege, and leave.

Neither the role of a foreigner in the planning of a trench nor the stories of negotiations and deception appear in the Koran. Despite the title, which suggests that the primary allusion would be to the Battle of the Trench, *Sūra Aḥzāb* has nothing to say on the subject. On the other hand, the *sūra* also concerns other matters of importance in the Prophet's personal life, as we will see.

The campaign against Banu Qurayzah is an appendix to the Battle of the Trench, but it is an important moment in the history of Islam in Medina. The campaign and its bloody end are far more important than the tangential references to them in the Koran seem to suggest. There are only a few verses in *Sūra Aḥzāb* that exegetes associate with the story of Banu Qurayzah.

No sooner had Quraysh and their allies lifted the siege and left the city than the Prophet turned his attention to Banu Qurayzah. The immediate action is dramatised in *ḥadith* literature: the Prophet had just returned home from the trenches and taken off his coat of arms when the angel Gabriel appeared before him and told him the angels had not disarmed and were marching towards the fortress of the Jewish tribe.[103] The Prophet quickly changed his mind – and it is easy to visualise him quickly altering course, without divine prompting – and set out to fight Banu Qurayzah. The tribe withdrew behind their walls, and the Muslims promptly laid siege to them.

---

[102] al-Tabarī, vol. 8, 24–25.

[103] al-Bukhāri, vol. 5, 269.

According to exegetes, the following verse is about the tribe:

> And those of the People of the Book who supported them, God did bring them down from their fortresses and cast terror into their hearts. Some you killed and some you took prisoner.
>
> (33:26)

And, as with Banu al-Nadir:

> He bequeathed on you their lands, their dwellings and their property, and a land you had not trodden before. And God has power over all things.
>
> (33:27)

The history of events surrounding the plight of the tribe is far more tragic, and the role of humans far greater, than these verses might suggest.

The circumstances leading to the Prophet's attack on Banu Qurayzah are not entirely clear. The tribe is said to have had a treaty of some kind with the Muslims, though the covenant between the Muslims and the tribes of Medina, the so-called Constitution of Medina, does not mention specifically either Banu Qurayzah or the two tribes already banished by Muḥammad.[104] As we have seen, this tribe neither sided with Quraysh nor aided the Muslims. Was sitting on the fence perhaps something that Muḥammad was unwilling to accept, especially given the strategic location of the tribe? Was he looking for a pretext to have the last major tribe removed from the scene? The following paragraph perhaps best sums up the circumstances of Muḥammad's campaign against the tribe:

> There were still a number of Jewish groups in Medina, but the only one of any importance was the clan of Qurayzah. During the siege of Medina this clan had probably preserved neutrality so far as outward acts were concerned, but they had engaged in negotiations

---

[104] W. Montgomery Watt, *Muḥammad in Medina* (London: Oxford University Press, 1956), Chapter 7.

> with Muhammad's enemies, and, could they have trusted Quraysh and their bedouin allies, would have turned against Muhammad. Immediately upon the withdrawal of his opponents Muhammad attacked Qurayzah, to show that the rising Islamic state was not prepared to tolerate such 'sitting on the fence'.[105]

The siege of Banu Qurayzah is said to have lasted twenty-five days. There was very little fighting, and the tribe soon realised the hopelessness of their circumstance. Muḥammad demanded and received unconditional surrender. Conversion to Islam would have saved them, but the tribe rejected the proposition out of hand. There were calls for leniency from the tribe of al-Aus, which had old ties with Banu Qurayzah, as well as being a staunch ally of the Muslims. The question of a mediator arose, and the Prophet asked, in a show of apparent magnanimity, whether al-Aus would be willing to accept mediation from someone among its members. Al-Aus agreed. The man Muḥammad appointed as mediator was S'ad b. Mu'ādh. S'ad was critically wounded in the Battle of the Trench by an enemy arrow; he was in agony and on the verge of death. His tough stance against the enemies of Islam was well known to the Prophet, having manifested itself at both Badr and Uḥud. His judgement was stunning. But it was also predictable, not least of all to the Prophet of Islam: specifically, that all men of Banu Qurayzah were to be killed, all of its property distributed, and all women and children taken prisoner. The Prophet lauded the decision, saying, 'You have judged according to Allah's judgment'.[106] There is little doubt that this was the judgement the Prophet himself would have made.

As the men of Banu Qurayzah surrendered, the Messenger of God had trenches dug in Medina's marketplace. The men of the tribe were then led to the trenches in batches, whereupon they were beheaded. The number killed was said to be six or seven hundred, though some sources put it as high as nine hundred.[107] The freshly dug trenches must have been full to overflowing with the blood from the great slaughter. The cries of the bereaved women and children must have risen to the high heavens.

---

[105] Watt, 214.

[106] al-Bukhāri, vol. 5, 271.

[107] Ibn Ishaq, 466.

It is said that two of the Prophet's companions, 'Ali and al-Zubayr, began the beheading of the male prisoners in the presence of the Prophet.[108] Only one woman prisoner was killed that day. Al-Tabarī reports she was accused of having killed a Muslim warrior during the siege of Banu Qurayzah, having thrown a millstone on him, presumably from the ramparts of the tribe's fortress. Al-Tabarī reports that the Prophet personally beheaded her.[109] He then divided the spoils of war – the wealth, women, and children of Banu Qurayzah – among the Muslims. Some of the captives were sent to Najd and exchanged for horses and arms. From among the captives he chose for himself a woman named Rayḥānah, who was made his concubine.[110]

The treatment meted out to Banu Qurayzah was so extraordinary that Muslim commentators have either kept silent about it or found elaborate justification for it. Of the latter, the commentary by Yusuf Ali on S'ad's judgement stands out.[111] S'ad, he explains, applied to the tribe the Jewish Law of the Old Testament, which requires an even more severe punishment in similar circumstances, namely ' ... thou shalt save alive nothing that breatheth.' (Deut. 20:16).

Yusuf Ali writes this without a trace of irony. Yet a two-part uncomfortable question must have lingered not far from his mind: why did Sa'd, a devout and hard-line Muslim, follow laws of the very religion that Muḥammad was out to supplant, and how could the prophet of the new religion go along with the judgement?

Sa'd died soon afterwards. It is said that when the Prophet's companions, Abū Bakr and 'Umar, visited him, he was on his last breath, and his imminent passing so distressed them that they cried aloud, a rarity for them. The Prophet himself was grief-stricken.[112] The scene was described by the Prophet's wife, 'A'ishah. She also said that it was just such tenderness for one of their own that was referred to in a verse of the Koran, reproduced below, in which God praises Muslims for

[108] al-Tabarī, vol. 8, 41.

[109] Ibid. vol. 8, 41.

[110] Ibid. vol. 8, 39.

[111] Qur'ān/Yusuf Ali, footnotes to verse 33:26.

[112] al-Tabarī, vol. 8, 40.

being 'compassionate among each other', while being 'hard against the unbelievers'.[113]

> Muhammad is the Apostle of God; and those who are with him are hard against the unbelievers but compassionate among each other ...
>
> (48:29)

The Battle of the Trench was followed by a number of relatively minor campaigns and raids. Among the latter, Muslims raided a rich caravan of Quraysh that was on its way from Syria. It resulted in a large booty in silver and other merchandise for the Muslims.[114]

The next campaign of some importance was against Banu al-Mustaliq. The Koran contains no direct reference to the campaign itself, but an event surrounding the Prophet's wife, 'A'ishah, at the end of the campaign had important consequences. (See Chapter 14.) The days of the campaign also saw an apparent manifestation of what the Muslims considered to be the true intentions of the Hypocrites.

Banu al-Mustaliq was a clan of the large tribe of Khuza'ah, whose territory lay to the south of Medina, along the Red Sea. Reports came that the clan, under its leader, al-Harith, was preparing for hostile action against the Muslims, probably under instigation of Quraysh who were again seeking to reopen the western trade route along the Red Sea. Muḥammad marched swiftly to face al-Mustaliq and routed them in a brief battle, with only light casualties to his men.

As in other campaigns, the spoils of war included property, livestock, and women and children. The booty is said to have included two thousand camels and five thousand sheep. Among the women was the daughter of the chief. She was called Juwayriyah and was a woman of exquisite beauty. She had originally fallen to the lot of one of the Anṣar, but the Prophet persuaded him to part with her, paid the required ransom himself, and married her.

It was also while the forces led by Muḥammad were camping after the battle that the tension between the Hypocrites and the Muslims came to

[113] Ibid. He refers only to the 'merciful' ('compassionate' in the translation used here) part of the verse. The other part is quoted here merely for completeness.
[114] Martin Lings, 235.

the fore. It resulted from a minor friction between two men, one of whom happened to be in the employ of ʻUmar, while the other belonged to one of the Anṣar tribes. Abdallah b. Ubayy, the leader of the Hypocrites and a prominent Medina man who had ambitions of his own to be leader of the whole region now apparently under the control of Muḥammad, lost no time in venting his feelings. He reportedly said, 'By God the proverb, "Fatten your dog and he will eat you up!" fits us ... By God, if we go back to Medina, those who are stronger will drive out the weaker from it.' Apparently, the dog here refers to the Muhājirūn, while the household where it was being fattened was that of the Anṣar. For a Muslim, few insults are worse than being compared to a dog. Another *sūra* of the Koran, 63, has been named after the Hypocrites, which suggests the importance of the activities this group. This particular incident is referred to in the *sūra*:[115]

> They say: "If we return to Medina, the mightier will expel therefrom the meaner." But might belongs to God and His Messenger and to the believers; but the Hypocrites know not.
>
> (63:8)

The report of the incident was shocking to Muḥammad and his associates. ʻUmar, known for his impetuosity, wanted Ubayy's head. Muḥammad kept his cool, his party returned to Medina, and the matter was laid to rest.

As with other expeditions, the one of al-Mustaliq led to the capture of many women; or, as such narratives as those of Ibn Ishaq and the *ḥadith* put it, God gave these women to the Prophet as part of the booty. A *ḥadith* in *Sahih Al-Bukhāri* reveals that having sex with women captives was taken for granted, an aspect of war that was typical of the time. In the *ḥadith,* some of the companions of the Prophet sought his permission to perform coitus interruptus with these captives.[116] The morality of sex with captives

---

[115] al-Tabarī, vol. 8, 52.

[116] al-Bukhāri, vol. 5, 278–79. The Prophet is said to have discouraged the practice. His reasoning was of course in consonance with the Koran: 'There is no person that is destined to exist, but will come to existence, till the Day of Resurrection,' he said. This can be better explained in these terms: human beings who are destined to be born till the Day of Resurrection will certainly be born, irrespective of human action.

was not in question. Apparently, divine intervention was not available here, just as it was not in a number of other important matters, as we will see. In fact, sex with captives was clearly permissible, according to the Koran.

The Khaybar campaign was a far more important affair. Khaybar, an oasis about a hundred miles north of Medina, was inhabited by a number of Jewish tribes generally known to be wealthy. Their number had swollen after the expulsion of their co-religionists from the neighbourhood of Medina. They were not a direct threat to the Muslims, and there is no evidence that that they planned an attack on Medina. That they would have been only too glad to see the Muslims vanish was to be expected, and some of their leaders had in fact instigated Quraysh against Muḥammad in the days leading to the Battle of the Trench. Muḥammad's decision to move against them, in AH 7, was thus partly motivated by his long-term goal to get rid of what he perceived as the Jewish threat. The other motive was undoubtedly pecuniary. He needed resources to support the growing community of Muslims, many of whom desperately poor. Booty from raids was just about the only way to meet this need.

Sūra 48(*Fāt-ḥ*) is said to have been revealed at or near Hudaybiyah, after the crucial treaty had been signed. It already talks of gains to be had from the Khaybar campaign soon to come. According to exegetes, the 'reward' of a 'speedy victory' in the following verse refers to the gains from the forthcoming campaign:[117]

> God indeed was well pleased with the believers when they swore allegiance to you under the tree … ; and He rewarded them with a near victory.
>
> (48:18)

While the above verse was inspired in the context of a critical treaty, the next two, inspired in the same context, have a starkly pecuniary theme:

> And many gains will they acquire: and God is Mighty and Wise.
>
> (48:19)

[117] Qur'ān/Muhiuddin.

> God has promised you many gains which you will acquire.
>
> (48:20)

In the same *sūra* and verse (48:16) that we saw earlier in this chapter, the desert Arabs were told that they would be accepted as fighters (in the campaign of Khaybar) if they showed obedience and that God would grant them goodly reward. The campaign of Khaybar was thus foreseen, and its worldly gains promised, well in advance.

The Jews were hardly a great fighting force, and their little fortresses fell one by one to the Muslim attackers. The property of the Jews was taken, as were some captives. Ibn Ishaq goes into considerable detail about the distribution among the Muslims. The fort of al-Sā'b b. Mu'ādh was said to be the richest in food in the whole of Khaybar, and its fall greatly added to the supply of food in the Muslim camps. The captured women were distributed among the Muslims. Among the captives was Safiyyah, the young daughter of the chief of al-Qamus and wife of Kinānah, a prominent member of the tribe. Also captured were two cousins of Safiyyah. One of the Muslims had asked for Safiyyah, but the Prophet chose her for himself, giving the man her two cousins.[118] *Sahih al-Bukhāri* says that the beauty of Safiyyah had earlier been mentioned to the Prophet.[119] It also reports that the Prophet married her on his way back to Medina.

The story of Safiyyah needs further elaboration. Her husband was killed soon after the fortress of al-Qamus fell, but not in combat. It is said that Kinānah was in the know of the treasures of Banu al-Nadir, as he was their keeper. To extract information about the treasure, the Prophet ordered his torture and finally his beheading, both of which were duly carried out. The marriage of Safiyyah to the Prophet assumes certain grotesqueness in the context of her marrying her husband's killer, and that too so soon after the killing. It also raises a vexing question. The Prophet started his return journey to Medina soon after the conquest of Khaybar, and that journey took only a few days. The Prophet married Safiyyah and consummated the marriage within that time, at the first

---

[118] Ibn Ishaq, 511; Al-Tabarī, vol. 8, 117.

[119] al-Bukhāri, vol. 5, 322.

halt on the return journey, by some accounts.[120] This appears contrary to law laid out in the Koran. Verse 2:234 specifies a hiatus – *'iddat* – of four months and ten days before a widow can marry again.

The Koran says little about these events. In fact, it contains very little of the story of the Khaybar campaign. At least one commentator thinks that if *Sūra Aḥzāb* was revealed in late AH 7, then verse 33:27, which we read earlier in connection with Banu Qurayzah, relates to Khaybar.[121]

Still, some of the events, such as the following, were no less significant than those explicitly narrated in the text of the Koran. The initial decision of the Prophet was to banish the Jews from their ancestral home. This was reversed, however, and he accepted a proposal of the Jews of Khaybar to let them stay on the land, now belonging to the Muslims, in exchange for half the produce of the property. This was perhaps the first time that Muslims concluded an arrangement of this nature with their enemies. Verse 33:27 seems to reflect these acquisitions in Khaybar, which was also a land not frequented by the Muslims before. Ibn Ishaq also relates that the Jews of Fadak, situated near Khaybar, also asked for and received the same kind of treatment. Fadak, however, became the exclusive property of the Prophet, while Khaybar belonged collectively to the Muslims.[122] The Khaybar campaign should be regarded as the first act in a long history of Muslim colonisation.

One other incident of some importance, also not mentioned in the Koran, was an attempt on the life of the Prophet. As told by Ibn Ishaq,[123] while Muḥammad rested after the battles of Khaybar, a woman named Zaynab, wife of a Jewish chief, offered to prepare a roast lamb for him. She asked him what part of a lamb he liked best, and the Prophet replied that he preferred the shoulder. The woman poisoned the whole lamb, taking care to put extra poison in the shoulders. At dinner, the Prophet took a bite of the shoulder, got suspicious, and spat out the food. He survived the attempt on his life, but a companion of his, who was sharing the lamb, died. When the Prophet asked the woman what made her do such a thing, she answered thus: 'You know what you have done to my people. I said to myself, if he is king I shall ease myself of him and if he is a prophet he will

[120] Martin Lings, 269.

[121] Qur'ān/Yusuf Ali, footnote to verse 33:27.

[122] Ibn Ishaq, 515–16.

[123] Ibid. 516.

be informed (of what I have done).' The latter part of the answer probably saved her life. The Prophet forgave the woman. The effect of the poison seemed to linger, however, and he complained about it later in life. Human susceptibilities are on display here. So of course is forgiveness. Some eight hundred years later, the Mughal emperor Babur had his alleged poisoner trampled by an elephant.

Unlike most other campaigns, the Battle of Ḥunayn is specifically named in the Koran:

> Certainly God helped you in many battlefields, and on the day of Hunayn, your great number pleased you, but they availed you naught and the earth for all its space shrank for you and you turned back in retreat.
>
> (9:25)

The battle was of great importance in that it helped consolidate the spread of Islam in the neighbourhood of Mecca. The year was AH 8, and Mecca had just been conquered by Muḥammad. But the tribe of Hawāzin remained stubbornly opposed to the Messenger of God. Alarm was added to hostility after the Muslim destruction of the temple of al-'Uzza at Nakhla. The tribe probably feared that their own temple of the sister goddess al-Lāt might meet the same fate.[124] Hawāzin and their ally, Thaqif, were also traditional enemies of Quraysh. The newly acquired strength of Quraysh, consequent of Muḥammad's conquest of Mecca and his consolidation of power there, could not have been to their liking. On the other hand, the news of impending hostility on their part raised in Quraysh a corresponding desire to fight them. A substantial number of men from the tribe willingly joined the Muslims. Muḥammad had been staying in Mecca after the conquest of the city and now marched out with some twelve thousand fighters to face an army of twenty thousand men assembled by Hawāzin. Malik, the chief of the tribe, assembled his forces in the valley of Ḥunayn.

The initial onslaught of Hawāzin was fierce, and Muḥammad's forces were on the verge of a rout. Many of them, particularly new converts from Mecca and those motivated by tribal animosity alone, ran from

[124] Martin Lings, 304.

the battlefield. A degree of overconfidence on the part of the Prophet at the beginning, as well as the initial setback, is well reflected in the verse quoted above. The difficulty of the terrain was described by historians.

The Prophet's frantic call to his forces to turn back, and a determined stand by some of his closest companions, saved the day. The Muslim forces rallied and won a decisive victory, with only moderate casualties. And as can be expected, divine help was later said to be at hand, and the defeat of the enemy was attributed to divine intervention. Thus, we have (following up on verse 9:25):

> Then God did send His calm on His Messenger and on the believers and sent down forces you did not see ...
>
> (9:26)

The forces referred to here were said to be angels, this time in the unlikely shape of ants that descended on the battlefield in black swarms.[125] Why angels were sent in the shape of ants is not clear, and the story, like many others of this genre, must be attributed to imagination of posterity.

Some of the retreating Hawāzin forces under Malik took refuge in the fort of Tāif. A long siege of the fort by the Muslims failed to dislodge them and had to be lifted. The Battle of Hunayn yielded a large number of captives and a huge booty: some six thousand women and children, twenty-four thousand camels and forty thousand sheep, as well as a huge quantity of silver.

Questions of the division of the spoils of war ranged from the venal, practical, and mundane, to the deliberately altruistic and noble. As a gesture of reconciliation, the Prophet gave some of the leading men of Mecca, including his former arch-rival, Abū Sufyān, generous portions of the booty. Some of them were given a hundred camels.

The practical importance of reconciliation, and the need for sealing it with gifts, was especially recognised in the following verse:

> Charity is for the poor and the needy, for those employed to administer it, for those whose hearts have been

[125] Ibn Ishaq, 572.

> reconciled, for freeing bondsmen, for those in debt, for spending in the way of God, and for the wayfarer …
>
> (9:60)

Several close companions of the Prophet were also given generous booty. The generosity shown to the Meccans, fellow tribesmen of the Prophet, did not sit well with some of the Anṣar from Medina who had supported Muḥammad those many years and fought battles with him. Apparently, they were initially given little booty and were therefore understandably disgruntled. There were instances of tempers fraying. Al-Tabari narrates that 'some Bedouin allies were so angry with the Prophet that they waylaid him, until they forced him back against a tree and his mantle was pulled away from him',[126] which looks like manhandling of the Prophet. Separately, the Prophet went to considerable lengths to assuage the feelings of the Anṣar, reminding them that it was he who brought God' guidance to them. His eloquence on this occasion is said to have brought tears to the eyes of the assembled Anṣar.[127] This still leaves open the question of why the people of Medina were expected to be happy with God's guidance alone, while the Meccans received both guidance and wealth. The disparity did not go away; neither did the resentment, as later history was to testify.

Soon a deputation of Hawāzin approached the Prophet for leniency of treatment. The tribe had embraced Islam; furthermore, as the delegates submitted, they were near kin of the Prophet. Muḥammad had probably been anticipating this and had reason to be elated by it because it meant the conversion of a large tribe of polytheists to Islam, with the consolidation of his power as a result. He agreed to return the captive women and children. There was a problem, however. Some of the women had already been distributed among the Muslims. Their new owners needed some compensation to part with them. Muḥammad then offered to give six camels for every woman captive returned, a barter that would jolt modern minds.

Among the captives was a woman who claimed that she was Muḥammad's foster sister. The woman was brought before him, and she

---

[126] al-Tabarī, vol. 9, 31.

[127] Ibid. vol. 9, 37.

was apparently able to prove that indeed she was what she claimed to be. The Prophet returned her to her folk with due respect and many gifts.

Muḥammad was probably also expecting that Malik would someday be reconciled to him. He sent word to Malik that if he were to become a Muslim, he would be given a hundred camels, and his family, still under siege, would be returned to him. Malik duly embraced Islam and received the reward. According to Ibn Ishaq, he became an excellent Muslim.

The expedition to Mu'tah in AH 8, soon after Khaybar, was memorable in Islamic history for two reasons: a serious miscalculation on the part of Muḥammad, and the valour and sacrifice on the part of his commanders. In fact, the expedition was a near disaster for the Muslims. The antecedents are somewhat unclear. Muḥammad had sent emissaries to a tribe near the border of Syria, ostensibly to invite it to enter Islam. All but one of them was killed in a battle with the tribe. At about the same time, another messenger sent by Muḥammad, this one to the Christian governor of Bostra, was intercepted and killed by the Christian tribe of Ghassān. The expedition of Mu'tah was said to be primarily against this tribe. The possibility that the tribe could call on Byzantine forces in Syria was evidently not considered by the Prophet. The Muslim force of three thousand men was met by a Byzantine army of as many as a hundred thousand, according to some accounts. The Muslims fought valiantly, and one by one, the commanders fell in battle. Among them were some of the dearest companions of the Prophet: Zayd, the Prophet's adopted son and former slave; his cousin, Ja'far b. Abū Talib; and Abdallah b. Rawāḥah. It was Khalid b. al-Walid who managed to extricate the Muslim forces from annihilation.

In the ninth year of the *hijrah* (AH 9), not long after the conquest of Mecca and the Battle of Hunayn, Muḥammad led a large expedition to Tabūk, situated close to the border of Syria. The army was said to be some thirty thousand strong, the largest expedition the Prophet ever led. It was also the longest, in terms of the distance covered, as Tabūk was some 350 miles from Medina. The reasons behind the decision to embark on the expedition were complex and not altogether clear. The threat of a Byzantine attack from Syria has been suggested as the most important factor. The fact that Muḥammad decided to march with a large army in an extremely hot season, over long distances, supports the hypothesis.

But this threat was greatly exaggerated, and no Byzantine army or its allies were about to mount an attack against the Muslims. Nevertheless, a potential threat from that direction, and a related strategy of neutralising some of the many tribes of that far-flung area, especially those with ties to the Byzantines, as well as subduing others, might have held weight with Muḥammad when he decided to march. His relationship with many of the tribes that inhabited the land between Medina and the borders of Syria still remained undefined at best. Perhaps Muḥammad desired a clearer relationship, one that suited his strategy of propagating and protecting Islam. Whatever the reason, however, there is no doubt that he attached great importance to the expedition. This is clear from the large number of tribes to whom he sent urgent appeals to contribute fighters and resources for the expedition. It was a very hot season, not one when men would willingly march long distances under a scorching sun. It was also a season of ripening fruit, which had its attraction. Yet Muḥammad insisted on the march. There were many who vacillated or declined to join. The Koran has verses on these people, as well as others who willingly marched. There are also verses on other aspects of the Tabūk expedition. The importance the Koran attaches to Tabūk, in *Sūra* 9 (*Barāat*), appears to parallel its importance to the Prophet Muḥammad.

While preparations for the expedition were afoot, Muḥammad happened to ask someone from among the so-called Hypocrites whether he was willing to join and fight. The man said, facetiously, that he would rather not because he was easily attracted to women, and if he came across Syrian women, he would not be able to restrain himself.

There were many others who were equally reluctant, though for other reasons. For example, there were seven Muslims who approached Muḥammad for mounts so that they might join the expedition. The Prophet had to turn them way, as he had no mounts to offer. These Muslims, who came to be known as 'the weepers' were reduced to tears. Of them, the Koran says:

> Nor is there blame on those who came to you for mounts … and you said: 'I cannot find any mounts for you.' They went back with their eyes overflowing with tears …
>
> (9:92)

Some of the desert Arabs came in for severe criticism for making all kinds of excuses to avoid joining the expedition.[128]

Sūra Barāat is replete with harangues for joining the expedition and denunciation of those who would not join:

> O you who believe! How is it that when you are asked to go forth in the path of God, you cling heavily to earth? Are you more pleased with life in this world than with life in the Hereafter? ...
>
> (9:38)

And once again:

> If you do not go forth, He will chastise with a grievous chastisement and put others in your place. And you can do Him no harm ...
>
> (9:39)

We see an unmistakable amount of sulking, threat of punishment, and enticement (putting 'others in your place') in the above narratives, all of which, once again, are all too human.

More enticement follows in this verse:

> If you do not help him, (it does not matter); God certainly helped him when the unbelievers expelled him[129] ...
>
> (9:40)

A clear tone of human complaint appears next:

> If the gains were near, and the journey short, they would certainly have followed you, but the journey seemed too long for them ...
>
> (9:42)

---

[128] Verses 9:90 and 9:101.

[129] This alludes to the circumstances that forced Muḥammad to flee Mecca and set out for Medina on the *hijrah*.

Denunciation of the malingerers continues:

> Those who were left behind rejoiced in staying back, against the wishes of the Apostle, and hated to struggle in the way of God with their possessions and their lives, and they said: 'Do not go out in this heat.' Say: 'The fire of hell is hotter still.' If only they understood!
>
> (9:81)

> Let them laugh a little; they will weep much, a recompense for what they earned.
>
> (9:82)

But there is also forgiveness (9:118). And then there is some more exhortation (9:120).

Finally, the expedition began. Even though a large majority of his forces were devoted Muslims, Muḥammad had to be on the lookout for treachery. The Hypocrites, especially their chief, Abdallah b. Ubayy, were not to be trusted. In any case, the Koran points out, they would only be trouble if they had joined:

> Had they[130] come out with you, they would only have increased you in trouble, running to and fro, seeking to sow dissention between you …
>
> (9:47)

There was no encounter with Byzantine forces because they simply were not there. Yet the Tabūk expedition was one of the most successful Muḥammad ever launched: it resulted in a significant consolidation of Muslim power and influence over a large area to the north of Medina. Given that ease of success, it is puzzling that the preparations for it were so elaborate, the call to arms so frantic, and the denunciation of the laggards so damning. If the Prophet's main goal was to confront the Byzantine threat, then his information about the purported enemy was wrong, in which case it must be presumed he had no divine guidance. Note in

[130] Those who vacillated, as well as the Hypocrites.

particular that most of the verses we read about Tabūk talk about an impending event, unlike, say, verses on the Battle of Badr which concern an event of the recent past. Given that these are supposed to be God's words, the question arises as to how He could have been so wrong about the enemy threat. On the other hand, the verses make perfect sense if they are words of the Prophet, a human haranguing over a threat about which he was ill-informed.

In Tabūk, the governor of Ayla, a Christian community on the Gulf of Aqabah, made a treaty with the Prophet. The treaty is said to have specified an annual tribute, or *jizya,* of three hundred dinars, in exchange for guarantee of the community's security by the Islamic state.[131] The Jewish communities of Maqna, Jarba, and Adhruh also came to similar agreements, involving considerably higher taxes, according to some accounts. The Prophet then sent Khālid b. al-Walīd, now one of his most prominent Muslim commanders, to Dumat al-Jandal, an important oasis situated at some distance to the east of Tabūk, also inhabited by Christians, with Ukaydir as king. The community was easily subdued. Ukaydir was brought to Medina, where he signed an agreement to pay *jizya.* Montgomery Watt thinks that by the late autumn of 630, Muḥammad had adopted the policy, as suggested by a verse of the Koran (9:29): 'Fight those who believe not in God … [even from among the People of the Book] until they pay the jizya … '.[132]

The expedition to Tabūk was the last major expedition led by Muḥammad.

There were many other expeditions from Medina, both those sent out by the Prophet and those led by him. Few of them form the background of a verse of the Koran. However, two expeditions that were very different in nature from those mentioned so far inspired a number of major verses: the Prophet's attempt at a pilgrimage to Mecca which was unsuccessful but which led to the crucial Treaty of Hudaybiyah, and the conquest of Mecca. For this, we go about three years back in history.

In the sixth year of the *hijrah,* in the month of Zul-qa'd, the Prophet set out on a 'lesser pilgrimage', the '*Umra,* to Mecca. It was, and still is,

[131] Watt, 115.

[132] Ibid. 116.

so called because the annual pilgrimage, the *ḥajj* itself, is made in the following month, Zul-ḥajj. The following verse of the Koran records the vision of the Prophet of the coming event:

> God did fulfil the vision for His Messenger with truth: You shall God willing certainly enter the Sacred Mosque, in security, your heads shaved, and hair cut short, without fear. He knows what you know not, and He has given, besides this, a speedy victory.
>
> (48:27)

Muḥammad wanted as large a number of his followers as possible to accompany him on this journey, which did not involve any fighting. Many of the Arab tribes, notably the desert Arabs, were not keen on the idea, presumably because it did not promise any material gains. The same *sūra* denounces those, particularly the desert Arabs, who found excuses not to join the expedition.[133]

Muḥammad's entourage thus consisted mainly of his more ardent followers. Quraysh, custodians of the holy precinct of Mecca, were in no mood to let him enter the city, even as a pilgrim. But neither could they fight a group of pilgrims.

When the news reached Muḥammad that Quraysh would not let him enter the city for the pilgrimage, he set up camp at a place below Mecca, called al-Hudaybiyah. Quraysh sent several emissaries to ascertain the true intentions of the Prophet. Finally, a leading man from the important tribe of Banu Khuzā'ah, which was inclined to friendship with Muḥammad, was able to convince Quraysh that the Muslims were not there to fight, that their intention was only to perform the pilgrimage. The chief of the Bedouin allies of Quraysh, called the Ahabish, also vouched for Muḥammad's intentions. A complex set of factors, including intertribal relationships and respect for the age-old tradition of not turning away pilgrims from the House of God, played a part in breaking down Quraysh obstinacy. Some of the emissaries of Quraysh reported back in vivid detail of how devoted Muḥammad's followers were towards him. That too might have impressed Quraysh.

Meanwhile, 'Uthman, the Prophet's companion, was sent to Mecca

[133] Verse 48:11.

with the message of the Muslim's peaceful intentions. He was told by Quraysh that he could perform the circumambulation of the Ka'ba if he liked, but as to allowing Muḥammad and his entourage to do the ritual, it was out of the question. 'Uthman declined the offer. Soon afterwards, news spread among the Muslims that he had been killed.

The news of 'Uthman's death turned out to be false. But the rumour had filled the Muslims with a sense of despair. According to some accounts, it was at this point that Muḥammad, sitting under an acacia tree, called for and obtained a special declaration of allegiance from his followers. This was the celebrated *Bai'at al-Ridhwan,* or the 'Pledge of God's Good Pleasure'. While the rumour of 'Uthman's death could be one reason behind a renewed pledge, the importance of solidarity in the Muslim camp was all too evident to Muḥammad on other grounds as well. While the appellation of the pledge was divine, its substance was crucially human. The results of the negotiations, for example, might not have been to the liking of everybody. This soon became all too apparent. Moreover, the Muslims were unarmed, or in some cases lightly armed, and would be at a great disadvantage if attacked. To a man of the Prophet's intelligence, a fresh declaration of allegiance would be of great value. And it was.

The Koran has this to say about the pledge under the acacia tree:

> God was well pleased with the believers when they swore allegiance to you under the tree, and He knew what was in their hearts, and He sent down tranquillity on them, and rewarded them with a speedy victory.
>
> (48:18)

This is followed, as we have read above, by God's promise of material gains in the near future: the booty that was to be had in the coming Khaybar expedition.

Finally, Quraysh sent a man called Suhayl b.'Amr, chief of Banu Amir, a clan of Quraysh, to negotiate an agreement with the Prophet. As he was approaching, along with two other men, the Prophet is reported to have said that God had made his business (of negotiations), easy as the man was one of his kinsmen.[134] He was mistaken. Suhayl proved a tough negotiator.

[134] al-Tabarī, vol. 8, 79.

The treaty that followed, the Treaty of Hudaybiyah, was one of the most celebrated in Islam's history. It bore the high watermark of Muḥammad's foresight and wisdom under difficult circumstances. The treaty prohibited armed hostility between the Muslims and Quraysh for ten years. Each party was free to enter into alliance with whomsoever it deemed fit to be allied with. In the event anyone from Quraysh came over to the Muslim camp without his guardians agreeing to it, he would be returned to his tribe, while anyone from among the Muslims returning to Quraysh would not be repatriated. As the treaty's provisions on alliances were being written, the tribe of Khuza'ah declared that they were now allied with Muḥammad, whereupon its traditional adversary, the tribe of Bakr, declared that it was allying itself with Quraysh. This too was incorporated into the agreement, and it would have important consequences, as we will see. As for the pilgrimage, the pledge obliged the Muslims to return home for the time being and come back next year, when Quraysh would allow them to enter the Holy Precincts and stay there for three days. The pilgrims would carry no weapons except swords in their scabbards.[135]

There was considerable unhappiness among the companions of the Prophet about the treaty and the way it was drawn up. For starters, when the Prophet asked 'Ali, who was acting as scribe, to begin the document with 'In the name of Allah the Compassionate', Suhayl objected. 'I do not recognise this,' he said, 'write only "In the name of Allah"'. The Prophet accepted this. He then asked 'Ali to write 'this is what Muḥammad, the Messenger of God, has agreed with Suhayl b. 'Amr'. Suhayl objected again. 'If I witnessed that you were God's Messenger I would not have fought you,' he said. Indeed. Nobody could argue on that. Suhayl would only accept 'This is what Muḥammad b. 'Abdullah has agreed with Suhayl b. 'Amr.' It was so agreed. This was enough to raise the hackles among some of the Muslims. The substantive parts of the document also seemed to put the Muslims at a disadvantage. They were to return home without performing the lesser pilgrimage; and they agreed to return to Quraysh any of its converts to Islam who joined the Muslims, while no reciprocity was required of Quraysh. 'Umar, one of the closest companions of the Prophet, broke into an open tantrum and had to be appeased by Abū Bakr.

But Muḥammad knew better. He sensed that it was only a matter

[135] Ibn Ishaq, 504. The paragraph that follows is also based on the same source.

of time before the Muslims would achieve victory over Quraysh. By appearing to be accommodating, he helped disarm Quraysh opposition, and at the same time, he favourably impressed other Arab tribes. He also knew that no Muslim belonging to the tribe of Quraysh would ever leave him and return to his tribe. Therefore, the lack of reciprocity on the part of Quraysh in the matter of repatriation was only technical.

There was no doubt in Muḥammad's mind that the mission was a success. This is reflected in the following verse:

> Verily We have granted you a manifest victory.
>
> (48:1)

Most exegetes agree that the above verse refers to the treaty. Towards the end of the *sūra* is a verse that spells out the nature of the victory:

> It is He Who has sent His Messenger with the guidance and the religion of Truth, that He may make it prevail over all religions; and enough is God for a witness.
>
> (48:28)

The Prophet returned to Mecca the following year, the seventh year of the *hijrah* (AH 7). In accordance with the terms of the treaty, he came on a pilgrimage, known as the Lesser Pilgrimage of Fulfilment, that is, making up for the pilgrimage from which the Meccan's turned Muhammad away the year before. The Meccans duly let the Muslims perform the pilgrimage, including the circumambulation of the Ka'ba. The Ka'ba was still surrounded with hundreds of idols. Its circumambulation by a Prophet committed to their obliteration must therefore be considered an extraordinary sight, even though ignored in the Islamic tradition. The Prophet stayed in Mecca for three nights before returning to Medina. His wish to stay a little longer was rather unceremoniously denied by the Meccans. During the short stay in Mecca, Muḥammad also married Maymūnah, a widowed sister-in-law of his uncle 'Abbas. He was at the time in the state of ritual purity of a pilgrim. The controversial marriage in a ritual state was said to have been consummated outside the city on his way back to Medina.[136]

[136] al-Tabarī, vol. 8, 136.

The lesser pilgrimage was an important landmark in the period of peace that followed. But, not unexpectedly, tension remained. There was always suspicion of foul play, and the need for vigilance persisted. A number of verses of the Koran refer to events that illustrate the tension. Thus, a migrant from Mecca, called Ḥatib, had secretly sent a letter to Quraysh, informing them of the preparation being made by the Prophet to launch an expedition to Mecca. The man probably did not want to harm the Muslim cause but wanted only to curry favour with the Meccans, as he had left behind his family in the city when he migrated. But the bearer of the letter, a woman, was caught, and the man confessed to having sent the letter. However, he was pardoned after he told the Prophet the truth about his family. The incident inspired the following verse, in quite another *sūra*:

> O you who believe! Take not my enemy and your enemy for friends, offering them love: They deny the Truth that has come to you and have driven out the Messenger and you …
>
> (60:1)

The *sūra* containing the above verse also has a number of verses that refer to an event having consequences for the repatriation clause of the treaty. Some Muslim women of Mecca were said to have fled the home of their nonbeliever husbands and sought refuge in Medina. Under the terms of the treaty, they were supposed to have been sent back. But the Prophet refused to send Muslim women back to their infidel husbands. Instead, the following rule was promulgated:

> O you who believe! When believing women come fleeing to you, examine them … If you conclude that they are believers, do not send them back to the unbelievers …
>
> (60:10)

It is easy to see that the rule brought under its purview those (husbands) who were not Muslim. There is no doubt that the ruling contained in the verse violated the treaty. But Muḥammad could not send back Muslim women to their unbelieving husbands, treaty or no treaty, and his stance is paralleled in the above verse.

The decision was not easy to rationalise, and this is reflected in the two very different exegetic points of view. One exegete argues that Quraysh had already broken the treaty, implying that the ruling was therefore justified under the circumstances.[137] Another exegete accepts that by this ruling, 'the scope of the Treaty was restricted', and the treaty could therefore be said to have been partly rescinded, but he simply states this as a unilateral fait accompli, without going into the niceties of binding obligations under a treaty.[138] The latter exegete places the event at soon after Hudaybiyah, which contradicts the first exegete, because the question of Quraysh breaking the treaty was to come much later.

The following verse also suggests payments of compensation to the nonbeliever husbands:

> ... And pay the unbelievers what they have spent (on their dower);
>
> and there is no blame on you if you marry them ...
>
> (60:10)

The Treaty of Hudaybiyah was supposed to remain in force for ten years. Its breakdown in a little less than two years was seen by Muḥammad as a *casus belli* leading to the conquest of Mecca. The treaty was said to have been breached through a renewal of an old feud between the two tribes of Khuzā'ah and Bakr, allied respectively to the Muslims and Quraysh. A party of Bakr raided Khuzā'ah and killed one of its members. This was apparently in retaliation of the killing of three men of Bakr by some members of Khuzā'ah sometime before the treaty had been concluded. Quraysh helped Bakr in the latest fighting and killing. Whether or not this was enough reason to launch an attack against Quraysh and conquer Mecca, Muḥammad decided to do exactly that. The treaty presumably did not specify the penalty for its breach, and Quraysh was not in a position to argue its defence.

It is remarkable that while the incidents relating to Ḥatib and the matter of the repatriation of Muslim women figured prominently in the Koran, and the latter issue even finds a place as a title of a *sūra* (*Mumtaḥana*, or 'The Woman to be Examined', *Sūra* 60), the feud between

[137] Qur'ān/Yusuf Ali, footnote to verse 60:10.

[138] Qur'ān/Muhiuddin, exegesis of verse 60:10.

the tribes, and the killing which led Muḥammad to invade Mecca, are nowhere mentioned. Nor for that matter is there a verse that foretells the conquest of Mecca that was soon to follow. For example, there is no verse comparable to 48:27 (see above) that presaged the unsuccessful pilgrimage which led to the Treaty of Hydaybiyah, even though the Meccan campaign was arguably at least as important as the conclusion of the treaty.

Neither does the Koran mention any of the events during the time Muḥammad decided on the expedition to Mecca and its actual conquest. These events need only a brief mention in the present context.

Muḥammad began preparations for the Mecca campaign in great secrecy. This was, in fact, one reason the Ḥatib missive was considered important. Even as he set out for Mecca, his destination was a matter of speculation. The Meccan tribes were already nervous about the consequences of the killing of the Khuzā'ah man. Abū Sufyān was hastily dispatched to Medina to find out what the Prophet was up to, and if possible, to see whether there was a way to mollify him. The trip was futile, and it was not long before Abū Sufyān himself became a Muslim under dire circumstances. It is said that al-'Abbas, the Prophet's uncle and confidant, who had accepted Islam, never migrated from Mecca. He was instrumental in goading Abū Sufyān to accept Islam. He brought Muḥammad's prevaricating cousin, a prominent leader of a sister clan, to his presence. Abū Sufyān accepted Islam just as 'Umar finally stopped clamouring for his head. Al-'Abbas' efforts were largely pragmatic. He wanted to avoid shedding of Quraysh blood.

The Prophet had a large army with him, probably some ten thousand strong. Quraysh were dispirited and divided, and there were only small skirmishes before he entered Mecca and declared victory. A general amnesty was declared, and almost all the inhabitants of Mecca became Muslim. The amnesty is reflected in the verse:

> And if anyone amongst the idolaters asks you for protection, grant it till he hears God's words, and escort him to safety. This is because they are a people who do not have knowledge.
>
> (9:6)

There are other verses which take a far less conciliatory view of the pagans, as we will see. Still, only a few Meccans were executed, including two or three women, a singing girl among them. The three implacable opponents of the Prophet, who had held out against the Muslim forces to the last – Suhayl b. ʿAmr, ʿIkrimah b. Abi Jahl, and Safwan b. Umayyah – were ultimately pardoned, and the latter two converted to Islam. A high watermark of mass conversion of Meccans to Islam was the Prophet's pardon of Hind bt. ʿUtbah, who had desecrated the body of his fallen uncle Ḥamzah during the Battle of Uḥud.

At a more personal level, according to al-Waqidi, as quoted by al-Tabari, the Prophet married Mulaykah bt. Dāwūd al-Laythiyyah.[139] She was a young and beautiful woman. After the marriage, one of the Prophet's wives confronted her and told her that she should be ashamed to marry a man who had killed her father. Al-Laythiyyah was killed during the conquest of Mecca. Mulaykah then asked for a separation, to which the Prophet agreed. The story brings to mind Muḥammad marrying Safiyyah, whose husband was killed on his orders at Khaybar. His twin act of marrying Maymūnah during the lesser pilgrimage to Mecca, followed by another marriage on his very next visit to the city, is perhaps no less remarkable.

One of the first acts of the Prophet after his entry into Mecca was to visit the Kaʿba, with cane in hand. There he recited the following verse:

> And say: Truth has come and falsehood has vanished:
> surely falsehood is bound to vanish.
>
> (17:81)

As reported by Ibn Ishaq, the Prophet pointed the cane at the 360 idols that surrounded the Kaʿba, whereupon they toppled, one by one.[140] That must be considered truly symbolic of the finality of Muḥammad's conquest of Mecca, accomplished in the month of Ramadan, in AH 8.

The pilgrimage to Mecca in the following year, AH 9, is of some importance in Islamic history of the period immediately after the conquest of Mecca. Muḥammad did not himself go on that pilgrimage; instead, he sent Abū Bakr at the head of pilgrims from Medina. We are

[139] al-Tabarī, vol. 8, 187.

[140] Ibn Ishaq, 552.

told that *Sūra* 9, *Barāāt* ('Immunity'), or most of it, had freshly been inspired in the interim.[141]

Abū Bakr was well on his way when Muḥammad hurriedly sent 'Ali to join the group, with a large number of verses from *Sūra* 9 and with instructions to read them out at the pilgrimage, to be heard by all pilgrims, Muslim or polytheist.[142] According to some accounts, Abū Bakr himself had been carrying the verses, and 'Ali took them from him. Irrespective of which version was true, Muḥammad is reported to have said that no one except himself or someone from his family should communicate the Declaration of Immunity. Abū Bakr was magnanimous. and while 'Ali read the proclamations of 'Immunity', he himself led the pilgrimage and gave the sermon. Nevertheless, the incident could not be without significance for the schism that was soon to appear in the Muslim community.

The *sūra* opens with the following verse (addressed to Muḥammad):

> Freedom from obligation (is proclaimed) from God and His messenger towards those of the idolaters with whom you made a treaty ... [143]
>
> (9:1)

Some commentators link the above verse with the violation of the Treaty of Hudaybiyah, by the Meccans.[144] Others do not necessarily link the abrogation to the Treaty of Hudaybiyah.[145] The nature of 'Ali's

---

[141] More fully, 'Declaration of Immunity', meaning immunity from, or dissolution of, treaty obligations. This is perhaps a more apt name, because dissolution (also described as dispensation) of such obligations is a major theme of the *sūra*.

[142] I have used al-Tabarī, vol. 9, 77–79; Ibn Ishaq, 618–19; and Martin Lings, 323, for the narrative on the pilgrimage and the related events. There is little difference between accounts in these sources.

[143] Koran/Pickthall. This is also close to the translation in Qur'ān/Muhiuddin. In essence, it means dispensation with obligations under a treaty or covenant.

[144] Qur'ān/Muhiuddin.

[145] Qur'ān/Yusuf Ali has this to say: The pagans and the enemies of Islam frequently made treaties of mutual alliance with the Muslims. The Muslims scrupulously observed their part, but the pagans violated their part again and again when it suited them.Yusuf Ali cites no specific instances of violation of the Treaty of Hudaybiyah in this context. None of the commentators I have read cite any specific instance of treaty violation.

proclamation contained in the verses that follow verse 9:1 also makes the link to that treaty rather tenuous.

In *Sūra* 9, the polytheists were given four months to travel through the land, after which Muḥammad would be free from any treaty obligations with the pagans. The following two verses say so:

> So go about in the land for four months, and know that you cannot defeat the will of God; and surely God will degrade the unbelievers.
>
> (9:2)

> And a proclamation from God and His Messenger to the people on the day of the Great Pilgrimage, that God and His Messenger are free of obligations to the idolaters. So if you repent, it will be good for you …
>
> (9:3)

This is a unilateral abrogation of treaty obligations. The verses make it quite clear who has the upper hand, treaty or no treaty. It is unclear exactly what kind of treaty obligations the verses abrogated. Presumably, the declaration banned pagans from the place of pilgrimage which were so far open to them by mutual understanding. Any ambiguity about this is fully dispelled by the following verse, in which the pagans are forbidden to approach the Sacred Precincts of the city in these unflattering terms:

> O you who believe! Truly the idolaters are unclean; so they shall not approach the Sacred Mosque after this years of theirs. And if you fear poverty, soon God will enrich you out of His Bounty, if He pleases. Surely God is All-knowing, Wise.
>
> (9:28)

The first part of the verse largely defines the status of the unbelievers in the eyes of Islam, in regard to visits to the Sacred Precinct. This has remained unchanged to this day. The second refers to the possibility that the absence of the polytheists from the Sacred Mosque would reduce the revenue the Meccans derived from the pilgrimage. The fear of pecuniary loss was soon to prove unfounded, and pilgrimage remained a major source of income for the Mother of Cities till recent times. About the verse's declaring the pagans unclean, we note the distance that had been travelled since the categorical statement in *Sūra* 2 (*Baqara*):

> Let there be no compulsion in religion …
>
> (2:256)

Verses 9:2 and 9:3 are said to apply to polytheists with whom there was no specific treaty or convention. For others the directive is rather different:

> But those idolaters with whom you made a covenant, and who have not failed you in anything, and have not aided anyone against you – fulfil your agreements with them till the end of their term. Surely God loves the god fearing.
>
> (9:4)

Then follows a verse with a clarion call to fight the idolaters:

> Then when the forbidden months are past, slay the idolaters whenever you find them …
>
> (9:5)

Coming immediately after a verse that allows fulfilment of covenants till the end of their term, the verse is puzzling. One commentator maintains that 9:5 does not apply to pagans mentioned in 9:4.[146] The question of why it is there still remains. We shall return to verse 9:5 in another context.

The conquest of Mecca was followed by a number of campaigns, as we saw earlier. Considerations of economic necessity and perceived security needs dominate the history of these wars and expeditions. As with any other campaign of this nature, human failures, guiles, as well as pursuit of

---

[146] Martin Lings, 323.

an idea, determined the outcome. There were great cruelties and excesses. As with any other military chief, Muḥammad's judgements were not always impeccable, but his overall strategy was a resounding success. By the time of his death, in AH 11 (632), Islam had established itself as a rising power in a large area of the Arabian peninsula. Further challenges and turmoil lay ahead. These are beyond the purview of the Koran.

Chapter 6
Relationship with the Unbelievers

> Surely those who believe, and those of Jewry, and the Christians and the Sabians, any who believes in God, and the Last Day, and the righteous, they have their reward with their Lord. And on them shall be no fear, and neither shall they grieve.
>
> (2:62)

Among the verses of the Koran that pronounce on how the nascent community of Muslims and its prophet should deal with those not sharing its faith, the above verse stands out: it emphasises the affinity between the believers in the Koran and the Judaeo-Christian believers, as all believe in one God. In recent times of rising religious fundamentalism, the verse has often been quoted to suggest that there is no real difference between the great monotheist religions of the world, and hence no cause for animosity among their adherents.

Most of the verses in the following paragraphs are far less sanguine about the commonality. Specifically, when it came to propagation of Islam, practical concerns, as opposed to spiritual affinities with peoples of other faiths, dominated. Hostility, doubt, and defensiveness better describe the relationship with the unbelievers. The verses often contradict each other. This is primarily because of changed contexts. In many cases the context is unclear, and exegeses are lacking. We shall read a fairly large number of verses concerning Islam's relationship with people of other faiths, roughly following the order in which they appear in the Koran, but with some inevitable reversal of that order.

The following verse could not be more different in tone and substance from verse 2:62 above. As in many places in the Koran, the verse below appears unconnected to the preceding as well as succeeding verses, and the context of its inspiration is not available. The *sūra* to which the verse belongs contains a number of references to the Battle of Badr and the Battle of Uḥud. Thus an atmosphere of hostility might have coloured the verse. The preference for a friendly believer over a friendly unbeliever is understandable, though, other things remaining the same. It is easy to visualise the Prophet counselling wisdom at a time when he had reason to be wary of the unbelievers.

Thus, we read:

> Let not the believers take the unbelievers for friends, rather than believers; and for one who does that, there will be no relationship with God, except when you guard yourselves against them ...
>
> (3:28)

Of similar import are the following two verses, with suspicion of the unbelievers added. The exact circumstances of their revelation are unclear:

> O you who believe! Take not for intimate friends other than from your own people: such men spare nothing to harm you. They love that which distresses you ...
>
> (3:118)

> You love them, but they love you not; and you believe in the whole Book; and when they meet you they say, 'We believe,' and when they are among themselves they bite the tip of their fingers at you ...
>
> (3:119)

The following verse, from a Meccan *sūra*, is remarkable in its mellow reasonableness. In the early years of the prophethood of Muḥammad, the Meccans were said to have been greatly upset by his cursing of the polytheists' gods. As reported by Ibn Ishaq, one day, Abū Jahl,

Muḥammad's uncle and an implacable enemy of Islam, was so angry that he waylaid Muḥammad to tell him, 'By God, Muhammad, you will either stop cursing our gods or we will curse the God you serve.'[147] The result was the verse below, which appears to be a strategy, rather than a universal expression of goodwill to people of other faiths. Muḥammad stopped cursing Mecca's gods and began to call the people to Allah instead. The verse is:

> Abuse not those whom they call god besides God, lest they, in their Ignorance, abuse God ...
>
> (6:108)

For a view that is altogether different, and unambiguous, read:

> Surely the worst of beasts in the sight of God are those who disbelieve; and then they will not believe.
>
> (8:55)

When opponents unite, strategy demands unity among the ranks of the believers:

> And the unbelievers are friends of another; if you do not do the same (among yourselves),there will be persecution in the land and great mischief.
>
> (8:73)

The following verse, which we read a few pages earlier (in Chapter 5), deserves to be re-read in the present context. There can be few expressions of greater antagonism, though it matches those in verse 8:55, above:

> O you who believe! Truly the idolaters are unclean; so they shall not approach the Sacred Mosque after this year of theirs ...
>
> (9:28)

---

[147] Ibn Ishaq, 162.

The following verse, also read earlier (again in Chapter 5), should be read against the background of Muḥammad's preparations for the conquest of Mecca and the unwise effort of Hatib, the Meccan living in Medina, to befriend some people in Mecca under those circumstances. The Prophet forgave him, but here we read unambiguous advice against making friends with those who reject the way of God:

> O you who believe! Take not my enemy and your enemy for friends, offering them love: They deny the Truth that has come to you and have driven out the Messenger and you ...
>
> (60:1)

Remarkably, the *sūra* containing the above verse also has a sharp change in tone. It comes with the impending conquest of Mecca. And it should be read in the context of the magnificence of Muslim victory and a natural desire on the part of those Meccans who migrated to Medina to be reunited with their fellow clansmen, especially when the possibility of their being driven from home again was now thin.

Thus, we read:

> Perhaps God will bring about friendship between you and those among them whom you consider as enemies ...
>
> (60:7)

> God forbids you not as regards those who fight you not, nor drive you from your homes, that you show kindness to them and deal justly with them. Surely God loves the just.
>
> (60:8)

The following, from *Sūra* 109 (*Kāfirūn*), are among the best known verses of the Koran:

> Say: O you that reject the faith!
>
> (109:1)

> I worship not what you worship;
>
> (109:2)

> Nor do you worship whom I worship;
>
> (109:3)
>
> Nor shall I worship that which you worship;
>
> (109:4)
>
> Nor do you worship whom I worship;
>
> (109:5)
>
> To you be your Way, and to me mine.
>
> (109:6)

The above verses have sometimes been quoted to bolster a liberal, non-coercive image of Islam, even in its early days. The last line – in Arabic, *lakum dīnukum wa liya dīn* – is said to represent the true face of Islam. Put in historical perspective, the verse would look far less radical. As we have seen, several years into Muḥammad's efforts at proselytisation, several influential Meccan leaders proposed to him an agreement under which they would worship Islam's God for a period of time, followed by a period when Muḥammad and the Muslims would worship the gods of the Meccans. Muḥammad finally declined the offer, to which *lakum dīnukum wa liya dīn* was a form of rebuff.[148] Any suggestion that the verse was a long-term hands-off approach would make Muḥammad's continuing proselytisation and his unflinching stand on *jihad* totally meaningless.

An uncommon attitude of non-confrontation and passivity, which would partly echo *lakum dīnukum wa liya dīn*, is to be found in the following verse. The righteous are those who, when God's words reach them, say, 'We believe therein' (28:53). Also:

... when they hear idle talk, they turn away from it saying:

> 'For us our deeds, for you yours. Peace be with you. We desire not the ignorant.'
>
> (28:55)

[148] Qur'ān/Muhiuddin.

This verse belongs to a Meccan *sūra* and is very likely to have been inspired during some brief hiatus in hostility, reflected in *Sūra* 109, above.

Relationship with Christians and Jews, the two monotheist groups that the Koran clearly distinguishes from the polytheist, occupies a number of verses. Some of these are reproduced below. It is useful to read them in context with the background of verse 2:62, given at the beginning of this chapter.

Thus, we read:

> O you who believe! Do not take Jews and Christians for friends: They are but friends of each other. And whoever among you makes them his friend is one of them. Surely God guides not people unjust.
>
> (5:51)

Although the polytheists come up for particular censure, in the next verse the Jews do not fare any better. The Christians fare remarkably well. This is perhaps related to the numerical strength, and hostility, of major Jewish communities, as compared with the Christian communities at that time. Still, it is rather hard to envisage many Christian eyes filling with tears while listening to God's revelation to Muḥammad, as the second of the following verses wants us to believe.

> You will find among the people most hostile to the believers the Jews, and the idolaters. And the nearest in friendship to the believers are those who say we are Christian: this is because there are among them learned men and men who have renounced the world and who are not arrogant.
>
> (5:82)

> And when they listen to the revelation received by the Messenger, you will see their eyes overflowing with tears because of the truth they recognise …
>
> (5:83)

The unbelievers had many questions to ask Muḥammad in regard to his message. Quraysh subjected him to verbal attacks while questioning his prophethood. In Medina, Jewish religious leaders often visited him, some challenging his mission. A number of verses allude to the opposition of the disbelievers and the nature of their arguments. Some of these verses purport to be rejoinders to the disbelievers' questions and doubts. A modern reader might find some of the responses less than adequate. Here are a few of these verses:

> And if they contend with you, say: 'God knows best what it is you do.'
>
> (22:68)

> 'God will judge between you on the Day of Resurrection concerning matters you differ on.'
>
> (22:69)

> And those without knowledge say: 'Why does not God speak to us or a sign comes to us?'
>
> (2:118)

The purported answer, in the same verse, is:

> That was what people who came before them said, in similar words. Their hearts are alike. Yet We have made the sign clear to people who have firm faith.
>
> (2:118)

This of course presents the existence of faith as the prerequisite for the ability to grasp the 'sign'. The verse is followed, in 2:119, by a further denunciation of the disbelievers as 'Companions of the Blazing Fire'. There is then the throwing up of hands instead of a direct answer to the unbelievers' question:

> Never will the Jews be satisfied with you, nor the Christians, till you follow their religion. Say: 'Surely God's guidance is the only guidance' …
>
> (2:120)

The unbelievers are quoted as saying, at the beginning of verse 39:3, 'We only serve them (the idols) in order that they may bring us nearer to God.' We would think this a valid position to take, and one requiring a valid response. But no such response comes, except only to say, in the rest of the verse:

... Surely God will judge between them in matters in which they differ. Surely God does not guide the liar, the ungrateful.

(39:3)

Similarly, in the following verse the unbelievers say:

> ... ' If it had been the will of the all- Merciful, we would not have worshipped them (the idols)' ...
>
> (43:20)

This may sound facetious, but it is still a legitimate statement. It is also difficult to answer. The response, in the same verse, is singularly inadequate:

> ... Of this they have no knowledge! They only lie!
>
> (43:20)

Again, the unbelievers would like to see a Koran sent down in its entirety, something certainly within God's power. On this we have:

> Nay, every one of them desires to be given scrolls spread out!
>
> (74:52)

The response is a retort and a resounding threat:

> By no means! But they fear not the Hereafter!
>
> (74:53)

Again, the unbelievers argue:

> If God had pleased we would not have set up partners to Him, nor our fathers, nor would we have forbidden anything ...
>
> (6:148)

This is not very different from what God himself might say, as we will see later (in Chapter 10) when we read verses on predestination. Here, the unbelievers are answered, in the same verse:

> ... So did those before them reject the truth until they tasted Our might.
>
> (6:148)

The next verse can well be seen as the final word:

> Say: 'With God is the final argument. If it had been His will He would have guided you all.' [149]
>
> (6:149)

To a modern reader with some knowledge of Arabic, the expression *Fa lillahil hujjāt-ul-bālega* – translated here as 'With God is the final argument' – will sound profound. It will still appear as a merely assertive response, rather than a rigorous answer to the various questions posed.

---

[149] *Fa lillahil hujjātul bālega* has also been variously translated as 'With God is the argument that reaches home' (Qur'ān/Yusuf Ali); 'To God belongs the argument conclusive' (Koran/Arberry); and 'For Allah's is the final Argument' (Koran/Pickthall).

Chapter 7
Jihad

In the Koran, *jihad* is the principal motivating force behind the expeditions Muḥammad led and the battles he fought. Many of the expeditions had undoubtedly pecuniary motives behind them, as we have seen. Still, the overarching design in most cases was propagation and defence of the new faith. Whether a battle was fought because the opportunity arose, as in Badr, or under grave threat of annihilation, as in Uḥud, or as a virtual walkover, as in the conquest of Mecca, the action was undertaken in the name of Islam: to establish the new faith, to please God, and to secure His mercy. Even assassinations, such as the ones we encountered in the accounts of battles and expeditions (in Chapter 5), were seen as means to attain the same objective of pleasing God and securing the faith. Death in such action was considered martyrdom, always guaranteeing a place in Heaven for the martyr. There were many who moved from unbelief to belief of their own volition. There were many more who became believers after losing in battle.

In popular mind today, *jihad* is clearly associated with force and violence. It so happens that, against the above background of *jihad* in the early days of Islam, the popular concept is also the right one. To some liberals and Islamic apologists, *jihad* is human 'striving', in the broadest sense, to further God's cause; as such, it is not restricted to violence (i.e. fighting with weapons). This view, however, does ignore the historical background of verses that call for 'striving'. As we have seen, verses like 9:41 or 9:81 talk of 'striving' in the context of the Tabūk expedition, with a clear call to arms.[150]

[150] See Chapter 5.

In an effort to distance the idea of *jihad* as an essentially violent action, some have even tried to cast it in spiritual terms. In an exegesis on verse 9:20, taken up later in this chapter, one liberal commentator maintains that while *jihad* may require fighting in the course of furthering God's cause, 'its essence consists in (1) a true and sincere Faith, which so fixes its gaze on God that all selfish or worldly motives seem paltry and fade away, and (2) an earnest and ceaseless activity involving the sacrifice (if need be) of life, person, or property, in the service of God' ... [151]

A modern Islamic scholar has viewed *jihad* in less abstruse terms:

> The Qur'an calls upon believers to undertake *jihad*, which is to surrender 'your properties and yourselves in the path of Allah;' the purpose of which in turn is to ' establish prayer, give zakat, command good and forbid evil' – i.e. to establish the Islamic socio-economic order ... [152]

In the Koranic context, surrendering properties and self in the cause of God has essentially meant fighting with weapons. And the fighting was not basically defensive:

... The most unacceptable on historical grounds, however, is the stand of those Muslim apologists who have tried to explain the *jihād* of the early [Islamic] Community in purely defensive terms.

In the aftermath of activities by Islamic extremists in recent years, there has been a revival of the Muslim apologist idea of *jihad* as 'striving' in its broadest sense. Still, mainstream Muslims would loathe being labelled *jihadists*. That appellation is usually reserved for Islamist advocates of violence as a means to establish an Islamic state of their choice. For their part, many from the latter group would wear the label willingly, even with pride. And they can even bring up an array of verses from the Koran to bolster their definition of *jihad*.

The number of verses of the Koran devoted to the idea of *jihad* is not very large. In the following paragraphs, we will examine most of the verses in the Book dealing with the subject. As with other themes in the Koran, the verses are scattered over many *sūras*, but are found

---

[151] Qur'ān/Yusuf Ali, exegesis of verse 9:20.

[152] Fazlur Rahman, *Islam*, 2nd edn (Chicago: University of Chicago Press, 1979), 37.

primarily in *Sūras* 2 (*Baqara*), 8 (*Anfāl*), and 9 (*Barāat*). All the verses are Medinan, and, as can be expected, many of them were inspired against the background of battles and expeditions.

Jihad was not an option for Muḥammad in Mecca. As a community, the Muslims were a weak lot, hardly capable of a fight. There are a number of Meccan verses that call for non-confrontation, even courtesy, on the part of Muslims in their relationship with the infidels. Thus, God advises Muḥammad:

> And when you see people engaged in finding fault in Our Signs, turn away from them till they turn into some other discourse ...
>
> (6:68)

And, good Muslims are those who:

> And when they hear idle talk, they turn away from it saying: 'For us our deeds, for you yours. Peace be with you. We desire not the ignorant.'
>
> (28:55)

This is virtually repeated in verse 42:15. There was soon to be a sharp reversal of attitude towards the unbelievers.

It is important to read the verses on the new faith's relationship with the unbelievers in historical context, as we have seen in the preceding chapter (Chapter 6). The historical context is perhaps even more important when reading verses on *jihad*. There are, however, a number of important verses for which the occasion of inspiration is not available, and so they are taken to be of general applicability. *Sūra* 2 (*Baqara*), the longest in the Book, also contains the largest number of verses on fighting. Exegetes chronologically place the *sūra*, or most of it, in the early Medina period, which was also when the two major battles, Badr and Uḥud, were fought. However, there are a number of verses in the *sūra* which are considered to be of a later vintage.

Among the earliest verses to be inspired on *jihad* are said to be the following two. They are from a *Sūra* 22 (*Ḥajj*), which is perhaps early Medinan:

> To those against whom war is made, permission is given to fight, because they are oppressed. And surely God is most able to aid them.
>
> (22:39)

> They are those who have been expelled from their homes without reason except that they say: God is our Lord …
>
> (22:40)

Here, Muslims are clearly urged to fight the enemy on the battlefield. Some exegetes consider the verses as giving permission for fighting, but only in self-defence. 'Those against whom war is made' are clearly the believers, and it is to them that permission is given to fight. They are also the people who suffered the wrong of having been expelled from their homes. There appears to be no particular incident occasioning the inspiration of the two verses. Still, there is little reason to doubt that, as some commentators have pointed out, there was a strong sentiment of hurt among the believers who had been forced out of their homes in Mecca by the hostility of the polytheists of the city. They were said to be keen to fight to return home and had been wishing the Prophet would soon approve fighting. Soon came divine approval.

The first word in Arabic that the following verse begins with is *qātelu*, meaning 'fight' (also translated as 'slay'), which is what the next verse also starts with. It is important to keep the historical background in mind here. Muḥammad and his companions made their way to Mecca for pilgrimage a year after the signing the Treaty of Hudaybiyah, and even though acting according to the terms of that treaty, they remained apprehensive. They could not be sure that Quraysh would not fight them or prevent them from entering the Sacred Precincts of Mecca. They also felt vulnerable because they were not supposed to fight in the prohibited month, while Quraysh might not be so constrained by custom.[153]

[153] Alī ibn Ahmad al-Wāhidī, (d. AH 468/AD 1075), *Asbāb al-Nuzūl* ('Occasions of Revelation') (Amman, Jordan: Royal Aal al-Bayt Institute for Islamic Thought, 2008). Qur'ān/Muhiuddin concurs.

> And fight in the way of God those who fight you; but do not transgress limits. Surely God likes not those who transgress limits.
>
> (2:190)

> And slay them wherever you find them; and drive them out from where they drove you; and persecution[154] is worse than slaughter. And fight them not at the precinct of the Sacred Mosque, unless they fight you there. But if they fight you, slay them …
>
> (2:191)

There is also a call for restraint, as in 2:190, and in 2:192, below:

> But if they desist, God is Forgiving, Merciful.
>
> (2:192)

But this is immediately followed by:

> And fight them on, until there is no *fitna*, and the religion established is God's. But if they cease, then there should be no hostility, except against the oppressors.
>
> (2:193)

It is important to see that, unlike in 2:190, cessation of hostility appears contingent on establishment of God's religion in the land.

The following verse is a general statement of principle which obligates the believers to fight:

> Fighting is enjoined upon you even if you dislike it. Perhaps you dislike a thing that is good for you, and you love a thing that is bad for you. God knows what you know not.
>
> (2:216)

---

[154] Some translators have given the Arabic word *fitna* (translated here as 'persecution') more inclusive definitions, such as 'tumult', 'oppression', 'anarchy', and 'civil war'. I shall use the Arabic *fitna* in what follows.

Following tradition, fighting was prohibited in the four designated sacred months of the Islamic calendar. The Koran upholds forcefully the sanctity of the sacred months. More forceful is the call to fight those who prevent access to God's path. The following verse is said to have been inspired after the Nakhlah expedition,[155] the first after Muḥammad's migration to Medina. As we have seen, a member of Quraysh was killed in the Muslim attack which took place during a prohibited month. The aggrieved Quraysh sent a delegation to Muḥammad to demand an explanation of the killing during a prohibited month. Verse 2:217, repeated below, was the response:

> They ask you about fighting in the Prohibited Month. Say: 'Fighting in it is heinous offence. But more heinous in the sight of God is to hinder men from the path of God, to deny Him and the Sacred Mosque, and turning people out of it. And persecution is graver than slaughter. And they will not stop fighting you till they turn you from your religion if they can …
>
> (2:217)

It is in connection with *jihad* that the word *irtada*, or 'turning back', is mentioned in the verse. From that word is derived *murtad*, or 'apostate', which Islamic militants have often used in recent times to denounce Muslim critics of Islam. The word appears in the last part of the above verse, continued below. It is worth noting that no worldly punishment is prescribed for those turning back from *jihad*. Punishment comes from God in the hereafter, as we read here:

> … And if some of you turn back from their religion and then die as unbelievers, their work will avail them nothing in this world and in the Hereafter. They are the companions of the Fire, wherein they will abide.
>
> (2:217)

Irtada appears in two more verses apparently not connected to *jihad*. Note again the absence of a threat of punishment to the *murtad*. In

---

[155] See Chapter 5.

fact, there is no verse in the Koran that prescribes punishment to an individual who has left Islam. In the following verse, Satan has a hand in instigating desertion from Islam. The sinner will presumably receive his comeuppance in the hereafter, as in the earlier verse:

> Surely those who turned back after guidance was shown to them, it was Satan who instigated them and give them false hope.
>
> (47:25)

The next verse appears unique in that, far from threatening those who turn back with worldly punishment, it only tries to entice the prospective sinner from turning back by pointing out what he would miss if he turned back:

> O you who believe! If any[156] among you turn back from his religion, certainly God will bring a people whom He loves and who love Him, who are humble towards the believers and hard against the unbelievers, who will fight in the way of God, and will not fear any reproach of the reproacher ...
>
> (5:54)

The following verse does not use the word *mān-yartādda* to mean 'who turns back'; instead, it uses *tawallau,* which has the same meaning. It is necessary to quote the verse in its entirety:

> They rather wish that you should disbelieve as they disbelieve, so that you are at par with them. So do not take from among them friends till they migrate to the way of God. If they turn back, seize them wherever you may find them, and slay them, and do not take friends or helpers from among them.
>
> (4:89)

[156] Qur'ān/Islamic Academy opines that the 'any' (*mān,* in Arabic) refers to a community, rather than an individual.

The phrase 'if they turn back' in this case suggests turning to hostility[157] and has not been used in the sense of turning back from religion, as in verse 5:54. The turning back and the killing need to be seen here in the context of war and not necessarily as part of *jihad.*

To return to the theme of *jihad* in *Sūra* 2, Muslims are again urged to fight:

> And fight in the path of God, and know that God hears and knows all things.
>
> (2:244)

The verse that follows is noteworthy as an easy-to-understand exhortation in terms of reward promised:

> Who will loan God a good loan? And God will increase it for him manifold …
>
> (2:245)

While *jihad* is fighting, all fighting is not necessarily *jihad.* The following two verses are remarkable in their implication that God will sometimes check one people by means of another, and that fighting among peoples is part of God's will. Within or without a context,[158] the two verses are among the most inscrutable in the Book:

> … And had God not checked some people by means of others, the world would have been full of mischief.
>
> (2:251)

In a similar vein:

> … If God had willed, succeeding generations would not have fought each other after clear arguments had come to them. But they disagreed, some believing and others

[157] Qur'ān/Muḥammad Ali.

[158] The context of the lines of the first verse is the way in which God helped David slay Goliath. The second verse refers to generations after Jesus.

> disbelieving. If God had willed they would not have fought each other. God does what He intends.
>
> (2:253)

Martyrdom is glorified in many of the verses, of which the following stand out:

> Think not of those who are killed in the way of God as dead. They are alive, receiving their sustenance from their Lord.
>
> (3:169)

> Let them fight in the way of God who sell life in this world for the Hereafter. To him who fights in the way of God, be he is killed or is victorious, shall We soon give a magnificent reward.
>
> (4:74)

The verse that follows makes a clear case for fighting against oppression. It is also puzzling to modern readers of the Koran. It attempts to portray men, women, and children waiting to be rescued while in the midst of townspeople who oppress them. Apparently, the oppressed here are the Muslim community in Mecca after the *hijrah,* and the oppressors are the polytheist majority of the city. The portrayal parallels the story of the Jews in Egypt waiting to be rescued by Moses. The parallel is ersatz and misleading. The difficulty is that nowhere else in the Koran are Muslims in Mecca so described, and there could not have been more than a handful of Muslims in Mecca after the *hijrah.* Some verses on *jihad* hark back to the flight of Muslims from their homeland, but none refer to the theme of Muslims stranded in their native city. The verse itself illustrates this best:

> And why should you not fight in the way of God, and for the weak among men and women and children who cry: 'Lord, rescue us from this town, whose people are oppressors, and give us from You a protector, and give us from You one who will help.'
>
> (4:75)

The true believer will always fight for the cause of God and against evil:

> Those who believe fight in the way of God, and those who disbelieve fight in the way Satan. Surely the cunning of the Satan is feeble.
>
> (4:76)

Sūras 8 (*Anfāl*) and 9 (*Barāat*), dominated by the theme of expedition and fighting, are naturally concerned with fighting for God's cause. Here is assurance of forgiveness for the unbelievers, but only after they have become believers:

> Say to those who disbelieve, if they desist their past will be forgiven them. And if they return to disbelief, there is the example of those of old.
>
> (8:38)

The verse that follows, almost identical to verse 2:193, leaves no doubt as to the consequences if they persist in disbelief:

> And fight them until there is no more fitna and there is God's religion entirely. And if they desist, God sees all they do.
>
> (8:39)

The verse immediately following is far more poetic in Arabic than in translation:

> And if they turn away, know that God is your Protector – the most excellent Protector, the most excellent Helper.
>
> (8:40)

In a remarkable descent, the very next verse is about booty, which is often not very far from the idea of fighting in the way of God:

> And know that out of whatever booty you acquire, a fifth is for God, His Messenger, next of kin, the orphans, the needy and the wayfarer …
>
> (8:41)

A cluster of verses in *Sūra* 8 (*Anfāl*) begins with a denunciation of the unbelievers as the worst of the beasts (8:55), reminds Muslims that the enemy often break covenants (8:56), and appears to provide what might be considered 'strategies' in the conduct of war:

> If you overtake them in war (deal with them so to) scatter the ones behind them …
>
> (8:57)

> Against them make ready whatever force you have, and strings of horses, to terrify thereby the enemies of God and your enemies, and others besides, whom you know not …
>
> (8:60)

Amazingly, the rest of the verse goes into an altogether different theme:

> … Whatever you spend in God's way, shall be repaid to you, and you shall not be wronged.
>
> (8:60)

Once again, there is call for peace, if the enemy is so inclined (8:61).

But soon comes one of the most rousing verses on fighting for God, though its proximity to verse 8:61 is puzzling. As we pointed out earlier, this was possibly inspired in the context of the Battle of Badr. The harangue resonated through Muslim minds over the centuries, and among some it still does. As such, is worth repeating:

> O Prophet! Rouse the believers to the fight. If there are twenty of you, all steadfast, they will defeat two hundred; if a hundred, they will defeat a thousand unbelievers …
>
> (8:65)

While many of the verses on *jihad* have historical backgrounds, here are four verses that are presented in the Koran apparently as statement of general principles. They are from an early Medinan *sūra, Muḥammad.* Verse 47:1 denounces those who reject God. Verse 47:2 promises help to followers of Muḥammad. In verse 47:3, God contrasts the unbelievers 'who follow vanities' with the believers 'who follow the Truth.' To a modern reader, these premises alone will not be enough reason to call for *jihad.* Nevertheless, verse 47:4, which begins with 'therefore' or 'so', makes exactly such a call:

> So when you meet the unbelievers (in battle), smite their necks; then, when you have overcome them, tie them in bonds, and thereafter it is time to set them free, either by grace or for ransom, till the war lays down its burdens. So shall it be. And if God had willed, He would have exacted retribution from them; but He (lets you fight) in order that He may try some of you by means of others.
>
> (47:4)

The above verse contradicts another important verse on the same theme, which we read earlier, verse 8:67. In that verse, the Prophet was reprimanded for taking prisoners at Badr, rather than killing them. Exegetes recognise the contradiction.[159] There are ample disagreements about whether one has been cancelled by the other. Verse 47:4 is said to have been inspired several years after verse 8:67. The conclusion follows that the latter was 'cancelled' by the former, if we accept the idea of cancellation, which itself entails differences of opinion among commentators.

Sūra 9 (*Barāat*) is said to have been very late Medinan. Inspired approximately in AH 9, it contains some major verses concerning *jihad.* Not unusually, there are differences of opinion on the time of inspiration of this *sūra.* Some commentators place it before the conquest of Mecca, which took place in AH 8.[160] Ibn Ishaq[161] and al-Tabarī [162]place the verses

[159] Qur'ān/Muhiuddin., commentary on verse 47:4.
[160] Qur'ān/Muhiuddin.
[161] Ibn Ishaq, 618.
[162] al-Tabarī, vol. 9, 77–78.

after the conquest of Mecca. The content of some of the narratives supports this view. It is necessary to remember the historical background of these verses.

As we have seen, at the annual pilgrimage to Mecca in AH 9 and under instructions from Muḥammad, 'Ali carried with him verses of the *sūra* that had just been inspired for the purpose of proclaiming on the day of sacrifice. Among other things, the proclamation gave the polytheists four months, roughly corresponding to the four traditional prohibited months, to make up their minds about accepting Islam (verse 9:3). All obligations under any covenant the Prophet might have made with the polytheists would stand dissolved at the end of the period. The following verse makes clear what would happen next, and is worth repeating:

> Then when the forbidden months are past, slay the idolaters whenever you find them, seize them, confine them, and lie in wait for them in every place of ambush. But if they repent, and perform regular prayer, practice regular charity, then leave their way free. Surely God is Forgiving, Merciful.
>
> (9:5)

It is essential to note that after the conquest of Mecca, and during the expeditions that followed, Muslims were practically in an unassailable position, and the call to fight in the above verse and elsewhere could not have been for defensive reasons. There is no instance of Muslims coming under serious threat. The sole purpose of these calls was to propagate Islam. General exhortation to fight for the cause of God continues in the *sūra*. Fighters have the highest station in His sight. They have His solemn promise of the Garden of Paradise in exchange for their lives and their worldly possessions:

> Those who believe and suffer exile and strive with their possessions and their lives in the way of God have the highest station with God: they are those who will triumph.
>
> (9:20)

In a change in tone, we read this about those who are the true believers:

> Who turn to God, those who serve Him, those who praise Him, those who journey, those who bow and prostrate themselves, those who enjoin good and forbid evil, and those who heeds the limits set by God: so give good tiding to the believers.
>
> (9:112)

But firmness against the enemy is once again emphasised:

> O you who believe! Fight the unbelievers who are near to you, And let them find firmness in you …
>
> (9:123)

Some of the strongest words on *jihad* are contained in the following verse from the same *sūra*:

> Fight those who believe not in God and the Last Day, and do not forbid what God and His Messenger have forbidden, nor follow the religion of truth, from among the People of the Book, until they pay the jizya out of hand, and feel themselves humbled.
>
> (9:29)

Once again, the idea of *jihad* as defensive war is absent in the above verse, in which the unbelievers are to be fought till they are subdued and are willing to pay the *jizya*.[163] The adversaries are also more broadly defined to include Christians and Jews. Most of the earlier calls to *jihad* had been directed against the polytheists; here, the foes to be fought

[163] A poll tax levied on unbelievers living in a Muslim land. The tax is purported to be for protection offered to them by the Islamic state.

include the People of the Book.[164] Noting that this is a late Medinan *sūra*, the expeditions to places like Khaybar come to mind.[165] It was also a time when many of the Jewish and Christian tribes had begun to pay *jizya*. Note also that the verse comes immediately after one that terms unbelievers 'unclean' and bans them from the Sacred Mosque (verse 9:28), and not long after 9:5 which dooms the idolaters. In the context of a ten-year campaign that saw the virtual abolition of idolatry and near-total submission of the Jews and the Christians to Muḥammad in much of the Arabian peninsula, verse 9:29 can perhaps be seen as the last word on *jihad* in the Koran.

The verse stands in striking contrast to some of the verses we read earlier, particularly the following:

> Surely those who believe, and those of Jewry, and the Christians and the Sabians, any who believes in God, and the Last Day, and the righteous, they have their reward with their Lord. And on them shall be no fear, and neither shall they grieve.
>
> (2:62)

---

[164] There is some confusion about whether the entire verse concerns only the Jews and the Christians. Some translators place 'those among the People of the Book' at the beginning of the verse and attribute to them alone the features of not believing in God, all the way to not following the religion of Truth, mentioned in the verse. That portrays only the Jews and the Christians as the enemy, to be fought till they are totally subdued. Other translators see the verse as concerning both the idolaters and the People of the Book, the latter appearing in the narrative, as in the Arabic, only after 'nor follow the religion of truth,' as I have done above, following Koran/Arberry and Qur'ān/Muḥammad Ali.

[165] See Chapter 5.

Chapter 8
Call to Piety

The primary aim of the exhortations in the Koran is to lead people to total submission to the will of God. That is the ultimate piety. The submission cannot be passive but has to be manifested in action, and the Koran lays down in considerable detail the codes of conduct for the believers. Islamic tradition, while emphasising the all-encompassing nature of these codes, has long placed five of them at the top of the list: faith, canonical prayer, fasting, pilgrimage to Mecca, and charity. Calls to these acts of piety are central to the Koran and traditional Islam.

In the following pages, we shall read a considerable number of Koranic verses describing these aspects of piety. The central importance of the theme of piety cannot be judged by the number of verses devoted to it. In the great variety of narratives and repetitions in the Koran, the number of verses concerning these aspects of piety looks relatively small.

In the Koran, unequivocal faith in God translates into total obedience to one God – one who has no partner, who was not begotten, and who does not beget. This is stressed over and over again in the Koran. Thus we have:

> And God has said: Take not two gods for worship. Surely He is just one God. So fear Me and Me alone.
>
> (16:51)

> Say: He is God, the One and only One. God, the Self-sufficient. He begets not and is not begotten. And there is none equal to Him.
>
> (112:1–4)

Obedience to God must show up in concrete action on the part of the faithful. Although the Koran does not expressly attach any order of importance to the several acts of piety it emphasises, tradition places the daily canonical prayer at the top of the list. Tradition obligates the faithful to say the prayer five times a day. As with much else in the Book, none of its verses specify these times clearly; they have been culled from a multiplicity of verses, revealed at different times. We shall read these verses with the utmost care.

One of the most important, and most quoted, verses related to prayer is the following:

> Establish regular prayers – at the sun's decline till the darkness of the night, and the morning prayer, and reading: for the prayer and reading in the morning carry their testimony.
>
> (17:78)

The above translation is by Yusuf Ali.[166] Note that the verse comes after a narrative on a host of themes not connected to it. The *sūra* also soon goes into other themes unrelated to the verse. From the verse itself it is impossible to determine the times of the five daily prayers the Koran is said to mandate. It does suggest praying in the evening, through night, and in the morning. But the precise timing is absent. So is the timing of the other two prayers of the day. For these, we must go to other verses. These verses will be taken up shortly. But it is worth our while to take a look at other translations of the above verse:

> Perform the prayer
> at the sinking of the sun to the darkening of the night
> and the recital of dawn;
> surely the recital of dawn is witnessed.[167]
> Establish worship at the going down of the
> sun until the dark of night, and (the

[166] Qur'ān/Yusuf Ali.
[167] Koran/Arberry.

> recital of) the Qur'an at dawn. Lo! (the
> recital of) the Qur'an at dawn is ever witnessed.[168]
> Establish prayer from the decline of the sun till
> the darkness of the night, and also the reading of the
> Qur'ān at dawn ... [169]

Note that in the translation by Yusuf Ali, above, the line 'and the morning prayer' is uncalled for; it does not exist in the Arabic. None of the other translations above use it. There is, however, a real problem with the translation of the phrase *wa Qur'ānal fajr* (whether translated as 'Recital at dawn' or '(the recital of) the Qur'an at dawn' or 'reading of the Qur-an at dawn'). Neither the original nor, naturally, the translations of the phrase make sense when read with the rest of the verse.

Perhaps the authors of the following translation, aware of the difficulty, provide their own interpretation:

> Establish prayer from the decline of the sun to the darkening of the night and establish prayer at dawn ... [170]

This makes sense, but only because it is an interpretation, rather than a translation of the Arabic text. The translators here take the *Qur'ān* in *wa Qur'ānal fajr* to mean 'prayer', which indeed is a considerable stretching of the meaning to fit the context. A modern reader trying to understand the narrative would naturally wonder why a simple phrase, such as 'establish prayer at dawn', is absent in the Arabic – especially in a book which claims to make things clear.[171]

The call to establish prayer 'At the sun's decline till the darkness of the night' also presents a problem. The difficulty lies in the word 'till'. An ordinary reading of the line would mean a single prayer stretching from sunset to well into night. In practice, there is the *Magrib* prayer, done immediately after sunset, and the *'Ishā* prayer, usually performed just over an hour afterwards, sometimes much later. What then is the explanation of the word 'till'? If the word intended was 'and', we would expect it to

[168] Koran/Pickthall.
[169] Qur'ān/Muhiuddin.
[170] Qur'ān/Islamic Foundation.
[171] As in verse 14:4, for example.

be used. Ordinary Muslims take the times of prayer for granted, given as they are by tradition. A modern reader studying verses relating to the most important act of piety in Islam could not help but wonder at the lack of clarity here.

Exegetes derive three prayer times from the verse: morning, early evening, and early night. For the times of the other daily prayers, we need to go to other verses. One such, in an altogether different *sūra,* is this:

> And perform regular prayers at the two ends of the day and the first hours of the night ...
>
> (11:114)

This, however, indicates almost the same prayer times as in verse 17:78 above. Among the other verses that concern prayer is this:

> So bear patiently what they say, and celebrate the praise of your Lord before the rising of the sun, and before its setting, and celebrate for parts of the night and at the two ends of the day ...
>
> (20:130)

It is important to note the beginning of the verse. It provides the context of the rest. The preceding verse (20:129) concerns punishment for those who do not believe in the signs of God. 'Therefore bear patiently what they say' should be seen in the background of the Meccans' hostilities to Muḥammad's message. As in many other places in the Koran, especially among the Meccan verses, it seeks to comfort a Prophet faced with the intransigence of the unbelievers. Seen against this background, the rest of the verse need not suggest any directive to perform canonical daily prayer. It may only mean what it says: 'celebrate the praise' of God. In fact, there is no mention of prayer in the verse, unlike in 17:78, for example, where canonical prayer is specifically enjoined. And in case the phrase 'celebrate them' does mean canonical prayer, we would wonder why such an important act of piety has been prescribed so coincidentally. Note further that the verse that follows has nothing to do with prayer, canonical or not:

> And do not strain your eyes towards things We have provided to different parties of them, the splendour of life in this world, that We may test them. And your Lord's provision is better and more enduring.
>
> (20:131)

To return to 20:130, exegetes have nevertheless drawn meaning from the verse, suggesting that it calls for prayers at midday and late afternoon, in addition to the dawn prayer which is specifically mentioned. Some exegetes suggest that the verse indicates all the five canonical prayer times: dawn, midday, late afternoon, sundown, and night. We would, however, find in the exegeses [172] an extraordinary stretching of meaning of the words of the verse and a fitting of prayer times into it from known practice, rather than a convincing interpretation.

No verses in the Koran prescribe the ritual to be followed in performing the canonical prayer. This stands in sharp contrast with the meticulous detail of the ritual of the washing, or ablution – *wudhū* – that must precede every prayer. The following verse describes the ritual of *wudhū*:

> O you who believe! When you prepare for prayer, wash your faces, and your hands up to your elbows, and wipe your heads, and your feet up to the ankles … [173]
>
> (5:6)

The verse goes further back and prescribes rituals for purification:

… And if you are in a state of ritual impurity, purify yourself. But if you are sick or on a journey, or if any one of you comes from a privy, or if you are in contact with women, and you cannot find water, then use wholesome dust to rub therewith your faces and your hands …

(5:6)

[172] For example, in Qur'ān/Yusuf Ali.

[173] A modern reader might face difficulty with the syntax here. Reading the Arabic text gives us the impression that the feet, like the head, should be rubbed, not washed like the face and hands. This is because 'and your feet' immediately follows the words 'rub your head'. Only a translator's use of a parenthetic 'wash', as in Qur'ān/Yusuf Ali, helps resolve the difficulty.

We can seriously wonder whether rubbing the face and hands alone is adequate cleaning, since the pollution is in other parts of the body, according to the circumstances described in the verse itself. But a more fundamental question can also cross the modern mind. If the rituals for ablution can be described in such detail, and a substitute for washing can be prescribed so unambiguously in contingencies, we would wonder why the verses on the timing of prayers, the ultimate object of these rituals, is so opaque that they needed elaborate human interpretation.

Neither is there any instruction in the Koran about the physical pose and posture – such as standing, bowing, and prostrating – required in the performance of ritual prayer. Once again, this contrasts with the elaborate instructions regarding the ablution that leads up to the prayer, as well as with the enormous prestige that canonical prayer enjoys in the hierarchy of pieties.

Finally, there arises the question of universality of the times of the daily canonical prayers. In the Koran, the words of God are addressed to the people of Arabia, as a number of verses in the Book clearly indicate. With the spread of Islam to other lands over the centuries, the tenets of the religion came to be seen as being of universal application. The occasional use of the word *naās* (which can mean 'mankind' as well as 'people') in the Koran's call to piety, seems to suggest universality. Traditional Islam has always claimed universality for itself. Practices that are prescribed to a people of a given geographic region were seen as being applicable in exactly the same way in other regions, however remote from the homeland of Islam.

This has some apparently incongruous implications, however. Because of its location in relation to the equator, the variations in the lengths of night and day according to the seasons are not extreme in Arabia, and of course, in other countries close to the equator. But the farther a country is from the equator, the greater these variations become. In the farthest countries in the northern hemisphere, the days are very long in summer and the nights are very short, and the exact opposite is true in winter. There are many places of human habitation far in the north, for example, where the winter means months of night, and the summer, months of daylight. In such places, it is impossible to divide day or night into prayer times as dictated in the Koran, or as interpreted from it. There are other countries in the less extreme north where very short days would mean a greater crowding of daytime prayers than in regions further south. Geography makes universality impossible. A parallel to the above scenario for the southern hemisphere is, of course, easy to draw.

The Koran's directives for fasting are given in a single chapter of the Koran, *Sūra* 2 (*Baqara*), although there are exhortations to fast elsewhere. Unlike the canonical prayer prescribed, fasting as an act of piety was already a part of Judaeo-Christian tradition. The Koranic directives on fasting are also more clear-cut than they are for prayer, perhaps because of its very nature. For instance, the directives designate the entire month of Ramadan as the month of fasting, and they lay down rules of observance, permissible practices, and specific exemptions. Thus we have:

> O ye who believe! Fasting is prescribed for you, as it was prescribed for those before you, so that you will be god fearing.
>
> (2:183)

> (Fasting is) for a fixed number of days. But if any of you is sick, or on a journey, then for a number of other days. And for those who find it extremely hard (to fast), a redemption by way of feeding an indigent. [174] …
>
> (2:184)

The next verse explains why Ramadan, as a month, is important:

> The month of Ramadan is the month in which was revealed the Koran, a guide to the people …
>
> (2:185)

A number of questions present themselves. It is not clear, for example, why the phenomenon of sending down the Koran should in itself call for fasting. More importantly, according to tradition, the Koran was revealed to Muḥammad over a period of twenty-three years. The verse pinpoints

---

[174] There are differences, and a great deal of confusion, in the interpretation of the third sentence. The translation accepted here is in conformity with Qur'ān/Muhiuddin and Qur'ān/Islamic Foundation.

Ramadan as the month in which the Book was revealed. The Koran offers no explanation for this apparent contradiction. Some exegetes maintain that the Koran was transferred from the *Lauḥ Maḥfūz* (or, the 'Preserved Tablet', on which the Koran was said to have been kept for eternity) to the skies above the earth on a Ramadan night, and was then revealed to Muḥammad over the next twenty-three years.[175] Such exegesis must belong to unbounded faith alone, and there is no verse of the Koran to substantiate it. A meaningful explanation is that the first verses of the Koran were inspired in that month.

The next verse has no relationship to fasting in the month of Ramadan.

> And when My servants ask you concerning Me, I am indeed near: I hear the prayer of the supplicant when he calls Me, so let them respond to my call, and believe in Me, that they may walk in right path.
>
> (2:186)

Particularly when read in the Arabic, the verse appears sublime: *wa eza sa'ālākā 'ebādi 'ānni, fā inni qārib: ūjibu d'awātad-dā'e ezā dā'āne*. We can also detect a touch of spirituality in it. But it is wholly unconnected to the preceding verse and to fasting, and thus appears meaningless in the context.

The sublimity of the above verse is also immediately followed by something singularly mundane, in the same manner of incongruous juxtaposition of verses that we encountered earlier. The question of sex is an obvious one to ask in the context of abstinence that fasting implies; its proximity to a sublime narrative is far from obvious:

> It is lawful to you, on the night of the fast, to go in to your wives. They are garments to you and you are their garments. God knows you have been deceiving yourselves, so He turned to you and pardoned you. So now lie with them and seek what God has prescribes for you …
>
> (2:187)

[175] Qur'ān/Muhiuddin.

Interspersed in the text of the long verse are lines granting permission to eat and drink, along with the important directive on the duration of the fast – exactly when fasting should begin and end. These are repeated here for completeness.

> ... And eat and drink, until the white thread of dawn appears distinct to you from the black thread (of night) ... [176]
>
> (2:187)

There can be disagreements about the exact meaning of some of the words of the long verse. The beginning and end of the day of fasting has not been clearly demarcated here; instead, they were left to practices developed and refined later. More important is a question relating to the meaning of 'the white thread' and 'the black thread'. As we have seen, these terms appear to have created considerable confusion at the beginning and, according to generally accepted *ḥadith* literature, the expression 'thread of dawn' was added to the verse sometime after the revelation.[177]

Ḥajj, the annual pilgrimage to Mecca, has been considered in the Koran in far greater detail than either prayer or fasting, though it comes third in the hierarchy of piety. The pilgrimage has a long history in pre-Islamic, pagan tradition. The history is opaque, but here in the Koran, Abraham is praying to God for his offspring in Mecca:

> 'Our Lord! I have settled some of my offspring in an unsown valley by Thy Sacred House, that they may perform regular prayer: so make the hearts of men incline towards them and provide them with fruits, that they may be grateful.
>
> (14:37)

[176] As translated in Qur'ān/Islamic Foundation. Translation from the Bengali is mine. There is a confusing array of translations from the Arabic in regard to the black and white threads.

[177] See Chapter 2.

In the Koranic tradition, the Sacred House was also built by Abraham (with his son Ishmael, according to legend):

> And when We settled for Abraham the place of the House, saying: You shall not associate with Me anything and shall purify My House for those who will go around it, stand before it, and bow and prostrate themselves.
>
> (22:26)

The verse below, from *Sūra* 22 (*Ḥajj*), the main chapter concerning pilgrimage, can be taken to be an introduction to the subject, even though it comes somewhat late in the *sūra*:

> And for every people did We appoint a holy rite, that they may celebrate the name of God on the four-footed beasts that He gave them as food …
>
> (22:34)

Particularly notable in the verse is the reference to the rites being prescribed to every 'people' (*ūmmah,* in Arabic), in this case the Arabs in particular, the implication being that other rites may have been prescribed to other peoples. Also, once again, celebrating the name of God is the sole purpose of the sacrifice. The reason behind the celebration of God's name is rather the mundane one of gratitude: it is He who has provided the people the sacrificial animal as food for their sustenance.

The Abrahamic tradition is continued after verse 22:26 (quoted above):

> And proclaim among men the Pilgrimage: they will come to you on foot, and on every lean camels, from every mountain roads and valleys. [178]
>
> (22:27)

> That they may witness the benefits to them, and pronounce the name of God, on the days appointed, over

[178] 'Mountain roads and valleys' is a literal translation. Some translators have interpreted this as people coming from far and wide.

> the four-footed beasts that He has given them as food. So eat of it and feed the wretched needy.
>
> (22:28)

> Then let them complete their act of cleansing, fulfil their vows and circumambulate the Ancient House.
>
> (22:29)

> So shall it be. And whoever venerates the sacred rites of God, it shall be better for him in the sight of his Lord. Permitted to you are the cattle except those mentioned to you (earlier); so eschew the abomination of the idols and shun false words.
>
> (22:30)

Animal sacrifice is an integral part of the *ḥajj*, and the Koran devotes a great deal of the narrative to it. The theme runs through a number of verses quoted above and is taken up in the following verses in considerable detail:

> And the camels, We have made them among the symbols of God: in it there is much good for you; then pronounce the name of God on them standing in a row. And when they are down on their sides, eat of them and feed those needy who live in contentment and those who are supplicants. Thus We have made the animals subject to you that you may be grateful.
>
> (22:36)

> Neither their meat nor their blood reaches God; it is your devotion to God that reaches Him. He has made them subject to you, so that you may glorify God for guiding you …
>
> (22:37)

Animal sacrifice to propitiate gods is as old as human history. The practice was alive and well in seventh-century Arabia. Mecca was a major place of pilgrimage, and animal sacrifice was always an important part of the rituals there. The Sacred Precinct of the Ka'ba and its surroundings housed a great many idols. The tribes of the city were mostly idolaters, as were the pilgrims, and it was to their idols that they made the animal sacrifices.

The Koran continued the pagan ritual of animal sacrifice, the difference of course being that the idolaters' sacrifice was meant to propitiate their many gods; whereas in Islam, the sacrifice is made to please God, the One and only One. The idea of propitiation is nevertheless common to both. As some of the above verses suggest, the purpose of the ritual is to 'celebrate the name of God' or to 'glorify God'. It is prescribed because 'it is good in the sight of his Lord.' Remarkably, the sacrificial animals have been called by God symbols of Him (verse 22:36), glorifying them in a way the pagans perhaps did not perceive their own gods doing.

The core of the ancient idea of sacrificing an animal to please a supreme being has remained unchanged. The ritual continues today, on an incomparably larger scale. It is an integral part of the annual pilgrimage to Mecca, when millions of animals are slaughtered, mostly in the course of a single day.

Muslims all over the world, especially in Muslim-majority lands, also sacrifice a huge number of animals on *'Īd-al-Aḏẖā*, celebrated during the *ḥajj*. They conduct these rituals in their own homes, far from Mecca. There is, however, no specific directive in the Koran to sacrifice animals outside the *ḥajj* ritual. The ritual of animal slaughter at the *'Īd* seeks to replicate the sacrifice at the *ḥajj*. This has come to be treated as a high religious obligation for those who can afford it. The rich often vie with each other to slaughter the most expensive beast, and the inability to slaughter an animal at *'Īd* even evokes self-pity among many Muslims. Yet a modern Muslim, venturing a little beyond ritual piety, would be hard put to find justification for the slaughter, either in the Koran or in his own reckoning.

The theme of *ḥajj* is taken up in another chapter of the Koran as well. *Sūra* 2 goes into considerable detail on *ḥajj*, beginning with this command, which we read earlier:

> And complete the *Ḥajj* and *'Umra* [179]for God. But if you are prevented, send whatever offering you may find, and

[179] *'Umra* is pilgrimage made on days other than during the *ḥajj*.

> do not shave your heads until the offering reaches its place of sacrifice …
>
> (2:196)

The sacrificial offering at the pilgrimage is a central theme in this long verse. After the above instruction on offering, the verse then elaborates on the rites and lays down rules of compensation if the offering cannot be made. These include fasting, feeding the poor, and offering the sacrifice at a later date. The remaining verses of the *sūra* (2:197–203) concerning the *ḥajj* elaborate on the rites, tell the pilgrims to fear God and seek his forgiveness, and permit them to seek His bounty during the pilgrimage.

Since the pilgrimage must involve travel, what could be the farthest geographic distance from which pilgrims are expected to journey to Mecca for the rites which must be performed within a short period of a few days? The question is relevant even today. Obviously, the pilgrimage is easy for people living in and around Mecca, not so easy for those living at some distance, more and more difficult as the distance increases, and impossible for those beyond the periphery. One part of verse 2:196, almost seeming not to appear to define the periphery, does exactly that. It asks the prospective pilgrim unable to make the journey to send the offering for slaughter and not shave his head 'until the offering reaches its place of sacrifice'. This clearly implies that the person on whose behalf the offering is being made must be living close enough to Mecca for him to receive news that the offering had reached the destination. In practical terms, we would expect this to occur within the very few days in which the rites have to be completed. In the days of travel on camelback through the desert, the implied distance could not have been long. At the most, it could have been only a few score miles, not hundreds of miles, and the conclusion must be that the Koran obligated only people living within that rather narrow perimeter. This does not mean that pilgrims did not come from great distances: they did come, perhaps in large numbers. But the notion of a narrow perimeter is built into the verse. It perhaps ruled out areas beyond the Hijaz, and certainly lands beyond the Arabian peninsula. Just as the Koran insisted that because it was written in Arabic, it was meant for the Arabs, it now defines a geographic Arabia for which the rule of animal sacrifice applies. A verse we read earlier reinforces the idea: 'And for every people did We appoint a holy rite … ' (22:34).

Verses on charity, defined broadly, outnumber those on prayer, fasting, and the *ḥajj*. In large part, the emphasis on charity is a reflection of a purely human concern for the poor and the destitute. In this, some of the pronouncements in the Koran share concerns expressed throughout human history, in all religions and by many individuals with little religious affiliation.

Poor relatives come in for special consideration. The fact that much of the newly emerging Muslim community was poor must also have enhanced the importance the Koran placed on charity. In the Koran, *zakāt* and *sadāqa,* both of which mean 'charity', have been used interchangeably. With the enlargement of the community, charity came to play a crucial role in the conduct of affairs of the nascent Muslim state. As institutionalised charity, *zakāt* meant a fixed proportion of an individual's wealth was given as charity to the poor or as tax to the state. *Sadāqa* remained a more inclusive term for giving. The Koran does not fix the proportion of an individual's wealth to be donated as charity.

Charity, especially in the form of alms, has been a trait of all human societies, and Arab societies were no exception. At its core lay individual acts of generosity, based on age-old traditions and concepts of morality. With the inception of the Islamic community, the communal aspect of charity grew in importance. In an environment of great poverty, the beginning of communal charity was not without friction and resentment. The following verse depicts this:

> And among them are those who find fault with you in the matter of the alms. If they are given some, they are pleased; and if they are not given, they are indignant.
>
> (9:58)

Sūra 2 (*Baqara*) contains the majority of the verses on charity. In many cases, calls to prayer and exhortations to give in charity are made in the same verse. Among them is this:

> And perform regular prayer, pay *zakāt*, and bow down with those who bow down.
>
> (2:43)

The following verse, though intertwined with other themes prescribes the amount of charitable giving in very broad and generous terms:

> … And they ask you how much they should spend. Say: 'Whatever you can spare.'
>
> (2:219)

Charity is much more than a personal choice; it comes close to compulsion. And then, each person can spend only out of what God has given him.

> O ye who believe! Spend out of what We have provided you before the day comes when there will be no bargaining, no friendship and no intercession …
>
> (2:254)

This is followed by gentle enticement in graphic terms:

> The parable of those who spend their wealth in the path of God is that of a grain growing seven ears, and each ear growing a hundred grains. God multiplies for whomsoever He pleases. He is Bountiful, All-Knowing.
>
> (2:261)

In a similar vein is verse 2:265, which compares the spender in the way of God to a fertile garden yielding rich harvest.

Charity given in silence is noble; generosity followed up by overt mention of it, or by rude words to the recipient, cancels out the act of charity:

> Those who spend their wealth in the cause of God, and follow not up their gift with reminder of the giving or with injury – their reward is with their Lord …
>
> (2:262)

And:

> Kind words and forgiveness are better than charity followed by injury …
>
> (2:263)

Also:

> O you who believe, do not cancel your charity by reproach and injury – like one who spends his wealth only to be seen by people and believes not in God and the Last Day. His parable is that of a hard rock with some earth on it, then heavy rain leaves it bare …
>
> (2:264)

Particularly noble is this:

> If you disclose acts of charity, it is well. And if you hide charity, and it is for the poor, it is best for you …
>
> (2:271)

Those really in need further include:

> … those poor who are so engaged in the way of God that they cannot move about the land (for a living); the ignorant think them rich because of their abstinence. You can recognise them by their mark: they beg not importunately …
>
> (2:273)

The verse in effect glorifies those modest Muslim souls in need, whose freedom has been limited in various ways.

Although it is the individual Muslim who is the focus of attention here and elsewhere, the following verse greatly increases the scope of charity to include such considerations as administration of charity, support to the new converts to Islam, freeing of slaves, absolution of debtors, and spending for the cause of God. We read this verse earlier, but it is worth repeating here:

> Charity is for the poor and the needy, for those employed to administer it, for those whose hearts have been reconciled, for freeing bondsmen, for those in debt, for spending in the way of God, and for the wayfarer ...
>
> (9:60)

While piety in the sense of devotion to God dominates Koranic texts, the importance of kindness and generosity to fellow human beings and next of kin, particularly parents, is proclaimed loud and clear. Thus we read:

> And when We made a covenant with the children of Israel: that you shall serve none but God; treat with kindness your parents and next of kin, the orphans and the needy; speak good to people; perform prayer; and pay *zakāt*.
>
> (2:83)

It is remarkable that treating parents with kindness appears in a verse right alongside devotion to God. In fact, filial piety has taken precedence over prayer and charity in the narrative, though this does not imply any order of importance.

The following verse goes even further in elaboration of piety to fellow humans:

> And serve God, and associate not any partner with Him. And be good to parents and the next of kin, to orphans and the needy, to a neighour who is of kin and neighbours who is a stranger, to the companion on a journey, to the wayfarer, and what your right hand possesses ... [180]
>
> (4:36)

Also remarkably, courtesy is emphasised. The following verse comes soon after one that calls for fighting in the way of God. The rationale for

[180] It is not evident from the verse that the command to be good applies when neighbours, companions on a journey, or wayfarers are unbelievers. However, from what we have read so far of the Koran, this is highly unlikely.

placing courtesy in such close proximity to fighting is hard to understand. But it is still noteworthy:

> And when you are greeted with courtesy, meet it with a greeting that is still more courteous, or with the same courtesy. God takes account of everything.
>
> (4:86)

Filial piety appears next to devotion to God in the verse below, even though the 'do' and 'don't' appear nixed up:

> Say: 'Come, I will recite to you what your Lord has forbidden to you: associate not anything with Him; and be good to your parents' ...
>
> (6:151)

The following two verses glorify filial piety, in terms far more appealing in the original Arabic than in translation:

> You Lord has decreed that you serve none but Him, and that you be good to your parents; if one or both attains old age with you, say not to them 'Fie!,' nor scold them, but speak to them with respect.
>
> (17:23)

> And lower to them the wing of humility out of kindness and say: My Lord, bestow on them mercy just as when they brought me up while I was little.
>
> (17:24)

There are few verses in the Koran, or perhaps in any holy book, that surpass the two verses above in expressions of filial nobility of the heart. There is, however, an important caveat. In instances probably not uncommon at the time of the advent of Islam, where parents followed polytheism and prevented their children from accepting Islam, such parents were not to be obeyed (verse 29:8). Filial piety and the caveat are repeated in verses like 31:14 and 31:15, with piety even more strongly emphasised.

Filial piety is repeated in greater detail in the following verse, which also has a remarkable melding of submission to God and filial piety:

> We have enjoined on man kindness to parents: His mother bore him in pain and in pain she gave him birth. Bearing and weaning him is thirty months. Until, when he is fully grown, and reaches the age of forty, he says: My Lord, grant me that I may give thanks for your favour which you have bestowed on me and on my parents, that I may do good deeds which pleases you.
>
> (46:15)

Verses on filial piety, nobility of the heart, and courtesy are strewn throughout a large number of verses of the Koran. They still account for just a tiny fraction of the more than 6,300 verses in the Holy Book of Islam. Their importance is noteworthy but should not be exaggerated. They are often overwhelmed by verses of very different nature and import, as we have seen and shall in the pages that follow. Note for now that while filial piety is emphasised, there is this verse in the Koran that explicitly forbids praying for forgiveness of unbelieving next of kin:

> It befits not the Prophet and the believers that they should ask forgiveness for the idolaters, even though they should be near relatives, after it was made clear to them that they were companions of the Fire.
>
> (9:113)

Chapter 9
God's Creation and His Signs

The text of the Koran is replete with allusions to God's creation. It is strewn with verses that describe, often in considerable detail, the physical world in its various manifestations, from the high heavens and the celestial bodies, to the origin of human life; from the clouds and rains from above, down to the seed grain in the soil; from life in the womb, to the beasts roaming the earth. To mankind, these are not mere phenomena; rather, they are signs from God:

> In the creation of the heavens and the earth and the alteration of the night and the day, are signs for men of understanding.
>
> (3:190)

Unlike the Old Testament, the Koran does not begin at the beginning. There is no equivalent of Genesis in the Koran. *Sūra* 2 (*Baqara*) takes off with a narrative of what the Book itself is about: a guide for those who fear God, those who believe in the unseen. Those who reject the faith, and their supposed mischief, comprise the central theme of the verses that follow. God's creation comes up, briefly, in verse 2:21, and is continued in the next verse, after which other themes are taken up. Like many other themes of the Koran, creation is taken up, elaborated upon, and repeated, in diverse contexts, or without any context, in a large number of *sūras*.

Looked at from beyond the realm of pure belief, the narratives of the physical world contained in these verses are broadly consistent with the stock of human knowledge some 1,400 years ago, as is the case with other major themes in the Koran. Over the centuries since then, that stock has grown to proportions unimaginable in seventh-century Arab societies, or in any other society at that time. Many of the concepts – biological, physical, or astrophysical – found in the Koran are at variance with the state of human knowledge today. The discrepancies have been large in many cases and have been viewed in many different ways. Those ordinary readers of the Koran who are aware of such discrepancies simply ignore them. This includes the vast majority of practising Muslims. Some would rather turn a blind eye to scientific evidence than ignore the affirmations of a Koranic verse. Traditional exegetes of the Koran have often sought, and found, confirmation of scientific explanation of natural phenomena in the words of the Koran.

Even among the traditionalists, however, there are those who have emphasised the futility of seeking scientific explanation of physical phenomena in the verses of the Koran. On the nature of the creation of God and the Koran, one commentator has this to say:

> Here it is essential to understand as a matter of principle that the Holy Qur'ān is not a book on science or astrology, whose scope of discussion is the nature of the created world or to describe the shape and motion of the heavens and the stars and planets. [181]

In a similar vein, a leading orthodox theologian ridicules the idea that the Koran is the source of all scientific knowledge:

> In fact, the Holy Qur'an is basically a spiritual book and in this it is unique. It is foolish to try to prove everything with reference to the Qur'an. [182]

Still other commentators, especially those of a liberal persuasion, often recognise the impossibility of squaring the circle and proceed to treat particular statements in the Koran merely as allegories. There are

[181] Qur'ān/Muhiuddin, commentary on *Sūra* 25 (*Furqān*). This, however, did not prevent the commentator from making many rather unscientific assertions elsewhere in his commentary on the Koran.

[182] Maulana Ashraf Ali Thanvi, *Ashraful Jawab, Part 2,* tr. into Bengali by Muḥammad Abū Ashraf (Dhaka, Bangladesh: Islamic Foundation Bangladesh, 1997), 69.

strict limits to the effectiveness of the device, however, as will be obvious as we proceed to read the relevant verses.

It is sometimes suggested that the Koran's repeated depiction of the natural phenomena is meant to urge man to 'study the universe -- the handiwork of God, which has been created for his benefit.'[183] This seems uncalled for. The objective in the Koran is not to coax man to study his physical environment in the manner of scientific inquiry, which is antithetical to the nature of the Book. The idea behind the Koran's texts on God's creation is solely to make man aware of God's great bounty and His power, so that he bows to Him in gratitude and submission. Some of the verses we shall read in this chapter make this abundantly clear. Often the glorification of God dominates the narrative of the verses on His creation.

Moreover, the themes under the rubric of God's creation are not developed systematically in the Koran, and there is a great deal of repetition. Here, I shall broadly follow the order of the *sūras* as they appear in the Koran, though it will often be necessary to backtrack. The verses below constitute the bulk of the Koranic narrative of the Koran on the subject of creation. These verses are scattered throughout a large number of *sūras*.

The first verse on God's creation, in *Sūra* 2, is prefaced by a cryptic call to man to serve God:

> O men! Serve your Lord, who created you and those before you,,.
>
> (2:21)

This is immediately followed by a narrative that is repeated in many verses:

> Who has made the earth your couch, and the heavens an edifice and sent down rains from the heavens, then brought forth therefrom fruits for your sustenance. So do not set up rivals to Him if you understand.
>
> (2:22)

[183] Fazlur Rahman, *Islam and Modernity* (Chicago: The University of Chicago Press, 1982), 50.

Creation of the heaven and the earth comes early in the narrative and is taken up again and again:

> (He is) the creator of the heavens and the earth; and when He decrees a thing, He says to it "Be" and it is.
>
> (2:117)

Elsewhere, creation takes time:

> Surely your Lord is God, who created the heavens and the earth in six days and was then sat himself on the throne. With night He covers the day, which it pursues incessantly.[184] And He created the sun, the moon, and the stars, all obeying his command. His is the creation, His is the command. Blessed be God, the Lord of all beings.
>
> (7:54)

As in the Old Testament, creation of the heavens and the earth and all therein takes six days, which is of course at colossal odds with what we know about the age of our universe. Most modern exegetes are aware of the difficulty of reconciling scientific knowledge with faith here, and some have come up with the idea that God's 'day' might be quite different from a twenty-four-hour day on earth. To make the distinction, in his translation, Yusuf Ali capitalises 'Day', and makes much of the idea taken from the Koran itself (22:47) that a Day in the sight of God is like a thousand years.[185] Elsewhere in the Koran (70:4), the heavenly day is like fifty thousand years on earth. These numbers, of course, still add up to a minute fraction of the age of the universe. The difficulty with defining God's day has led one translator to use the term 'period' instead.[186] The idea that God's day is much longer than it is for mortals on earth also conflicts with the idea of instant creation implicit in the 'Be and it is', in verse 2:117, above.

---

[184] There are large differences over the translation of the sentence in Arabic. I have followed Qur'ān/Muḥammad Ali.

[185] The verse is … 'verily a day in the sight of thy Lord is like a thousand years of your reckoning' (22:47).

[186] Qur'ān/Muḥammad Ali.

The idea of God sitting on a throne has long been a contentious issue among commentators on the Koran. Since, in the Islamic tradition, God has no physical embodiment, He cannot be envisaged as seated on a throne. Some translators, therefore, would like the throne to be a mere allegory.[187] The artifice does not always work, however. For example, take the following verses, where, of necessity, the throne has to have a physical dimension. In a verse reminiscent of the Old Testament, God's throne rests on the primal waters:[188]

> He it is Who created the heavens and the earth in six days
> and His throne was on the waters ...
>
> (11:7)

Elsewhere, we read:

> And the angels will be on its sides. And eight will that day
> bear the throne of your Lord above them.
>
> (69:17)

The vexing question of the throne as a physical phenomenon therefore remains, and it can only be resolved by resorting to unadulterated faith alone. The problem echoes in the following statement of a major eighth-century Islamic jurist. Asked about the difficulty of envisaging God sitting on a throne, an irate Mālik Ibn Anas is said to have retorted: 'The sitting is well-known, its modality is unknown, belief in it is obligatory and questioning it is heresy.'[189]

Narratives on God's creation, followed by repose, appear in several other verses in the Koran, such as 10:3, 25:59 and 32:4.

Narratives on the creation of the heavens and the earth, and the time it took God to complete the work, continue:

---

[187] Qur'ān/Yusuf Ali uses the expression 'Throne (of authority)', while Qur'ān/Muḥammad Ali uses 'Throne of Power'.

[188] 'And the Spirit of God moved upon the face of the waters' (Genesis 1:2).

[189] Majid Fakhry, *Averroes (Ibn Rushd): His Life, Works and Influence* (Oxford: Oneworld, 2001), xii.

> Say: Is it that you disbelieve in Him who created the earth in two days? ...
>
> (41:9)

> And He set in it (the earth) mountains standing firm above it, and He blessed it, and He ordained therein its sustenance, in four days ...
>
> (41:10)

> Then He lifted Himself to the heaven,[190] and it was smoke. So He said to it and the earth: 'Come together, willingly or unwillingly!' They said 'We come willingly.'
>
> (41:11)

> So He completed them as seven heavens in two days, and He assigned each heaven its duty. And We[191] adorned the lower heavens with lights ...
>
> (41:12)

We note that the total length of time of creation in these verses adds up to eight days, which is at odds with the total of six days in verse 7:54 and elsewhere. Some exegetes acknowledge this but attribute it, rather unconvincingly, to a kind of overlap in the act of creation, leaving the actual time at six days.[192]

The uniqueness of the heavens thus created is underlined:

> It is God who raised the heavens without any pillars that you can see; ...
>
> (13:2

---

190 Qur'ān/Yusuf Ali uses this extraordinary expression, 'He comprehended in His design the sky', in his translation, presumably to avoid any suggestion that God would lift Himself or direct Himself to the sky.

191 Note, once again, the 'We' succeeding 'He' in the same verse.

192 Qur'ān/Muhiuddin, exegesis to *Sūra* 41(*Fussilat*). The exegesis also narrates a *ḥadith* that purports to quote the Prophet of Islam as having specified the exact days of the week, starting with Sunday, on which specific tasks were performed by God. (Sunday and Monday were devoted to the making of the earth; Thursday, to creation of the heavens, for example.)

The narrative on the wonders of heavenly creation and their purpose continues:

> It is He who makes the stars for you that you might guide yourselves by them in the darkness of the earth and the sea …
>
> (6:97)

> It is He who made the sun a shining brightness, and the moon a light and ordained stages for it that you might know the number of the years and the reckoning …
>
> (10:5)

Old Satan is still around to contend with as well. In the following verse, God adorns the heavens with lamps, but He also uses the lamps for a special purpose:

> And We have adorned the lowest heavens with lamps, and made such (Lamps) as missiles to chase the Evil Ones and We have prepared for them the punishment of burning.
>
> (67:5)

We have here the extraordinary spectacle of shooting stars used by God to prevent the 'Evil Ones' from reaching the higher heavens. The scene is repeated elsewhere and is not a passing narrative:

> And surely We have set in the sky constellations and We have decked out them for the beholders.
>
> (15:16)

> And We have guarded them from every accursed Satan.
>
> (15:17)

> But any that steals a hearing is pursued by a manifest flame.
>
> (15:18)

'Stealing a hearing' in 15:18 is presumably an allusion to Satan trying to listen to what might have been going on in the upper heavens of God and the Angels. The narrative on the stars as guards against the evil spirits continues into yet another *sūra,* in very similar terms (37:6–10). Scientific evidence gives us a rather different explanation of the phenomenon. These are meteorites with which the earth is being constantly bombarded, harmlessly in the vast majority of cases, but on rare occasions with devastating results, under nobody's direction. An allegorical interpretation of the verses would be unconvincing.

Down on earth, the narrative extends to the mountains, wide tracts of land spread out like carpet, the rivers, the rains, and the seas. Mountains figure rather prominently in the narrative:

> And it is He who spread out the earth, and set on it firm mountains and rivers …
>
> (13:3)

Mountains appear again in the following verses and are said to have been set in order to prevent the earth from shaking, or perhaps tilting in some way, from the movement of people inhabiting it, an idea that would confound the modern mind:

> And He has set on the earth firm mountains lest the earth should shake with you; and rivers and roads, that you may guide yourselves.
>
> (16:15)

In the verse above, 'you' refers to the human multitude.
Similarly,

> And We have set on the earth mountains standing firm, lest it should shake with them …
>
> (21:31)

'Them' here refers to the unbelievers.

It is perhaps not surprising that there is no mention of volcanoes, which actually do shake the earth's crust from time to time. Active volcanoes are absent from Arabia, and so they are also absent from the pages of the Koran. On the other hand, deserts have an overwhelming presence in Arabia, and yet their majesty is not a part of the landscape here, except for a fleeting mention in some of the short Meccan *sūras*; perhaps this is because the narrative emphasises God's bounty. Oil, the great unsung treasure lying beneath the desert sands, would await discovery for well over a millennium, and so, naturally, does not get a mention in the Koran.

All of God's creation on earth must of course perish someday. Only God Himself will abide:

> All that is on earth will perish: but forever will abide the
> Face of your Lord, Majestic, Splendid.
>
> (55:26–27)

The eschatological question of the end of creation goes far beyond the destruction of the earth. Celestial bodies too will perish, and the Koran dwells on this spectacle in a number of verses, such as the ones below, which provide the beginning of a long build-up to a final question:

> When the sun is folded up. [193]
>
> (81:1)

> When the stars fall.
>
> (81:2)

The *sūra* then goes on to describe further apocalyptic scenes. A modern mind will have little difficulty envisioning the destruction of the universe, perhaps many billions of years hence, in a scenario that began many billions of years ago. But what could the Koran have meant in these verses? Here again, the answer lies in the state of human knowledge at the time of its inspiration. Thus, on the matter of the folding up (*ku'werat,* in Arabic) of the sun, some exegetes have taken the verse to mean that the sun will be thrust into the ocean. *Sahih Al-Bukhāri* is invoked to suggest

[193] Some translations (Qur'ān/Islamic Academy among them) have used 'the sun will lose lustre', instead, though accepting that the literal meaning is 'folding up' of the sun.

that the Prophet himself explained the end of the sun and the moon in those terms.[194] The sun is of course a hugely larger body than the oceans of the earth, and the infeasibility of the prophetic scenario only points to the stock of man's knowledge of the physical world at the time.

On earth again, there are a number of sweeping verses in the Koran which depict God's bounties for mankind:

> In the creation of the heaven and the earth, the alteration of day and night, the ship that sails on the sea with what benefits people, and the rains that God sends down from the sky, that the earth comes to life after it was dead, in the scattering of beasts of all kinds through the earth, in the change of the winds, and in the clouds directed between the heaven and the earth, there are surely signs for people who understand.
>
> (2:164)

> It is God who causes the seed-grain and the date-stone to split and sprout. He brings forth the living from the dead, and the dead from the living. That then is God, so how are you deluded?
>
> (6:95)

> And it is He who sends down water from the clouds; then We bring forth shoots of every plant; and We bring forth green foliage from which We produce grains in clusters; and, out of the spathes of date-palm tree, clusters of dates easy to reach; and gardens of grapes, olives, and pomegranates …
>
> (6:99)

Verse 6:141 has a similar narrative, with gardens, some even trellised, added as gifts of God.

The narrative of God's bounty continues:

[194] Qur'ān/Muhiuddin, commentary on *Sūra* 81 (*Takwir*).

> It is He Who sends the winds bearing good news ahead of His mercy, till, when they have carried the laden cloud, We drive it to a dead land, then We send down rains on it, and We bring forth thereby fruits of all kinds ...
>
> (7:57)

> And in the earth are tracts neighbouring to each other and garden of vines and fields sown with corn, and palms growing out of single or distinct roots, watered by the same water, yet We make some of them to excel others in fruit.
>
> (13:4)

> And We send the rain-laden winds, then send from the sky water for you to drink, and you are not its treasurer.
>
> (15:22)

> And We send down water from the sky in due measure and preserve it in the soil; and We are able to drain it too.
>
> (23:18)

In Arabic, many of these verses are poetic. This is absent from the translation, as is the sweep of the narrative. On their substance, one feature stands out. The wind, the clouds, and the rains are all instruments of God. That indeed is the essence of the narrative. It emphasises the benevolence of God, the sustainer of the world. The rain brings the dead lands back to life. Rain also nourishes the seed grain, and makes the date-stone split and sprout. After the rain, the land is wrapped in green, and crops pile up on the field. The sprawling gardens, some trellised, and all God's handiwork, add to the idyll.

And yet, the wind and the rain that bring all that goodness often also do enormous harm. Wind turns into hurricanes that destroy the very crops the wind-blown clouds help produce. Cyclones kill people and demolish their homes. Rain does not always come in due measure; it turns torrential, causes floods, and wipes out crops. Or it rains too little, and the land turns into shards of baked earth under a scorching sun. The Koran does not concern itself with the often devastating phenomena – floods, tsunamis, and cyclones – that are the flipside of the benevolence of the rain and the wind. The Book does not have much to say about the devastations of droughts either.

Neither does the Book consider other natural phenomena, such as earthquakes, which often visit God's creation with devastating effect. Earthquakes and tsunamis take a colossal toll on humanity, yet there is no mention of them in the Koran. However, we do read verses that allude to natural calamities. Among such verses is one that attributes these catastrophes to man's disobedience and impiety:

> Disaster[195] has appeared on land and sea because of what men's hands have wrought, that He may make them taste some part of what they have done, so that they may return.
>
> (30:41)

This of course discounts innocents, such as children, who also get killed in earthquakes and landslides. The devastating tsunami of December 2004 killed hundreds of thousands, a large majority of them Muslim, many of them women and children. Earthquakes have devastated Iran and Pakistan, both Muslim countries, in recent years, sparing neither children nor women, nor the sick and the elderly.

The very second verse of the earliest *sūra* revealed, *Sūra* 96 (*Iqraa,* also called *'Alaq*), calls attention to the biological development of man, even if very briefly. God, it says, created man from *'alaq*, a clot of congealed blood (96:2). The narrative then turns abruptly to themes which are difficult to connect with the idea of clots of blood. But the beginning of human life crops up in many other verses of the Koran. We shall read quite a few of these verses:

> O people! If you are in any doubt about Resurrection, consider that We created you from dust, then out of sperm, then out of a clot of congealed blood, then out of a lump of flesh, partly formed and partly not, that We

[195] The Arabic word *fasād* has also been translated as 'mischief' and 'corruption'.

> may make clear to you (our power); and We cause whom please to rest in the wombs for an appointed time …
>
> (22:5)

These verses begin with the primal creation of man from clay and quickly switch to biological developments:

> And certainly We created man from an extract of clay.
>
> (23:12)

> Then We placed him as a drop of sperm in a firm place of rest.
>
> (23:13)

> Then We made the sperm a clot of congealed blood, then We made the clot a lump of flesh; then We made out of the lump bones, then We clothed the bones with flesh, then We caused it to grow into another creation …
>
> (23:14)

The creation of man from out of nothing more than clay, and then from a despised human fluid, is stressed in the following verses:

> He Who has made beautiful everything He created and began creation of man from clay.
>
> (32:7)

> And then made his progeny from an extract of a mean fluid.
>
> (32:8)

> Then He shaped him and breathed into him something from His spirit. And He gave you hearing and sight and the heart. Little thank you give!
>
> (32:9)

There are several more narratives on the subject. Verse 40:67 almost duplicates verse 22:5, which gives a fuller description of the biological development of man than some of the other verses. The despised sperm and the leech-like clot appear again, in a few more short verses: 75:37, 75:38, and 76:2.

Long and repetitious though the list of verses on the beginning of human life is, some of the narratives are at serious odds with scientific evidence. The difficulty in accepting some of the narratives as fact starts with the Arabic word '*alaq*. The word has always been translated as 'blood clot' or 'congealed blood'. The embryo, as we know now, is not a blood clot. At about the age of seven weeks, the embryo, less than an inch in length, already has the rudiments of all the human limbs as well as the beginning of the heart and lungs. Apparently, the stock of human knowledge in the seventh century lacked this information. The presence of blood in the embryo in any appreciable amount actually presages its destruction, leading to a miscarriage.

Neither is there a concept of a foetus in the verses on the beginning of life. The parenthetic mention of 'foetus' along with 'lump of flesh' (*muzgat*, in Arabic) in 23:14, in some translations, is merely a translator's discretion. It is absent from the Arabic Koran. Some translators have restricted themselves to 'lump'. The concept of bones being made out of that lump and then clad in flesh also goes against scientific evidence. The development of the bones is an integral part of the overall development of the embryo and the foetus. The bones are not 'clothed' in flesh, except in the figurative sense.

A great lacuna in the narrative on life in the Koran is the absence of any mention of the ovum. It is the fertilisation of the ovum that begins conception, starting the process of development of life in the womb. While the Koran repeatedly mentions sperm drops, nowhere in it is there any mention of the ovum. Human knowledge had yet to extend to it at the time.

Some traditional exegetes still seem to exude ignorance here. In verse 76:2, God creates man from a drop of 'mingled sperm',[196] a term that is not easy to understand. Here is an extraordinary exegesis by a

[196] Qur'ān/Yusuf Ali. Both Qur'ān/Yusuf Ali and Qur'ān/Muḥammad Ali) seem to think that the 'mingling' implies fertilisation. This is unacceptable, because the concept of ovum itself is absent from the Koran.

traditionalist commentator: 'By the term here is meant the mixing of men's and woman's semen. Most *tafsirists* agree on this interpretation.'[197]

The work just cited is a recent publication (from the late twentieth century). It is also strikingly similar in nature to other statements on biological conception and development in the womb, made over 1,400 years ago by the chief interpreter of the Koran, Muḥammad himself. According to *Sahih Al-Bukhāri,* while talking to his companions, the Prophet said:

> (As regards your creation) everyone of you is collected in the womb of his mother for the first forty days, then he becomes a clot for another forty days, then a piece of flesh for another forty days … [198]

The rest of the *ḥadith* then describes how an angel determines the length of the human life, and much else.

Finally, while human sperm is actually created in the testicles, the Koran says it is produced from between the backbone and the ribs:

> He is created from water emitted, issuing from between the backbone and the ribs.
>
> (86:6–7)

---

[197] Qur'ān/Muhiuddin, commentary on *Sūra* 76. The author seems blissfully unaware of the non-existence of female 'semen'. *Tafsirists* are translators/exegetes.

[198] al-Bukhāri, vol. 4, 129.

Chapter 10

The Insignificance of Man

The sweep of glorification of God in the Koran is interspersed with a corresponding emphasis on the unimportance of man and his efforts. If everything exists because God wishes it to exist, then, evidently, human effort is worth very little. There is, however, a further reason for the insignificance of man's efforts: not only what happens today but also what will happen in the infinite future, is predetermined by God. And all of this is an integral part of God's scheme, where the temporal world is so much inferior to life in the hereafter.

Liberal Islamic commentators often make much of man supposedly being the viceroy of God on earth, as in the expression appearing in the following verse:

> It is He who has appointed you viceroys of the earth and raised some of you in rank above others, that He may try you in what He has given you ...
>
> (6:165)

If man is no less than a viceroy of God on earth, he could not possibly be truly insignificant. The first part of the verse does seem to elevate the status of man in the eyes of God. This is, however, followed by a statement that has no bearing on that status and only alludes to ranking of some in society above, or below, others. On the other hand, the long series of verses we shall read in the following pages make the insignificance of man abundantly clear.

The sentence below would seem at first blush to suggest that man was created great:

> Surely We created man in the best of moulds.
>
> (95:4)

The next verse nullifies man's greatness in unflattering terms:

> Then did We reduce him to be the lowest of the low.
>
> (95:5)

There is a caveat in the next verse:

> Except those who believe and do good: so they have a reward unfailing.
>
> (96:6)

As with other themes in the Koran, the narrative on the role of man is scattered throughout the Book and brought up in very different contexts. Sometimes no context seems to exist. These parts of the Koran are best read together, and a substantial number of them have been collected below. Many of these verses are self-explanatory, needing little commentary.

The Koran does not belittle worldly human activity; in fact, that activity is important enough to require elaborate Koranic directives. Neither does the Koran forbid people to enjoy the good things in life; after all, these things are God's bounty. On the other hand, life in the hereafter is far more important than life on earth.

Thus, we read:

> And life of this world is nothing but sport and amusement. And certainly for those who are righteous, the abode of the Hereafter is the best …
>
> (6:32)

> And know that your possessions and your children are a temptation and with God is the best reward.
>
> (8:28)

> Whatever you are given is but a provision of the life in this world; and what is with God is better and more lasting for those who believe and put their trust in their Lord.
>
> (42:36)

Against this background, man's endeavour to improve his lot must look miniscule. Much of his needs are met by divine intervention:

> It is God Who has created the heavens and the earth and sent down rain from the skies, then brought forth with it fruits for your sustenance; and made the ships subservient to you that they may sail on the sea by His command. And the rivers too He made subservient to you.
>
> (14:32)

Remarkably, even the shirt on man's back is not something that he makes. It is made for him:

> And of things He made for you, He has created shades, and given you mountain refuge, and provided for you garments as protection against heat, and coats of mail as protection in fighting. Thus does He complete His favour for you that you may submit to Him.
>
> (16:81)

The ship, the mode of transport on the oceans, sails only at the command of God:

> See you not that God has subjected to you all that is on earth, and the ships that sail through the sea by His command?
>
> (22:65)

It is the wind that swells the sails that propel the ship, and it is God's command that makes this possible:

> Among His Signs is: that He sends the winds bearing good news, giving you the taste of His mercy, and that the ships sail by His command, that you may seek His bounty …
>
> (30:40)

> See you not that the ships sail through the ocean by the grace of God, that He may show you His signs? …
>
> (31:31)

As we saw earlier, it is God who creates the orchard, tends the date palm, and irrigates the land. Man's hands have little contribution to make, not even in splitting the land for cultivation, and far it is for him to produce anything in great abundance. God produces and distributes, and He does so in due measure, so that man does not transgress:

> And We layout in it orchards of date-palm, and grapes and We make the springs flow therein:
>
> (36:34)

> That they may eat the fruits thereof. And it is not their hands that made it. Will they not give thanks?
>
> (36:35)

Even more specifically:

> Then let man look at his food.
>
> (80:24)

> We pour forth water in abundance;
>
> (80: 5)

> And We split the earth in fragments;
>
> (80:26)

> And produce therein corn;
>
> (80:27)

> And grapes and nutritious plants;
>
> (80:28)

> And olives and dates.
>
> (80:29)

> And if God were to enlarge the provisions for His servants, they would indeed transgress in the land; but He sends it down in due measure, as He pleases. Surely, He is knowledgeable and all-seeing with His servants.
>
> (42:27)

Rain delights the peasants, but they must look on helplessly when crops on their land wilt and crumble:

(... Here is a similitude:)

> How rain and the vegetation it brings forth, delight the peasants;[199]soon it withers; you see it turning yellow; then it becomes chaff ...
>
> (57:20)

Man must therefore learn to be humble.

Once again, the majestic, smooth-running ships that ply the oceans are some of His signs. The ships, with sailors on board, are powerless without the wind that blows only at His wish:

> And among His signs are the ships like mountains on the sea.
>
> (42:32)

> If it is His will, He can still the wind, so that they would lie motionless on the ocean's back. Verily these are signs for

[199] The Arabic word used here is *kuffar*, which usually means 'unbelievers'. Its use to mean 'tillers' is rare, and other translators have used 'unbelievers' when translating the term. In the context of the verse, however, the use of 'peasants' makes more sense. Qur'ān/ Muhiuddin agrees.

> everyone that is patient and grateful.
>
> (42:33)

In an age when man-made roads were uncommon, God not only spread the earth like a carpet for man's convenience, He also made roads for his movement to distant lands:

> (God is also He) who had the earth spread out, and made for you ways therein that you may be guided.
>
> (43:10)

Given that man has so little control over his known environment, it is no wonder that it is futile for him to think of the unknown, much less probe it. Throughout history, exploration of the unknown has been the motive power of every dynamic human civilisation. Thus, man invented the steam engine and the light bulb, discovered new lands, and explored hitherto unknown depths of the ocean. Man has unlocked the doors of innumerable unknowns. In the static world of the Koran, however, it is God alone who knows the unknown. The following verse says this in no uncertain terms:

> And with Him are the keys of the unseen: none knows it but He. And He knows what is in the earth and in the sea. And not a leaf falls without His knowledge …
>
> (6:59)

Man's status of insignificance appears to have been finally sealed by predestination: man is not only seen to be insignificant but also is destined to be so.

In the early days of Islam, a long, hard battle raged between the protagonists of what might be called, with some risk of oversimplification, free will and predestination. Orthodoxy, in the main, upheld the doctrine of predestination, claiming the Koran was on its side. And they could come up with chapter and verse from the Koran which, according to them, proved their point, though the arguments on both sides went far beyond just quoting the Holy Book.

The Koranic narratives on man's capacity or incapacity to do good or commit evil of course have a lapsarian background which the Holy Book alludes to more than once. *Sūra* 15 (*Hijr*) has this remarkable though familiar exchange between God and Iblis (Satan). As the accursed Iblis is being expelled from Heaven, he asks God:

> "O my Lord! As you have put me in the wrong, so shall I make wrong seem fair to them on earth. And I will put them all in the wrong.
>
> (15:39)

He then added a critical exception:

> Except thy servants among them who are devoted.
>
> (15:40)

And God decrees:

> This is the Way that leads straight to Me.[200]
>
> (15:41)

> Over My servants you shall have no jurisdiction, except such perverts who follow you.
>
> (15:42)

> And surely, Hell is the promised place for them all.
>
> (15:43)

It would thus seem that there will be servants of God predestined to be sincere and pure, and others who will inevitably follow Satan and, just as inevitably, enter hell. Nevertheless, those who see a role for free will, in the glorious ambiguities worked out in Heaven, can still come up with a fair number of verses to back up their stand.[201]

The verse below suggests that man has a choice to act righteously:

---

[200] 'The way' refers to devotion to God, alluded to in 15:40.

[201] To search verses on the subject, I have used, not exclusively, Fazlur Rahman, *Major Themes of the Qur'an* (Chicago: University of Chicago Press, 1980).

> Whoever does good it is for the benefit of his soul; whoever does evil, it goes against his own soul.
>
> (41:46)

The verses below emphasise man's ability to distinguish between right and wrong, and thereupon make an effort to purify his soul:

> Truly he succeeds who purifies himself, and he fails who corrupts himself.
>
> (91:9–10)

The following verse seems to make a bolder case for human action to improve his lot, and it has often been quoted in the present context:

> Surely God never changes the condition of a people, until they change what is in themselves,
>
> (13:11)

As is often the case, however, the beginning of the verse bears little relationship to the lines above, leaving them devoid of context. Neither are the lines that follow quite unequivocal. The verse in its entirety is:

> For him are angels in succession before him and after him: they watch over him by the command of God. Surely God never changes the condition of a people until they change what is in themselves. And when God desires evil for a people there is no turning back, and there is no protector for them except Him.
>
> (13:11)

The following verse is a clearer statement on free will than some of the others. Muḥammad is asked to say:

> … And no soul earns except on its own account, and no bearer of burden can carry another's burden …
>
> (6:164)

Furthermore, has not God given man a pair of eyes, a tongue, and a pair of lips (90:8-9), and

> And shown him the two highways?
>
> (90:10)

It is up to each human to choose a highway. One highway leads to vice and an easy life. The life of virtue, which is far more difficult, requires the use of man's better faculties:

> But he attempts not the steep way.
>
> (90:11)

The verses that follow are a remarkable rendering of the virtues man can strive for:

> And what will explain to you what a steep way is?
>
> (90:12)

Verses 90:13–16 list the virtues: freeing a slave, and giving food to the needy, the orphaned, and the indigent. Note, however, that while these are certainly acts of piety, they are not meant to be instruments of improvement of man's lot.

Verses with a strong flavour of predestination far outnumber those seeming to suggest free will. The former are also clearer in their import than the latter. Of the verses of the Koran dwelling on particular themes, those on predestination are also among the most numerous. We shall read a fairly large sample of them in the following pages. As with other themes, these verses appear in a wide variety of contexts and are scattered throughout a large number of *sūras*. Sometimes it is difficult to comprehend the context of a verse; often a verse comes without any apparent context. There are a number of verses where God tells His Messenger it is He who decides whether or not the unbelievers finally turn to the right path. Neither Muḥammad's effort nor man's free will is of any avail. It might sometimes seem that some of the narratives of this nature are reflections of divine frustration and anger, as we have seen earlier.[202] Yet there are numerous verses that bear heavy imprints of predestination.

People who reject the faith are not merely denounced in the Koran; they are doomed by God's wrath. We have already read the following verses appearing at the beginning of the first substantive *sūra* of the Koran. They are apt to read again here:

> God has set a seal in their hearts and on their hearing, and on their eyes is a covering; and a severe penalty awaits them.
>
> (2:7)

> In their hearts is a sickness; and God has increased their sickness …
>
> (2:10)

In the following verse, man is responsible for his evil deeds but gets no credit for his good actions:

> Whatever good happens to you is from God; whatever evil happens is from your own soul …
>
> (4:79)

No amount of coaxing would turn unbelievers into believers, unless this is predestined by God:

> … Whom God wills, He leaves in error; whom He wills, He puts on the straight path.
>
> (6:39)

The above theme is repeated many times, such as in verses 16:93, 39:23, 70:39, and 74:31.

Here are some variations on the theme that appear in the narrative:

[202] See Chapter 3.

> Those whom God wishes to guide, He expands their breasts for Islam; those He wishes to leave straying, He makes their breasts narrow ...
>
> (6:125)

> Whom God guides, he is on the right path; and he whom He leaves straying, is the loser.
>
> (7:178)

> Whom God leads astray, there is no guide for him ...
>
> (7:186)

In the same vein are verses 13:33 and 39:23.

And again:

> If it had been your Lord's will, they would all have believed, all those who are on the earth ...
>
> (10:99)

Here, God Himself lets disbelief, reflected in the attitude of people towards messengers in earlier times (verse 15:11), work towards the same end:

> Thus do We let it creep into the hearts of the guilty –
>
> (15:12)

> (Thus) They do not believe in the Message ...
>
> (15:13)

In two verses addressed to the Prophet, the disbelievers are destined not to listen to the Koran:

> When you recite the Koran, We put between you and those who do not believe in the Hereafter, an invisible screen.[203]
>
> (17:45)

[203] The *ḥijab*, in Arabic.

> And We put coverings over their hearts lest they comprehend it, and deafness in their ears ...
>
> (17:46)

Even if the unbelievers manage to hear the admonition:

> They will not remember it except as God wills ...
>
> (74:56)

Furthermore, not only man's actions are predestined, but so are his misfortunes. On this there can be no stronger statement than the following:

> No disaster can happen on earth or to you but as it is decreed, before We make it to happen. That is easy for God.
>
> (57:22)

Finally, here is a *ḥadith* from *Sahih Al-Bukhāri* that leaves no doubt over where the Prophet of Islam stood on predestination. A person's destiny, he says, is written down by the angels at the command of God:

> ... And by Allah, a person among you (or a man) may do deeds of the people of (Hell) Fire till there is only a cubit or an arm length distance between him and the (Hell) fire, but then that writing (which Allah has ordered the angel to write) precedes, and he does the deeds of the people of paradise and enters it; and a man may do the deeds of the people of Paradise till there is only a cubit or two between him and Paradise, and then that writing precedes and he does the deeds of the people of the Fire and enters it. [204]

There appears to be no last word on predestination versus free will. But the following *ḥadith* from *Tirmizi,* one of the collections of *ḥadiths* considered most authentic, sounds like one:

[204] al-Bukhāri, vol. 8, 316.

From Hazrat Abu Hureira: One day the Apostle of Allah (Peace of Allah on him) came to us while we had been debating predestination. At this he became so angry with us that his face turned red as if it had been daubed with pomegranate juice. Then he said: "Have you been told to do nothing but this? Or have I been sent (by Allah) to you to deal with this (subject) alone? Peoples in earlier times were destroyed whenever they fell into debating this matter. I swear, and I swear, Beware! Never fall into debating on this matter."

(Source: *Tirmizi*)[205]

[205] Azmi, Maulana Nur Muhammad, *Meshqat Sharif: with Bengali Translation and Commentary,* vol. 1. (Dhaka, Bangladesh: Imdadia Library, 1978), 116. The *ḥadith* can be read on Sunnah.com, *Jami at-Tirmidhi,* Chapter 33 (Al-Qadar).

Chapter 11
Heaven and Hell

In *Sūra* 11 (*Hūd*), verse 119, God promises to fill hell with unbelieving human beings and jinns. The verse leaves no doubt about the enormity of the number of sinners destined for hell. At the same time, it reiterates predestination: that men will not cease disputing the true religion:

> Except those on whom thy Lord has bestowed His mercy; to that end did He create them; and the word of your Lord shall be fulfilled: "I shall fill hell with jinns and men all together."
>
> (11:119)

In case ambiguity arises regarding the identity of 'them' in the verse, one exegete[206] clarifies that it refers to those deprived of God's mercy: the disputants have been created to dispute, and hell has been created for them. The inevitability of hell for so much of humanity stands out in this verse. And yet, the Koran is replete with verses that call upon man to do good deeds and shun evil. And a life of pleasure in Heaven is described, often in considerable detail, in order to goad man to good deeds. The kind of punishment in hell awaiting the perpetrators of evil is similarly narrated. Sometimes reward and retribution are described in contrasting juxtaposition.

In this chapter, we shall read a selection of verses on Heaven and hell, without following any particular order of the *sūras* in the Koran, and starting with Heaven. I shall skip verses which have only passing reference

[206] Qur'ān/Muhiuddin.

to it. It is remarkable that most of the *sūras* that have more than a few verses on Heaven and hell are Meccan.

> And give glad tidings to those who believe and do good deeds, that for them are the Gardens beneath which flow the rivers. Every time they are given fruits to eat, they will say: This is what we were given for food before; and they will be given the like of it; and for them there will be pure female companions; and there they will forever abide.
>
> (2:25)

Note the emphasis on food, especially of the kind the inhabitants of the Gardens[207] were familiar with on earth, but of which many of them had been deprived because of scarcity and poverty. In a reversal of the imagery of Heaven on earth, the translation of the earthly idea of a good life into an actuality in Heaven is repeated in many other verses. In the early days of Islam, Heaven was held out as the ultimate reward for martyrs in the cause of Islam. In recent times, Islamist extremists have often found suicide bombing an attractive device to gate-crash into Heaven. But the allure of Heaven has been a constant with Muslims ever since the Koran began to be propagated. It has been the primary motivation behind acts of piety enjoined by the Holy Book of Islam. The pleasures of Heaven reach hedonist proportions in later verses.

The following verse substantially raises the status of Heaven as a lucrative abode. Here we read about those who worked righteously on earth:

> For them will be perpetual Gardens beneath which flow the rivers; they will be adorned with bracelets of gold; and they will wear green attire of fine silk and thick brocade, reclining on raised couches …
>
> (18:31)

---

[207] I have used Gardens and Heaven interchangeably.

In the Islamic tradition, men are forbidden to wear gold and silk. Exegetes have tried in vain to justify the words in the above verse. The scene turns distinctly hedonistic in the following series of verses on the delights of the Gardens:

> For them awaits known sustenance:
>
> (37:41)
>
> Fruits. And they in honour and dignity;
>
> (37:42)
>
> In Gardens of delight;
>
> (37:43)
>
> On thrones, facing each other;
>
> (37:44)
>
> A drinking cup will be passed round to them from a flowing spring;
>
> (37:45)
>
> White, delicious to the drinkers;
>
> (37:46)
>
> Wherein there is no sickness; nor will they be intoxicated therewith.
>
> (37:47)
>
> And besides them will be wide-eyed maidens, restraining their glances.
>
> (37:48)

The delights of the Gardens are truly remarkable in their sensuousness. These delights are repeated and enhanced; in some verses, the scene becomes distinctly sensual.

In the verse below, the believers are again placed in the Gardens and beside springs, decked in silk and brocade, and in the company of beautiful *houris.*[208] They will be:

> Among Gardens and Springs;
>
> (44:52)

> Dressed in fine silk and rich brocades, facing each other;
>
> (44:53)

> ... and We shall join them to chaste companions with big, beautiful eyes.
>
> (44:54)

Wine, the drinking of which is denounced in the Koran itself, appears in the following verse, along with milk and honey:

> Here is a parable of the Garden the godfearing have been promised: In it are rivers of clear water; rivers of milk, unchanging in taste; rivers of wine, delicious to the drinkers; and rivers of honey, pure and clear ...
>
> (47:15)

Wine (*khamr,* in Arabic) has been spoken against in strong terms in at least three verses of the Koran.[209] In Islamic *shari'a,* drinking is enough of a sin to call for flogging of the offender.[210] And yet a drink, so decried in Koran when it comes to life on earth, is glorified for life in Heaven. A human craving denounced on earth finds ample favour in the hereafter.

Narratives of Heaven continue, with minor variations on the theme. In a *sūra* ringing with high rhetoric, the virtuous are once again found in the Garden:

---

[208] These are said to be female companions, young, large-eyed, and especially beautiful.

[209] See Chapter 12.

[210] Sadakat Kadri, *Heaven on Earth: A Journey Through Shari'a Law from the Deserts of Ancient Arabia to the Streets of the Modern Muslim World* (Farrar, Straus and Giroux, 2012). It provides an interesting discussion on wine and the *shari'a.*

> Surely the god fearing will be in the Gardens in bliss,
> (52:17)
>
> Rejoicing in what their Lord has given them. And their Lord saved them from the punishment of Hell.
> (52:18)
>
> (It will be said to them:) Eat and drink with relish (as reward) for what you have accomplished.
> (52:19)
>
> Reclining on thrones placed in rows and We shall join them with wide-eyed *houris.*
> (52:20)

The early Meccan *Sūra* 55 (*Raḥmān*), known for its rhythmic quality – particularly the refrain 'Then which of the favours of your Lord will ye deny?' – contains a familiar list of favours that God promises for the righteous in Heaven. The *sūra* actually speaks of two Gardens; or, more precisely, two groups of Gardens, though the precise significance of the difference between the two Gardens is rather unclear.[211]

For those nearest to God, the Gardens will contain all kinds of trees and delights, though there are identical pleasures in both categories of Gardens.

> In them will be two springs flowing free.
> (55:50)
>
> Therein will be every kind of fruit in pairs. [212]
> (55:52)

[211] Qur'ān/Yusuf Ali states that the 'best opinion' among exegetes is that verses 55:46–61 describe the abode and pleasures of those who are nearest to God, while verses 55:62–76 are for the lesser ones in righteousness, though still immensely blessed ones.

[212] Qur'ān/Yusuf Ali has this unconvincing explanation of fruit coming in pairs: 'The Duality of Fruits is for the same reason as the Duality of the Garden.'
The missing verse Between 55:50 and 55:52, and among the verses that follow, is the refrain 'Then which of the favours of your Lord will you deny?'.

> They will recline on couches, lined with brocades; and the fruit of the two gardens will be easy to reach.
>
> (55:54)

> Therein will be maidens restraining their glances whom no man or jinn has touched before them.
>
> (55:56)

Noteworthy is the emphasis in the above verse on the virginity of the female companions of the virtuous. This appears to be the ultimate in sensuality in Heaven, and is expressed as such in the narrative of the Holy Book. Modern readers will find it amazing.

The other Gardens, for the righteous who are just below the first category in rank, will be:

> Dark-green in colour.
>
> (55:64)

> In them will be two springs of gushing water.
>
> (55:66)

> In them will be fruits, dates and pomegranates.
>
> (55:68)

> In them will be maidens, good and beautiful.
>
> (55:70)

> *Houris*, confined to the pavilions,
>
> (55:72)

> Whom no man or jinn has touched before them.
>
> (55:74)

> Reclining on green cushions and beautiful carpets.
>
> (55:76)

Once again, the beautiful young women are a major feature of the narrative, as is their virginity. It is difficult to see the difference between the two groups of Gardens, and the distinctions offered by exegetes appear quite forced and unconvincing.

The next *sūra*, *Waqiʿa*, said to have been inspired at about the same time as *Raḥman*, takes the pleasures of Heaven to new levels of sensuality. It should strike us that while the theme of both *sūras* is the same Heaven, the narratives vary significantly. It starts with the Gardens for those nearest to God:

> And the foremost are the foremost.
> (56:10)
>
> Those are the nearest (to God).
> (56:11)
>
> In Gardens of Bliss.
> (56:12)
>
> Many from among the ancients
> (56:13)
>
> And a few from those of later times.
> (56:14)
>
> On thrones wrought.
> (56:15)
>
> Reclining on them, facing each other.
> (56:16)
>
> Round them will serve ageless youths,
> (56:17)
>
> With goblets, beakers, and cups filled from clear fountains.
> (56:18)

> No headache will they suffer therefrom nor will they be intoxicated.
>
> (56:19)

> And fruit of their choice.
>
> (56:20)

> And the flesh of fowls they may wish for.
>
> (56:21)

> And wide-eyed *houris*.
>
> (56:22)

The narrative continues for a few more verses in the same vein, but we shall skip them.

As for the righteous other than those nearest to God, they will be:

> Among thornless Lote trees.
>
> (56:28)

> Among Talh trees[213] with serried flowers.
>
> (56:29)

> In shades long extended.
>
> (56:30)

> Besides water flowing,
>
> (56:31)

> And fruit in abundance.
>
> (56:32)

> Never interrupted, never forbidden.
>
> (56:33)

[213] Some exegetes have translated this as 'banana trees'. This is strange because they were not a familiar sight in the desert. A dictionary meaning is 'acacia'. Qur'ān/Yusuf Ali points out that the Arabic word for banana is *mauz*, and *talh* is perhaps a variety of acacia.

And on upraised couches.

(56:34)

There are companions who have been created especially for the pleasure of the inhabitants of theses Gardens. It is not clear, though, why the superior group mentioned above is deprived of the company of this special creation.

Surely We have created them as a special creation.

(56:35)

So We have made them virgin. [214]–

(56:36)

It is worth repeating here the background of two pairs of the verses in *Sūra* 56 (*Wāqi'a*), as quoted above. A traditional exegesis suggests that verses 56:13 and 56:14, above, were said to have pained the companions of Muḥammad, since the words appear to suggest (or, the Prophet's companions interpreted the verses as suggesting) that the inhabitants of the Gardens from generations preceding his will form a larger group than those belonging to his generation. And then, after what amounts to a human-divine bargain, came verses 56:39 and 56:40, whereupon the companions felt placated.[215] The change does once again suggest the amenability of the Holy Book to human sentiments.[216] The new verses inspired appear below. It is extraordinary that both the old and new verses stand in the *sūra*, and traditional exegeses do not seem to see this as an incongruity, as it would be any other texts. The two new verses are:

Many from among the ancients.

(56:39)

[214] Modern sensibility would be jolted by the following exegesis of the Arabic word *abkar*, translated as 'virgin': '*Abkar* is plural of *bakr*, meaning 'maiden'. The idea here is that the women of the Gardens will be so created that they will revert to being virgins after each sexual intercourse.' Translation is from Qur'ān/Muhiuddin.

Perhaps not all exegetes will agree on this interpretation of the verse. The stress here on the extra sensuality implied for virginity is nevertheless unmistakable.

[215] Qur'ān/Muhiuddin.

[216] See Chapter 2.

> And many from later times.
>
> (56:40)

For comparison, read again:

> Many from among the ancients
>
> (56:13)

And:

> And a few from those of later times
>
> (56:14)

Sūras 76 (*Dahr*) and 77 (*Mursalāt*) contain a fairly large number of verses on Heaven. These are minor variations and repetitions of the above verses, which must suffice here.

A remarkable feature of the narrative on Heaven in the Koran is the total absence of women among its residents. There are women companions, presumably meant for male residents alone. But these are mere companions and not those who, by dint of their virtuous conduct on earth, were also entitled by God to a place in the Garden. There is no mention of such women anywhere in the narratives.

The Koran's narratives on hell are almost as extensive as those on Heaven and are often given as an exercise in contrast. The righteous go to a perpetual life of sensual bliss. Unmitigated suffering is the lot of those who rejected God during their time on earth. We shall now read a selection of the verses on hell, which broadly follows the order in which they appear in the Koran.

The following is a categorical promise of unrelenting punishment for all those who reject Islam:

> Those who reject our Message, soon shall We cast into the Fire. Every time their skins are roasted, We shall give new skins in their place, that they taste the penalty …
>
> (4:56)

The following verse has an unmistakable biblical flavour, though in a very different context:

> To those who reject our Message and treat them with arrogance, there shall be no opening for them of the doors of Heaven and nor shall they enter the Garden until the camel passes through the eye of the needle. Thus We reward the guilty.
>
> (7:40)

The pleasures of Heaven are sometimes juxtaposed with the pains of hell. Here is a tongue-in-cheek address from the companions of Heaven to the companions of hell:

> The companions of the Garden will call out to the companions of the Fire: We have found that what our Lord had promised us is true. Have you found the promise of your Lord true? They will say, yes. Then a crier will cry out among them: the curse of God is on the wrongdoers.
>
> (7:44)

The companions of hell will plead with the companions of Heaven for help:

> The companions of the Fire will call out to the companions of the Garden: pour down on us some water or from what God is giving to you for food. They will say: surely God has forbidden both to the unbelievers.
>
> (7:50)

The pleading will be in vain:

> ... This day shall We forget them as they forgot the meeting of this day of theirs, and they denied our Signs.
>
> (7:51)

Idolatry is the greatest of sins, and so the idolaters suffer the gravest penalties:

> And We wronged them not: they wronged their own souls. And those whom they invoked besides God availed them not …
>
> (11:101)

> They will abide therein as long as the heavens and the earth endure, except as your Lord please …
>
> (11:107)

Instead of the sustenance craved (as in 7:50), the unbeliever will have only boiling, fetid water to drink:

> He only sips it but is not able to swallow it; and death comes to him from every direction yet he will not be dead.
>
> (14:17)

Here is a graphic description of punishment for the unbelievers:

> And that day you will see the sinners chained together.
>
> (14:49)

> Their garments are of tar[217] and their faces are enveloped in fire.
>
> (14:50)

In *Sūra* 15 (*Ḥijr*), after an exchange with Satan, God promises his followers hell, which will have seven gates:

---

[217] Tar, as we know it, was unlikely to have existed at the time. Based on the dictionary meaning of the Arabic *Qateran*, the tar referred to here was perhaps an extract of a tree, such as juniper.

> It has seven Gates; to each gate a set of the sinners is assigned.
>
> (15:44)

The sinners and Satan will be assembled on their knees around hell (*Sūra* 19:68, *Maryam*), and everyone in obstinate rebellion against God will be dragged from every sect (19:69). Everybody (apparently, even the righteous) will have to pass over hell.

> And We shall save those who are god fearing and We shall leave the wrongdoers on their knees.
>
> (19:72)

Elsewhere in the narrative (Sūra 22, *Ḥajj)*, for the unbelievers and those who deny God:

> … For them will be cut out garments of fire; on their heads will be poured boiling water.
>
> (22:19)

> With it will be melted what is inside their bellies and their skin.
>
> (22:20)

For further punishment:

> And there will be maces of iron.
>
> (22:21)

> Every time they wish to get away from it, from the agony, they will be turned back (and it will be said to them): Taste the punishment of burning.
>
> (22:22)

They could have had eternal life in the Garden, but while on earth, they chose to deny the very existence of the Day of Judgement:

> They deny the Hour, but We have prepared, for those who deny the Hour, a blazing fire.
>
> (25:11)

The wrongdoers will quarrel among themselves, laying the blame for their plight on those whom they worshipped and on one another. But (*Sūra* 37, *Sāffāt*):

> Truly, that Day, they will share in the punishment.
>
> (37:33)

> For, when they were told that there was no god but God, they were indeed scornful.
>
> (37:35)

> And said: "What! Shall we give up our gods for a poet gone mad?
>
> (37:36)

And while the righteous enjoy good food and lead lives of honour and dignity, as well as great pleasure (narrated again at length in 37:41–49), at same time, they observe the fire of hell; the entertainment prepared for the wrongdoers is the bitter tree called Zaqqum:

> For it is a tree that springs out of the bottom of Hell.
>
> (37:64)

> Its spathes are like the heads of Satans.
>
> (37:65)

> Surely they will eat it and fill their bellies with it.
>
> (37:66)

Graphic contrasts between the reception given to the unbelievers at the gates of hell and that accorded to the righteous at the gates of Heaven are repeated (*Sūra* 39, *Zumar*):

> The unbelievers will be herded towards Hell, until they arrive, its gates are opened, and its keepers say to them: Did not Messengers come among you, reciting to you signs of you Lord and warning you of the meeting of this day of yours? They will say yes ...
>
> (39:71)

> It will be said to them: Enter the gates of Hell, to abide there. Evil is the abode of the conceited!
>
> (39:72)

The narrative contrasts this with:

> And the god fearing will be taken to the Garden in groups until they come to it, and its gates are opened, and its keepers say: Peace be on you! You have done well! So enter it to dwell in it forever.
>
> (39:73)

In *Sūra* 55 (*Raḥman*), the refrain 'Then which of the favours of your Lord will you deny?' follows verses on hell, including those of total humiliation of its denizens. The refrain is repeated just as it is after verses on Heaven. The intention perhaps is Godly sarcasm, of which there are many instances in the Koran. Thus we read:

> The guilty will be known by their marks; and they will be seized by their forelocks and by their feet.
>
> (55:41)

This is termed a 'favour', hence the refrain:

> Then which of the favours of your Lord will you deny?
>
> (55:42)

Once in hell:

> They will go round between it and between boiling hot water.
> (55:44)

The refrain again:

> Then which of the favours of your Lord will you deny?
> (55:45)

In *Sūra* 56 (*Wāqi'a*), narratives of a sumptuous dinner and sensual pleasure are juxtaposed with these narratives of hell:

> And the Companions of the Left? O the Companions of the Left!
> (56:41)

> They will be in the searing wind and boiling water.
> (56:42)

> And in shades of black smoke.
> (56:43)

Now they will be told:

> Eat of the tree of Zaqqum.
> (56:52)

> Fill your bellies with it.
> (56:53)

> Then after that have a drink of boiling water.
> (56:54)

> And drink like the thirsty camel.
> (56:55)

Here, in *Sūra* 74 (*Mūddaththir*) is a rare occasion in the Koran where punishments are prescribed for specific sins. These verses are exchanges between the righteous residing in the Garden and sinners being led to hell.

The residents of the Gardens will ask:

> What brought you to Hell?
>
> (74:42)

> They will say: We did not pray.
>
> (74:43)

> Nor did we feed the poor.
>
> (74:44)

> But we indulged in vain talks with vain talkers.
>
> (74:45)

> And we denied the Day of Judgment.
>
> (74:46)

> Until the inevitable caught up with us.
>
> (74:47)

Their fate is surely an admonition (to the living):

> Nay, this surely is a reminder.
>
> (74:54)

> Let any who wills remember it.
>
> (74:55)

Yet the *sūra* ends with a verse where predestination makes a comeback:

> But none will remember unless God wills. He is worthy to be feared, worthy to forgive.
>
> (74:56)

However, whether forgiveness will extend to those who failed to keep the admonition in remembrance, as they were destined to, is not clear.

Chapter 12

Virtue, Equity, and Justice on Earth

Back on earth, the Koran lays down codes of conduct for the private and social lives of the believer, and prescribes retributions for infringement. Righteous living is the goal.

> And let there arise from you a nation that will invite to good, enjoin what is right, and forbid what is wrong: They are the ones who will prosper.
>
> (3:104)

The following verse goes much further and is perhaps the most comprehensive definition of righteousness in the Koran:

> It is not righteousness that you turn your faces towards East or West. It is: to believe in God and in the Last Day, in the angels, the Book, and the Prophets; to spend your wealth out love for Him, for the kinsmen, the orphans, the needy, the wayfarer, those who ask, and for ransoming a slave; to perform regular prayer, and give in charity; to fulfil contracts made, and to be patient in distress and affliction and in times of conflict.They are the god fearing.
>
> (2:177)

Canonical acts of piety naturally receive the greatest attention in the Koran. Prayer, fasting, and charity appear in the above verse, and they have been emphasised in many other verses. Yet righteousness is more than these acts of piety. In the Koran's widely discursive narratives, we find a number of verses emphasising kindness to parents and fellow believers, caveats notwithstanding. Similarly, there are verses that stress a measure of equity, sometimes indistinguishable from the kindness of the heart. The disapproval of usury in the Koran can be seen as a censure of exploitation, even though its rationale can be questioned, especially in the context of the role of money and finance in a modern economy. A debtor in difficulty calls for humane treatment. It is remarkable too that the above verse considers patience in distress a virtue.

Yet there are aspects of righteous living envisaged in the Koran that will be at huge variance with accepted codes of individual and societal behaviour today. A life with 'those whom your right hands possess', an oft-used expression in the Koran, was considered quite virtuous, other things remaining the same. The expression is, however, a euphemism for captives of war, or slaves, and more often than not, it is used to refer to bondmaids. In the Koran, slaves, captives, and bondmen are part of the social fabric, as they were in many other societies around the world – contemporary, ancient, and still to come.

There can be few human conditions of iniquity and inequality more egregious than slavery. Though there are verses in the Koran that call for humane treatment of slaves, bondmen, and captive women, it does not call for abolition of the system. Nor is any retribution prescribed for cruelty to slaves. Righteousness in this case did not extend beyond individual acts of kindness. Apparently, slavery was too important a part of the social system to be tampered with, even by divine intervention. It would be more than a millennium before secular and liberal ideas and economic forces finally ended the system.

Of the various forms of slavery, captive women receive the most mention in the Koran. The following verses clearly permit the master to have a sexual relationship with the captive woman he possesses.

Thus, the Koran declares that among the righteous are those:

> Who restrain their sexual passion,
>
> (23:5)

(An important proviso immediately follows in the next verse:)

> Except in the case of their spouses, or those whom your right hands possess …
>
> (23:6)

Apparently, the relationship need not be consensual. A captive woman can be expected to have little choice. In the following verse, the system is not only accepted but also given divine imprimatur. It is God himself who assigns captives for possession of the believers. The following verse is addressed directly to Muḥammad:

> O Prophet! We have made lawful to you your wives to whom you have paid their dowers, and those whom your right hand possesses from the prisoners of war that God has given to you …
>
> (33:50)

Again, echoing 23:5–6, above, the righteous are those who fear God:

> And those who guard their chastity,
>
> (70:29)

> Except with their wives and those whom their right hand possess …
>
> (70:30)

Having confirmed captive women in their position, the Koran also calls on believers to treat them with kindness. A major verse (4:36) lists kindness to captive women among righteous deeds, which also include serving God, doing good for parents, kinsmen, orphans, and neighbours, among other acts. The directive about kindness to captive women is not without its ironies, as seen below.

While the kindest thing to do was to set them free, arguably the next-best thing was to be kind to them, which in effect also helped to perpetuate the system itself. There is also advice to marry captive women in some circumstances:

> If any of you have not the means to marry free believing women, let them marry believing maidens from among those whom your right hand possess. … so marry them with the permission of their masters …
>
> (4:25)

In the verse, marrying such women is recommended only as the last resort, and even then, only to guard the believers from 'falling into evil'. It is not advocated out of any consideration for the welfare of the slave girl. It is strange, though, that the women are also required, in the same verse, to be 'chaste, not fornicating, and not receiving paramour.' Since these women are those whom 'their right hands possess' (with 'their' referring to the masters), the stringency of the requirement must look wholly ironic.

Married women cannot be remarried till they are separated from their husbands. In the case of captives, this rule is relaxed. The master can marry a captive woman even if she has a husband:

> Also (prohibited for marriage are) women already married, except those whom your right hand possesses …
>
> (4:24)

Here, it is easy to picture a captive woman, pining for her husband, but still giving herself in marriage to her captor and master; meanwhile, the forlorn husband sighs and sheds tears in some distant land. That of course is a tale told a million times in the course of human history, not just in the deserts of ancient Arabia.

A verse of the Koran asks the masters not to force their captive women into prostitution:

> … But when your slave -girls desire chastity, do not force them into prostitution in order to seek gain in goods of this life of this world. But whoever compels them, then, after their compulsion, surely God is Forgiving, Merciful.
>
> (24:33)

Exactly whom is God forgiving here? It is not obvious. From the construction of the sentence, starting with 'whoever compels', it would appear that God is forgiving the person doing the compelling. Exegetes seem to see it differently: it is on the slave girls who have been forced into prostitution that divine pardon is bestowed here![218]

There is little need for explicit statements about the social inferiority of slaves. However, the following verse makes their position abundantly clear, and quite reasonably too, while simultaneously attributing the exalted status of the master to the bounty of God:

> God strikes a similitude: a slave, in servitude, with no power over anything; and one (the master) whom We have provided from us goodly provisions, out of which he spends in secret or openly. Are the two equal? Praise be to God! No! Most of them do not know.
>
> (16:75)

And yet, while consigning the slave to a system impervious to change, the Koran calls for freeing him, at a price. Inexplicably wedged between a sentence on the desirability of abstinence, and the injunction we just came across against forcing slave-girls into prostitution, is the following verse:

> ... And if any of your slaves prays for a written deed of freedom give it to them, if you know any good in them, and give them from the wealth that God has given you ...
>
> (24:33)

As one exegete explains, this involves the slave being allowed to earn enough money, while still serving his master, to pay for his manumission.[219] That such a process of earning freedom can be prolonged and extremely arduous is easy to see. The verse has sometimes been offered as evidence of Islam's commitment to freeing slaves. The question then arises as to why the directive is ensconced parenthetically between two quite unrelated themes, in a single verse.

There are several other verses in the Koran where the freeing of slaves is

---

[218] Both Qur'ān/Muhiuddin and Qur'ān/Yusuf Ali explain it in this manner. Apparently, the reasoning is that since the girls commit the immoral act, it is they who are in need of forgiveness. The person compelling them goes scot-free.

[219] Qur'ān/Yusuf Ali.

mentioned. These verses, along with the above verse, have sometimes been offered as sufficient evidence of Islam's humane attitude to slaves. A close examination of the verses would show them as falling far short of a call for an end to the system. In some of the verses, the freeing of a slave is listed among acts of piety (as in verse 2:177, above), along with belief in God, performing regular prayer, and practising charity. But the freeing of a slave is certainly not in the same category of righteousness as belief in God or performing prayer. Any infringement of the two edicts of righteous acts just mentioned would call for severe penalty. There is no such penalty for not freeing a slave. Similarly, verse 9:60, which we read above, only lists the freeing of slave as one of the areas where money for *zakat* could be spent. Verse 90:13 also lists the freeing of slaves along with other acts of piety. Among the other verses treating the subject is 24:33, which we just read. The rest of the verses that mention the freeing of slaves are 4:92, 5:89, and 58:3. All of them mention it only as an individual act of atonement for some sinful acts, including breaking a vow, certain killings, and a special case of unintended divorce. There is no verse in the Koran which calls on the believers to free slaves in the same sense that it calls for fasting or waging *jihad.*

As in other areas, it is necessary to traverse the Koran for verses on specific wrongdoings and the corresponding retributions called for. A hugely elaborate and complex system of Islamic justice, the *shari'a,* has evolved over the centuries. Its authors all claim to have derived the laws of *shari'a* from the Koran and *ḥadith.* The Koran itself has a surprisingly limited number of deliberations on crime and punishments, popular ideas of its prolixity notwithstanding. We shall read a selection of verses under the broad headings of apostasy and blasphemy; waging war against Islam; gross sexual improprieties; homicide and the code of equality; intoxication; and slander. This just about exhausts the Koran's express concern with crime and punishment.

In recent years, apostasy has received an inordinate amount of attention from Islamic fundamentalists all over the world. Calls for killing the apostate – the *murtad,* in Arabic – have become frequent in the Islamic world, and so has actual killing. As we have seen, the Koran does not use the epithet *murtad,* much less call for killing him.[220]

---

[220] See Chapter 7.

Whatever authority the proponents of *shari'a* may invoke in support of the persecution of whomsoever it considers an apostate, it is not likely to be found in the Koran itself.

Throughout the ages, the makers of the *shari'a* have tried to find precedence elsewhere to punish apostates, howsoever defined. For example, they could cite the case of Ạbdallāh b. Sa'd, a companion of the Prophet who became a Muslim and then reverted to polytheism. After the conquest of Mecca, he sought refuge with 'Uthmān, one of the Prophet's closest companions. 'Uthmān brought him to the Prophet and pleaded for his forgiveness. At the time, the Prophet was surrounded by his companions. He remained silent for a long time and then said yes. After 'Uthmān had left with Ạbdāllah, the Prophet reportedly said to the companions around him, 'By God, I kept silent so that one of you might go up to him and cut off his head !'[221] To some makers of the *shari'a,* this might have been sufficient precedence to condemn the likes of Abdallāh b. Sa'd. In modern times, individuals have been condemned as apostates for far lesser crimes, such as indiscretions of being merely critical of Islam.

If the above story is true, however, it brings up an important question. If Muḥammad really intended to have Ạbdallah b. Sa'd killed for apostasy, he could have done so only under an edict of the Koran. The Koran forbids all killings except those in accordance with its laws, and there is no verse in the Koran that prescribes killing for apostasy. He would have violated Koranic laws if he had ordered Ạbdallah's killing. On the other hand, as we have seen, the Prophet was supposed to know each and every verse of the Holy Book; they all came to his heart, and he memorised each verse under Gabriel's guidance. If he was unaware of the verses we just read, where apostasy is mentioned and decried but for which no earthly punishment has been prescribed, then who wrote those verses? The question remains just as pertinent for the myriad *ḥadiths* which *shari'a* proponents are said to have found in support of killing apostates. An alternative hypothesis is of course that the above story and its *ḥadith* variants are apocryphal.

Insulting Islam, its personalities (especially Muḥammad), and its institutions, has long raised the hackles of ordinary Muslims; among Islamists, it has retained the status of a heinous crime. The Koran itself

[221] al-Tabarī, vol. 8, 178.

does not prescribe punishment for what could be called blasphemy. However, this has never prevented defenders of literal Islam from asking for the blasphemer's scalp.

Matters are very different when it comes to waging war on Islam. The Koran's pronouncements here are clear, and the punishment prescribed unmistakable:

> The penalty for those who wage war against God and His Messenger and goes on making mischief in the land is: they shall be slaughtered, or crucified, or their hand and foot shall be cut off from alternate sides, or they shall be banished from the land. This shall be a disgrace for them on earth and severe punishment awaits them in the Hereafter.
>
> (5:33)

The harshness of the punishments prescribed would outrage the modern mind. It is easy to lose sight of the harsh reality of an era of history when the retributions described above were all too common, not only in Arabia but also in much of the rest of the world.

The verse that follows, addressed to the Prophet, provides an escape route through timely repentance. The above punishments have been prescribed,

> Except for those who repent before you overpower them. And know that God is All-forgiving, Most-merciful.
>
> (5:34)

The Koran specifies punishments for certain categories of sins. These punishments are said to be divine requirements and are not deemed subject to human discretion. Called *hādd*,[222] this is applied to only four types of sins: waging war against Islam; theft; fornication; and sexual slander, or false accusations of sexual impropriety. To these four, Islamic jurists have added a fifth category: the penalty for intoxication, although

[222] Among the dictionary definitions of *hādd* (plural: *hudud*) are the following: 'a penalty', 'a limit', or 'bounds set by God or the law of God' (as in *hudud Allah*).

it is not clear how humans could add to laws which God himself has promulgated and which are considered to be beyond human discretion.[223] There are a number of *ḥadiths,* however, suggesting that the Prophet did on some occasions have drunks lashed with date-palm stalks and shoes. Makers of the *shari'a* used these precedents to call for the punishments they desired to mete out, and then they interpret it as a *hādd.*

The verse prescribing punishment for theft comes rather abruptly after calls to the believers to do their duty to God and warnings to the unbelievers of dire consequences on the Day of Judgement:

> As to the thief, male or female, cut off their hands: punishment by way of example, from God, for what they have earned. And God is Mighty, Wise.
>
> (5:38)

The verse is followed by one that appears to offer a respite:

> But whoever repents after his crime, and makes amends, God will turn to him. God is All-forgiving, All-merciful.
>
> (5:39)

We would normally conclude from the above verse that the sin will be forgiven if the thief is genuinely repentant. However, that is not the conclusion of the *shari'a* (or versions of it), which considers *hādd* sins unpardonable even after repentance, except in the case of waging war, as mentioned above.[224] This leaves the meaning of 5:39 hanging in the air. Islamic jurists would rather argue about how much of the thief's hand needed to be cut off; repentance could wait till after the punishment.

There is no ambivalence about the *hādd* punishment for adultery. The Koran unambiguously forbids the practice in the following verse:

> And do not come near adultery: it is an obscenity and an evil way.
>
> (17:32)

[223] I have used the exegeses in Qur'ān/Muhiuddin for the fifth *hādd.*

[224] Qur'ān/Muhiuddin.

As for punishment:

> The adulteress and the adulterer – flog each of them with a hundred stripes. And let no pity move you in matters God' religion, if you believe in God and the Last Day. And let a party from among the believers witness their punishment.
>
> (24:2)

It is perhaps no accident that while in most narratives of the Koran where men and women are mentioned together, man comes first; in this case, woman precedes man. More importantly, the critical consideration of evidence of guilt does not appear in the verse at all. It appears in an altogether different *sūra,* in verse 4:15; and we see it again in verse 24:4, which considers slander against chaste women, but not in the context of adultery or fornication in general.

The plight of such men and women does not end with the above description, though:

> Let no man guilty of adultery marry any except an adulteress or an unbelieving woman. An the adulteress cannot marry any except an adulterer or an unbelieving man. To the believers it is forbidden.
>
> (24:3)

Punishment can, however, be more severe for women than for men:

> And as for those of your women who commit acts of lewdness,[225] gather four witnesses from among you. If they testify (against them), confine them to the house until death claims them or God find a way for them.
>
> (4:15)

This contrasts with the following:

---

[225] This is 'indecency', in some translations, giving the Arabic word *fāhishat* a wider significance.

> If two men among you commit such acts, punish them both.[226] Then if they repent and amend their conduct, leave them alone ...
>
> (4:16)

Though the critical question of evidence as to the guilt of adultery is absent in the major verse relating to the guilt (verse 24:2, above), exegetes treat the requirement of evidence (of four persons) specified in verse 4:15 as applicable to adultery. Confusion arises, however, because first, verse 4:15 talks of 'lewdness', which probably means sexual impropriety other than adultery or fornication, with a hint of homosexuality.[227] Second, if indeed adultery is meant, why is it not mentioned specifically? Third, why is the matter of evidence not specified in verse 24:2 (on adultery), when it does appear in verse 4:15 (on lewdness)? These questions did not prevent exegetes from maintaining that it was adultery which was meant here, and that the punishment prescribed in 4:15 was later altered to the hundred stripes by verse 24:2.[228] We thus have punishment prescribed in one *sūra* (in verse 24:2), but nothing on the crucial matter of evidence. And the matter of evidence then appears in a quite different *sūra* (in verse 4:15), where the guilt itself requires reinterpretation; consequently, the guilt mentioned in the latter verse is made to fit the punishment prescribed in the former.

While sexual propriety is upheld, false accusations of sexual misconduct are severely dealt with and are punishable under *hādd*.[229] Thus we read:

> And those who accuse chaste women but cannot produce four witnesses, flog them with eighty stripes, and do not ever accept their evidence. They are the transgressors.
>
> (24:4)

[226] It is not at all clear what sort of punishment is meant here. Exegetes are silent about it.
[227] Qur'ān/Yusuf Ali supports this conjecture but points out the generally accepted view that lewdness includes adultery and fornication.
[228] According to Qur'ān/Yusuf Ali, most commentators accepting the above view consider that the punishment was altered to 100 stripes by the later verse 24: 2.
[229] The historical background of the stricture against slander is given in Chapter 14.

> Except those who repent and amend their conduct …
> (24:5)

Exegetes point out, however, that this does not protect the offender from the punishment. Rather, this ensures that the chastised person would return to his place in society and would be eligible for giving evidence, for example.[230]

Note, however, that verse 24:4 does not specify the kind of sexual misconduct, or breach of chastity, in question here. Coming as it does immediately after verses on adultery (24:2 and 24:3), the presumption is that it in fact refers to that particular kind of impropriety. It is nevertheless puzzling that the matter of evidence of four persons is not brought up in the main verse (24:2) on adultery, and is mentioned only when it comes to false allegation of unspecified misconduct.

The requirement in 24:4 that charges of sexual misconduct must be backed up by four witnesses should virtually ensure that the offence would rarely be proved to have occurred. In practice, there are numerous instances in Muslim-majority countries of *shari'a* convictions secured under dubious circumstantial evidence. In almost all cases, it is the women who end up on the wrong side of justice.[231]

On charges of conjugal unfaithfulness, there is remarkable even-handedness. In cases where there is no witness, verses 24:6 through 24:9 state that a husband can swear by God four times, and invoke His curse if he has told a lie, in support of his accusations of infidelity against his wife. The wife is given exactly the same rights.

There are also directives in the Koran that allow violent justice to be meted out, not necessarily by a judge, but by those who have been subjected to violence. Called *qisas*, or retaliation, this kind of violent tit for tat has its origin in Jewish traditions. The two oft-quoted verses, given below, propound the concept. The idea of 'equal' retaliation for injuries suffered or for death inflicted was perhaps not alien in societies attuned to rough justice. Modern societies will certainly reject such retaliation as a form of justice and consider it inhumane. Islamic exegetes note the element of mercy in the Koranic imprimatur. Mercy, however, is highly

[230] Qur'ān/Yusuf Ali.

[231] For a succinct treatment of the state of justice here, see Sadakat Kadri.

discretionary and cannot be relied upon to alleviate the consequences of *qisas*.

The following are major verses on the theme of retaliation:

> O you who believe! Retaliation is prescribed to you in case of murder: the free for the free, the slave for the slave, the woman for the woman. But if remission is made by the brother (of the slain), then let the payment be according to usage and done in a good manner. That is a lightening (of burden) and a mercy from your Lord.
>
> (2:178)

As for the Jewish tradition:

> Surely We revealed the Torah, wherein is guidance and light ...
>
> (5:44)

And:

> We prescribed therein for them: Life for life, eye for eye, nose for nose ear for ear, tooth for tooth, and wounds in retaliation. But if one remits the retaliation, that will be an expiation for him ...
>
> (5:45)

Khamr is the word used in the Koran for wine, whereas the dictionary definition extends to all intoxicating drinks. The Koran clearly discourages drinking and decries the intoxication that it might cause. But the injunction does not fall in the category of prohibition, such as the eating of pork, for example. In a number of verses, for example, in 2:173, the eating of pig meat is categorically forbidden. No such prohibition applies to wine. And even though drinking has been condemned in strong terms, no penalty has been prescribed for flouting the injunction. The following verses appear in different *sūras* of the Koran, and although some exegetes see a chronology and a progression from a relatively mild discouragement to an actual injunction, no such sequence necessarily exists.

> They ask you about wine and gambling. Say: "In them is great sin, and some use for men: but the sin is greater than the use …
>
> (2:219)

> O ye who believe! Approach not prayer when you are intoxicated till you know what you say …
>
> (4:43)

> O you who believe, wine, gambling, dedication of stones, and divination by arrows are abominations from Satan's handiwork: so shun it that you might prosper.
>
> (5:90)

These verses do not prescribe any punishment for drinking. This did not deter makers of the *shari'a* from writing laws of their own under which the offender can be administered up to eighty lashes.

Readers of the Koran who have pondered over its gamut of crime and punishment might be perplexed by the absence of earthly retribution for a practice denounced repeatedly in the Holy Book: usury.

The following verse plainly forbids usury:

> O ye who believe! Devour not usury, doubled or redoubled; fear God, that you may prosper. [232]
>
> (3:130)

Perhaps the strongest denunciation of the practice is this:

> Those who devour usury will not rise except as one whom Satan by his touch has driven to madness.
>
> (2:275)

Also:

[232] Compare: 'Take thou no usury of him, or increase: but fear thy God; that thy brother may live with thee.' (Lev. 25:36)

> God will blot out usury but will cause charity to grow.
> God does not love any ungrateful sinner.
>
> (2:276)

Note here the vehemence with which usury has been condemned. Yet no punishment is prescribed for the usurer. We must conclude that the practice was too widespread and, even so more than slavery, too important for the social fabric and economic structure to be tampered with. An outright prohibition of the practice of usury as a punishable offence would have led to social and economic collapse. The Koran clearly recognised the danger and, we might say, the limits of divine intervention.

Chapter 13
Women in the Koran

The Koran has a chapter on women, *Sūra* 2 (*Nisāa*) (literally meaning, 'Women'); it is one of the longest chapters in the Book. But there is at least as much written on women in other chapters of the Koran as there is in *Nisāa,* which also deals with a host of matters other than those concerning women. As with other issues in the Koran, it will be necessary to go well beyond the *sūra* for an adequate reading on women in the Koran.

A whole range of issues concerning women are dealt with in the Koran: from sexuality, to respect for mothers; from marriage and divorce, to purdah. Sexual and marital relationships dominate the narratives on women. This was perhaps inevitable at a time when these relationships were at the centre of family and society. In the absence of the diversity of ideas and activities, physical and intellectual, that was to emerge in human societies over time, preoccupation with marriage, sex, and procreation was natural.[233] So natural was it that sexuality indeed found a prominent place in the Koranic narratives on Heaven too, as we have seen. Elsewhere, the Koran reflects these all-too-human preoccupations in its narratives that take us to questions of women to marry and many other subjects, not excluding menstruation. As with other issues in the Koranic narrative, verses concerning women tend to appear without any particular order and are often interspersed among diverse subject matters. The following pages cover a large number of these narratives. There have been endless debates on the place of women in society, as

[233] It is perhaps no mere coincidence that the Arabic word *nikah* ('marriage') has an additional and explicit sexual connotation. Other ancient and mediaeval societies where sex played a prominent role are not far to seek.

seen in the Koran. It is useful to keep the major aspects of these debates in mind while reading the verses appearing below.

There is a group of verses in the Koran that clearly underlines women's position of inferiority to men – or which subordinates women to men, some by implication, others quite explicitly. Thus, we read:

> And they assign daughters to God! - Glory be to Him - and for themselves what they desire.
>
> (16:57)

'They', above, refers to the idolaters, and what they desire is sons. Similarly:

> Or has He only daughters and you have sons?
>
> (52:39)

Also similar is this:

> Or does He take daughters from what He creates, and favours you with sons?
>
> (43:16)

These verses leave no doubt about the inferiority of women in the eyes of God Himself. And He depicts women as those brought up among trinkets:

> (Is then one to be associated with God who) is brought up among trinkets and is unable to make a plain speech in a dispute?
>
> (43:18)

God even mocks the idolaters for their own aversion to daughters:

> And when news is given to any of them (of the birth of) one whose likeness to God All-merciful he sets up, his face darkens, and he chokes with rage.
>
> (43:17)

This complicated sentence merely suggests that the birth of a daughter is seen as a highly unwelcome event. The human perception of the event is of course well portrayed here.

The verses above, except the last, allude to an episode in Muḥammad's life when Satan is said to have tried to lure him to polytheism, and to praising some of the goddesses of its pantheon.[234] To the idolaters, the goddesses worshipped were no less than the daughters of God. To God in the Koran, saying such a thing is an extreme insult to Him. For one thing, He is not begotten, and neither does He beget. More important in the context, though, how can He have the inferior females for progeny while mere mortals have the superior males? The narratives in these verses are clearly meant to confirm that women are in a position of inferiority. There are verses in the Koran that elevate the position of women, as we will see. None of them changes the perception of women reflected in the verses above; and some, in fact, only strengthen women's status of inferiority.

Celibacy is not encouraged either in the Koran or in the *ḥadith,* and marriage has a prominent place in both. The Koran clearly specifies those it is not permissible to marry, the list largely conforming to age-old traditions in most human societies:

> Forbidden to you are: your mothers, daughters, sisters; father's sisters, mother's sisters; brother's daughters, sister's daughters; foster mothers (Who gave you suck); foster sisters; your wives' mothers; your step daughters under your guardianship, born of your wives, to whom you have gone in, – no blame if ye have not gone in; – wives of your sons proceeding from your loins; and two sisters in wedlock at one and the same time, except for what is past; ...
>
> (4:23)

These prohibitions extend to women who are already married (4:24). The exception, as we have seen, is captives of war; in such cases, the master can marry a captured woman, if he is so inclined, even if she has a husband.

---

[234] See Chapter 2.

Also:

> And do not marry unbelieving (idolater) women, till they believe; a slave woman who believes is better than an idolater woman, even though she allures you. Nor marry your girls to unbelievers until they believe. They call you to the Fire, while God calls you to the Garden ...
>
> (2:221)

Verse 2:221 forbids a Muslim from marrying an unbelieving woman. It similarly prohibits his daughters from wedding unbelievers. The Koran allows a Muslim to wed a Jewish or Christian woman. Here, inexplicably tagged to issues of permissible food, is the permission to marry women from among the People of the Book:[235]

> This day are all things good are permitted to you. The food of the People of the Book is lawful to you ... Permitted to you in marriage chaste women from among the believers and chaste women from among the People who have been given the Book before you, when you give them the dowers, taking them in marriage, not for immoral ends, nor taking them as secret lovers ...
>
> (5:5)

How many wives is a Muslim is allowed to take? The answer to that much-discussed subject is embedded in a single verse, which turns out to be far from simple:

> And if you fear that ye shall not be able to act justly to orphans, marry such women of your choice: two,

[235] Exegetes are quick to note caveats. Qur'ān/Yusuf Ali, for example, points out, 'A Muslim woman may not marry a non-Muslim man because her Muslim status would be affected: the wife ordinarily takes the nationality and status given by her husband's law. A non-Muslim woman marrying a Muslim husband would be expected eventually to accept Islam.' The asymmetry of treatment between a Muslim man marrying, say, a Christian woman, and a Muslim woman marrying a Christian could not have been lost on the exegete.

> three, or four. But if you fear that you will not deal with them equitably, then only one, or what your right hand possesses. So it is likelier that you will not be partial.
>
> (4:3)

The verse is one of the most difficult to understand in the Koran, and there have been widely different interpretations. We must wonder why the question of the maximum number of wives a man can have at any one time could not be answered in a straightforward manner, and without bringing in the orphans, which can of course be an important issue by itself. The background of the verse is said to be the Battle of Uḥud, which left many orphans as well as widows among the Muslims. There was a community obligation to take care of them and protect their interest, while selfish interest in their property was not lacking. One interpretation of the narrative is: marry the orphans if you are quite sure that you will in that way protect their interest and their property.[236] A second interpretation is entirely different: since there is no paucity of women, marry women other than those among the orphans.[237] Yet another interpretation is that the women to marry are the widows of war, the reasoning being that marrying them would be the best way of protecting the interest of the fatherless children.[238]

On the question of how many women a man can marry, the directive in the verse is a maximum of four wives at any time, and only if the husband can treat them with impartiality.

The clarity dims, however, in the following verse:

> You are never able to be fair between wives, even if this is what you wish. But turn not away from one woman altogether so that you leave her hanging …
>
> (4:129)

One can fairly ask why, when men are 'never able to be fair between wives,'(4:129) is there a provision for four wives (4:3) at all. There is no suggestion among the exegetes that the verse nulls verse 4:3.

---

[236] The sentence is from Qur'ān/Yusuf Ali.

[237] Qur'ān/Muhiuddin. Qur'ān/Islamic Foundation concurs.

[238] Qur'ān/Muḥammad Ali.

There is little doubt that the Koran enhanced the position of women in the family in some important ways: principally, by defining the obligations of husbands towards their wives and enunciating women's rights in terms of inheritance and divorce. To start with, there is the emphasis on the dower, referring to the gift of a husband to his bride. There are many verses where the requirement of the dower is mentioned, among others aspects of a marriage. The following verse is entirely and clearly on the dower:

> And give women their dower as a free gift; but if they give you a part of it, out of pleasure, then take it and enjoy it.
>
> (4:4)

The system of dowry prevailing in many societies – Muslim and Hindu, for instance – obliges parents of the bride to offer a sumptuous dowry to the groom or his family. Too often the system takes the form of cruel extortion. The Koran obliges the groom to make a gift to the bride instead. The following verses again underline the importance of the dower, as well as offering remarkable counsel to the husband to be good to the wife:

> O you who believe! It is forbidden to inherit women by force. Nor should you treat them with harshness in order to take away what you gave them, unless they are guilty of open indecency. Live with them honourably. If you are averse to them, perhaps that is because you hate something, and God has put in it much good.
>
> (4:19)

> But if ye decide to take one wife in place of another, and if you had given one (the present) a load of treasure, take not a bit of it back …
>
> (4:20)

Similarly, the Koran defines women's rights to property, inheritance, and divorce, at a time when these were alien concepts not only in Arab societies but also elsewhere in the world. It was many centuries before these rights were recognised in Western societies.

The following verse starts with what the husband's share of the wife's property will be at her death and then goes on to prescribe the wife's share when the husband dies:

> Of what your wives leave, your share is half if they have no children. But if they have children, your share is a fourth of what they leave, after payment of legacies and debts. And for them is a fourth of what you leave if you have no children. If you have children, their share is an eighth of what you leave ...
>
> (4:12)

About the other inheritors:

> For men a share of what parents and near relatives leave; and for women a share of what parents and near relatives leave; be the property little or large – an apportioned share.
>
> (4:7)

> God instructs you as regards your children: to the male, a portion equal to that of two females; but if only daughters, and they are more than two, two-thirds of the inheritance, and if only one daughter, half ... [239]
>
> (4:11)

The woman's share in the property in question was equal to half of the male's, which has been much highlighted in modern times. Verse 4:11 clearly short-changes the female. The claim often made that the greater family responsibility of males justifies their getting double the female share of the inheritance was weak even then; it is unacceptable now. Still, it is hard not to acknowledge that few societies of the time recognised the right of women to any inheritance, and thus the provision of the verse should be seen as an advance for women.

[239] I have avoided going into the details of the verse, since they are not entirely relevant in the present context.

Verse 2:282, in *Sūra Baqara,* is by far the longest in the Koran. The entire verse is devoted to contractual matters of doing business. It begins with: 'O you who believe, when you deal with each other on contracting debt for a fixed period of time, document it' ... It then recommends that there should be witnesses to the deal:

> ... And get two men to witness the deal: and if you cannot find two men, find a man and two women whom you choose for witness ...
>
> (2:282)

The words 'If you cannot find two men, find a man and two women', wedged in a single verse on contractual obligations, is the source of the much-discussed traditional Islamic thinking that in matters of legal evidence two women equal one man; in other words, a female witness is half as reliable as a male witness. And this appears to conform to God's words in verses like 43:18, above.

The Koran places considerable importance on another subject that affects the family and especially the life of women: divorce. This is spelt out in considerable detail throughout a large number of verses. The following narratives must suffice here.

Divorce is apparently recommended as the last resort:

> And if a wife fears misbehavior or desertion on the part of her husband there is no blame on them if they arrange an amicable settlement between themselves; and a reconciliation is better ...
>
> (4:128)

A pronouncement of divorce is effective only after three monthly periods of the wife divorced. Considerable importance is given to reconciliation and equity:

> O Prophet! When you divorce women, divorce them by their prescribed periods, and count the period. And fear God, your Lord. Do not turn them out of their houses.. .[240]
>
> (65:1)

> Then when they have reached their term, either retain them with kindness, or part with them honourably, and call in to witness two just men from among you, and establish the evidence before God …
>
> (65:2)

> Lodge them (in *'iddat*) where you live,[241] according to your means, and do not press them in order to straighten them. And if they are with child, expend on them until they lay down their burden. If they suckle your child, give them their wages, and do each other good; and if you disagree, let another suckle it.
>
> (65:6)

The following verse, from a different *sūra* altogether, is essentially a variation of the above themes:

> And divorced women shall wait for three monthly periods. And it is not lawful for them to hide what God has created in their wombs, if they believe in God and the Last Day. And their husbands have a better right to take them back in that period, if they seek reconciliation. And the women have rights similar to their obligations in a just manner; and men have a station a degree above the women's. And God is All-mighty, All-wise.
>
> (2:228)

---

[240] According to exegetes, although the verse is addressed to Muḥammad, it is applicable to all Muslims. The 'prescribed period' (*'iddat,* in Arabic) is three menstrual cycles (see verse 2:228, below), the length of time the divorcee is required to wait for the divorce to be effective; otherwise, she is taken back by the husband, nullifying the divorce.

[241] Some have translated this as 'let them live in the same style as you' (for example, Qur'ān/ Yusuf Ali).

Remarkably for a society of that time, there is a recommendation of provision for the divorced woman, though opinions differ regarding the length of the time period over which it should be made:

> For divorced women, maintenance (should be provided) on a reasonable (scale). This is a duty on the righteous.[242]
>
> (2:241)

And yet the Koran also has the following verse, a jarring one to the modern mind:

> So if a husband divorces his wife (irrevocably), he cannot after that remarry her until she marries another husband. If he divorces her there is no fault if they return to each other (in marriage) …
>
> (2:230)

While the provision for marriage to another husband might have been made in order that divorce is taken seriously by men and not trifled with, it is easy to see that the consequences can be heart-rending for the former husband as well as his former wife.

The following verse, on the other hand, provides considerable latitude for husbands and wives to avoid the irrevocable outcome. It allows divorces twice before the divorce becomes irrevocable:

> Divorce can be (pronounced) only twice: after that, the parties should remain together with good relationship or separate with kindness. ..
>
> (2:229)

The issue of women's rights in matters of inheritance and divorce sometimes seems to take second place in some modern Muslim-majority countries, and even elsewhere, to another set of rules of conduct for

---

[242] Translation in Qur'ān/Yusuf Ali. There is a good deal of difference of opinion over the period covered, as well as on whether the verse has been overridden by some other verses. Some exegetes maintain that the period covered is only the period of the '*iddat* (Qur'ān/Islamic Foundation).

Muslim women said to be found in the Koran: purdah. Defined as both 'seclusion' and 'veil', purdah has long had its hold on Muslim societies, and of late, it has seen a resurgence in many countries, especially in its latter form. The term, practically the same in some of the major languages of the Indian subcontinent, with minor variations in intonation, is derived from the word 'screen.' This screen refers to various materials, especially cloth, and it is also used on the subcontinent for various modes of seclusion of women from the male gaze. Seclusion may take the form of confining women to home; out of doors, it requires them to wear clothes that hide them from public view. The requisite apparel involves different degrees of elaborateness: from the skimpy *ḥijab* (headscarf), to the elaborate *burqa* (the loose shroud hat covers a woman's entire body, often including the eyes); from the mask-like *niqab,* to the all-engulfing *abaya,* to the *chador.* All such garments and accoutrements receive the nomenclature of the veil.

Exponents of the purdah, in the sense of both seclusion and the veil, claim the *shari'a* on their side. Wearing the veil is often considered an act of piety; by the same token, being without a veil is viewed as something impious and even punishable. The Koran, on the other hand, has little to say about the veil, per se. The Book broadly emphasises modesty, and its pronouncements on seclusion of women were directed at a specific group of women, as we will see.

Ḥijab, the term often used interchangeably with the veil, is used in a number of places in the Koran, but only once in the sense relevant here. The following verse, from the territory of predestination, illustrates the use of the term *ḥijab* in the general sense of a screen:

> When you recite the Koran, We put between you and those who do not believe in the Hereafter, an invisible screen.[243]
>
> (17:45)

In the sense of the screening of women, the antecedents of the following verse are given in the next chapter of the present volume (Chapter 14). It suffices to note here that the companions of the Prophet

[243] 'An invisible screen' is *ḥijabūn mastūra,* in Arabic.

are urged to remain behind a screen separating them from the wives of the Prophet, if they needed to speak to them. This is where the word *ḥijab*, translated as a 'screen', is used in the Koran:

> … And when you ask (of the Prophet's wives) anything, ask from
>
> before a screen: that is purer for you hearts and purer for theirs …
>
> (33:53)

The word *ḥijab* has not been used in the Koran in its modern sense of a headscarf. Purdah, in the sense of women covering themselves, and the manner in which this should be done, comes up in a later verse in the same *sūra*, which makes no reference to covering the head (the *ḥijab*, in the modern sense):

> O Prophet! Tell your wives and daughters, and the believing women to cast their outer garment over their person (when abroad); so it is likelier that they will be known, and not molested …
>
> (33:59)

In the above translation, the Arabic word translated as 'outer garments' is *jalabeeb*. Other translators and exegetes have used 'shawls', 'scarves', or an equivalent. There is no necessary implication that the wearer of these pieces of apparel would also cover their heads with them. The long verse below should be considered as a major pronouncement of the Koran on the subject. Note, first, there is no requirement for covering the head; rather, the importance is on covering the bosom. Perhaps most important is the emphasis placed on modesty:

> And say to the believing women that they lower their gaze and guard their modesty, and not display their ornaments except what (normally) appears thereof; and let them cast their veil on their bosoms. And let them not reveal their adornment except to their husbands, their fathers …
>
> (24:31)

The next verse relaxes the above requirements of purdah for elderly women, who are defined as those past the age of marriage. In some modern Muslim societies, this should come as a surprise. Many women in these societies seem to have suddenly discovered the purdah and taken to the veil, often of the most concealing variety, and the enthusiasm is most clearly visible among women who are well past their prime and who did not care much about the attire in their younger days.

Once again, the emphasis is on modesty:

> And as for elderly women who are past the age of marriage, there is no blame if they lay aside their outer garments without displaying their beauty; but it is better for them to be modest …
>
> (24:60)

There is, on the other hand, no absolute standard of modesty in dress or degree of exposure of an individual to fellow humans; there has never been any in human history. In many societies, codes of dress that were deemed correct at some point in time were once considered outrageous. For example, knee-length skirts on women were perfectly modest in Western societies in the twentieth century. In the Middle Ages, they would have been unimaginably immodest. Whatever interpretation we put on verses of the Koran regarding dress codes for women must also be seen in the context of the time. Women's attire that would have been considered morally provocative at that time may be perfectly normal and devoid of any unethical overtones today.

In a remarkable verse, modesty is required of men too. The verse, in fact, comes before the one (above) where women are required to lower their gaze:

> Say to the believing men that they should lower their gaze and guard their modesty: that is purer for them …
>
> (24:30)

The narratives in 24:30–31 are preceded by verses (24:27 and 24:28) that emphasise privacy in general, and these are worth noting. The recommendations were perhaps all the more remarkable in the social milieu of the time. It is not clear whether the two verses below are connected with a similar verse concerning entry into the Prophet's house, which we shall return to in the next chapter (Chapter 14). For now, here is verse 24:27:

> O ye who believe! Do not enter houses other than yours, until you Have asked permission and saluted the inmates ...
>
> (24:27)

In both 24:30 and 24:31, modesty has markedly sexual connotations, a nexus that characterised societies of the time. In fact, the Arabic words for 'guard their modesty'[244] in both verses have been translated elsewhere as 'guard their private parts'. Thus, in Arberry, we have:[245]

> Say to the believers, that they cast down their eyes and guard their private parts ... And say to the believing women, that they cast down their eyes and guard their private parts ...
>
> (24:30–31)

One translator puts the idea in even more explicit sexual terms:[246]

> Say to the believing men that they lower their gaze and restrain their sexual passions ...
>
> (24:30)

> And say to the believing women that they lower their gaze and restrain their sexual passions ...
>
> (24:31)

Despite some of the improvements in the position of women in society and family, women's status remained as one of total subordination to

---

244 I have followed Qur'ān/Yusuf Ali in using 'guard their modesty'.

245 Qur'ān/Arberry.

246 Qur'ān/Muḥammad Ali. Qur'ān/Muhiuddin uses the term 'and guarding their sexual organs'.

men, and this was designated to be so in the Koran. Seen in modern terms, many of the narratives of the Koran diminish women. This was true of many other societies around the world as well. To a modern reader of the Koran, the portrait of women in its narratives would nevertheless be striking.

Except for the references to relationships with women captives and slaves, verses like 33:55 and 24:31 are almost prudish to modern readers. The following verse stands in remarkable contrast:

> They ask you about women's courses. Say: it is a hurt; so keep away from women during their the monthly course, and do not approach until they are clean. Then when they have cleansed themselves, you can go in to them in any manner commanded by God. Surely God loves those who turn to Him, and He loves those are clean.
>
> (2:222)

The importance given to menstruation is also reflected in the *ḥadith* literature. The *Sahih Al-Bukhāri* has over forty *ḥadiths* concerning the subject. In the Islamic tradition, menstruating women are not permitted to perform obligatory rituals of canonical prayer and fasting, even though the Koran is silent on the subject. The restriction certainly diminishes women for merely being subject to a natural function of the female body, especially when the performance of these obligatory rituals does not involve contact with other human beings.[247]

Along with diminution comes passivity. Perhaps the most striking imagery of women's passivity in the Koran is the verse below. Coming immediately after the above verse, the narrative has clear sexual connotations. The Arabic word *harth* in the first sentence is rightly translated here as 'tilth', with such minor variations in other translations as 'tillage' or 'land under the plough'. Thus, we read:

> Your wives are a tilth to you; so approach your tilth as you will, and do some good act for yourselve beforehand;

[247] The Jewish tradition too considers contact with menstruating women as something of an abomination, only more so. See, for example, Lev. 15:19, 15:20, 18:19, and 20:18.

> and fear God; and know that you will meet Him; and give good tidings to the believers.
>
> (2:223)

All exegetes plainly interpret 'approach your tilth' as sexual intercourse, though some with a liberal bent have been defensive about it, choosing to be philosophical instead.[248] Others, following up on the instructions in the preceding verse (2:222), have interpreted the phrase as 'a man may go in to his wife when he likes and as he likes.'[249] A *ḥadith* in the *Sahih Al-Bukhāri* makes this abundantly clear.[250]

'Tilth' also provides apt imagery. The conjugal relationship here is not based on mutuality and reciprocity of feelings and passion. The female is an entirely passive partner. The time and mode of approach are decided by the male alone. This again reflects the life of women in society at that time.

The clarity of the verse thus far is marred for us, as modern readers, once we try to understand the rest of it, beginning with 'and do some good' ... The proviso is a perplexing one, and it has been translated in diverse ways, none of them throwing light on the intended meaning. One translator has put this as 'but do some good act for your soul beforehand.'[251] Others have translated this as 'and forward for your souls,' 'send (good) beforehand for yourself,' or 'make provision for your own future.'[252] Available exegeses do not help. The puzzle only increases, with some translators using 'your soul', and others using 'yourself', for the Arabic *nafsikum*. And one wonders why the husband is asked to fear God in this context and what good news he is intended to give the believers.

In the following verse, women's subordination to men is emphasised in no uncertain terms:

---

[248] Qur'ān/Yusuf Ali.

[249] Qur'ān/Muḥammad Ali.

[250] al-Bukhāri, vol. 6, 51–52.

[251] Qur'ān/Yusuf Ali.

[252] Koran/Arberry, Qur'ān/Muḥammad Ali, and Qur'ān/Muhiuddin, respectively. Qur'ān/Islamic Foundation's translation is virtually the same as that of the latter. Koran/Pickthall translates this as 'and send (good deeds) before you for your souls'.

> Men have authority over women, because God has bestowed more bounty on the one than on the other, and because they support them from their means. So the righteous women are those who are obedient, and who guard in the absence (of the husband's) what God guards. As to those women on whose part you fear disobedience, admonish them, refuse to share their beds, and beat them. But if they then obey you, do not seek a way against them: Surely God is Most Exalted, Great.
>
> (4:34)

In sum, the total authority of the husband over the wife is emphasised in the verse, as is the corresponding obedience of the wife. Beating of the intransigent wife is clearly recommended.

The very next verse recommends reconciliation:

> If you fear a breach between the two, appoint arbiters, one from his family one from hers. If they both desire agreement, God will cause their reconciliation. God is All-knowing, All-aware.
>
> (4:35)

Of course, this does not annul the directives in 4:34 above, and neither does this abrogate a verse like 2:223.

Chapter 14
Wives of the Prophet

Prophet Muḥammad's wives have been the subject of a great deal of attention from both his followers and his detractors, going back to the earliest days of Islam. Explicit reference to Muḥammad's wives is limited to a small number of verses in the Koran. There are, however, verses behind which lie important events relating to Muḥammad's wives and which can be understood only against the background of such events. There are also important directives of the Koran, such as those on slander and the purdah, that emerged from events involving the Prophet's wives. And no less important is the light which many of these verses shed on Muḥammad the man.

There are few other verses of the Koran which bring into sharper focus the non-pietistic and human dimensions of the Koran as in the narratives concerning Muḥammad's wives, even though this might seem odd; after all, the narratives concern the household of no less a person than a Prophet of God. In several verses, tensions in the relationship between the Prophet and his wives were important enough for God to address the wives directly. These addresses are so strongly worded that traditional exegeses seem less than adequate to explain the circumstances that provoked them. The directness of these addresses also calls into question the nature of the revelations. A particular marriage of the Prophet was so out of the ordinary at the time that it comes up repeatedly, in apparently unexpected places, throughout the length of a whole *sūra*. The number of wives he could take comes up explicitly in the narrative. Together, the number of these verses is quite significant. These are contained mainly in three *sūras* of the Koran: 24 (*Nūr*), 33(*Aḥzāb*), and 66 (*Taḥrim*).

The Koran does not contain any references to any of Muḥammad's wives other than Zaynab bt. Jaḥsh. It does not even mention the Prophet's wife, Khadījah, whom he married when he was about twenty-five years old and she was forty. But this was Muḥammad's most important marriage. Khadījah bore him six children. Muḥammad did not marry another woman while Khadījah was alive, but he did take a good number of wives after her death. According to Ibn Ishaq, he married thirteen women, consummating the marriage with eleven of them.[253] The youngest of his wives was 'A'ishah, daughter of his close companion, Abū Bakr. The Prophet married 'A'ishah when she was perhaps seven years old; he was past fifty at the time. There was a mix of the elderly and the young –and the beautiful – among the women in the Prophet's household. None of his wives besides Khadījah bore him any children. This is truly puzzling, given the large number of his wives who were of childbearing age. Apart from the children that his first wife bore him, a captive woman, Māriyah the Copt (a gift to the Prophet from the ruler of Egypt), bore him a son who died in infancy.

Aḥzāb is an extraordinary *sūra*. It has at least two major themes that could not be more different from each other. Called 'The Confederates', the *sūra* is largely concerned with the threat that the Muslims saw coming from an alliance of their enemies, the pagans and the Jews. By far the largest number of its verses have, as their background, the Battle of the Trench.[254] Yet a recurring theme of the *sūra* is Muḥammad's marriage to Zaynab bt. Jaḥsh, wife of his adopted son, Zaid. The Koran is notable for its juxtaposition of themes that would not normally be juxtaposed. In *Sūra Aḥzāb,* the themes of war and the marriage are intertwined throughout, in unexpected ways. A few other themes of considerable importance also crop up in the narrative, among them the seclusion of Muḥammad's wives, and God talking directly to them. There are verses in which a theme is difficult to pinpoint, and there are those for which the connecting link with others is impossible to establish.

The *sūra* starts with this extraordinary verse:

[253] Ibn Ishaq, 792. According to this source, the prophet left nine wives at the time of his death.

[254] See Chapter 5.

> O Prophet! Fear God, and do not listen to the unbelievers and the hypocrites; verily God is All-knowing, All-wise.
>
> (33:1)

God's call continues:

> And follow what comes to you by inspiration from your Lord; surely God knows well what you do.
>
> (33:2)

> And put your trust in God; and enough is God as a guardian.
>
> (33:3)

Verses 33:1 and 33:2 are extraordinary in that the Prophet himself is told to fear God and to follow only what comes to him by way of inspiration from God. One should have thought this was the essence of prophethood and that Muḥammad would need no reminder of it so late in his prophetic life. The oddity of seeing the Prophet asked to fear God may have prompted some translators to use an alternative, such as 'keep thy duty' to God.[255] That these verses would lead to the theme of the Prophet's marriage to Zaynab might seem no less intriguing at first blush; on a close reading of the *sūra*, though, the device appears to be merely a build-up to support for the marriage.

There are several versions of the story of the marriage. Zaid was a freed slave whom Muḥammad had adopted as his son. Zaynab was Zaid's cousin, and the two knew each other since childhood. At one point, Muḥammad himself was instrumental in arranging Zaynab's marriage to Zaid.

The following is from the well-regarded work on Muḥammad by Martin Lings:

> It happened one day that he [Prophet] wanted to speak to Zayd about something and went to his house. Zaynab

[255] As in Qur'ān/Muḥammad Ali and Koran/Pickthall. The Arabic word *attaqi* used in the verse usually means both 'fear' and 'do God's duty'.

> opened the door, and as she stood in the doorway telling him that Zayd was out but inviting him none the less to enter, a look passed between the two cousins which made each one conscious of a deep and lasting bond of love between them. In a moment the Prophet knew that Zaynab loved him and that he loved her and that she knew that he loved her. But what could this mean? Surprised at the strength of his feeling, he refused the invitation, and as he turned to go she heard him say: 'Glory be to God the Infinite! Glory be to him who disposeth men's heart!' When Zayd returned she told him of the Prophet's visit and the glorification she had heard him utter.[256]

It is said that Zaid immediately went to Muḥammad and offered to divorce Zaynab in order for the Prophet to marry her. Muḥammad initially refused the offer. One reason given by tradition was that he disapproved the practice of divorce. The other reason must have been that it was taboo to marry the wife of a son, even an adopted son. But soon enough, Zaynab was divorced, and the Prophet married her. In the repeated return to the theme in the *sūra,* we see an unmistakable *ex post facto* justification for the marriage.

The first explicit reference to the affair in *Sūra Aḥzāb* comes in the fourth verse:

> God has not made for a man two hearts in his breast: nor has He made your wives whom you divorce by *zihar*[257] your mothers; nor has He made your adopted sons your

[256] Martin Lings, 213.

[257] Exegetes point out that the system of *zihr* was one of the traditional ways (though perhaps not very widespread) for a husband to divorce his wife by comparing her to his mother. The word *zihr* is derives from an Arabic word for the back of the human body. The husband wishing to divorce his wife would declare that his wife's back was like his mother's. Such comparison with someone the husband could not possibly marry was said to render the wife ineligible for conjugal status; thus, it was in fact a divorce. The verse decries the custom and asserts that *zihr* does not make a mother out of a wife. The idea is put forward as a parallel to the really important point of the verse: that to adopt someone as a son does not actually make him a real son.

> sons. Those are only your words of the mouth; and God tells you the truth and shows you the way.
>
> (33:4)

In this verse, God is telling Muḥammad, in effect, that both the traditional concept of an adopted son and the position of an adopted son in relation to the man who adopted him are wrong. Some traditional commentators have even called the practice evil, though a modern reader will find it difficult to see how. The point of the verse is that if the adopted son is no son at all, there cannot be any calumny in marrying his wife (after divorce).

In the following two verses, the concept of adoption is again denounced, the closeness of the relationship between the believers and Muḥammad the Prophet is emphasised (even though this appears far-fetched, given the context), and the ties of blood are decreed as the true relationships among human beings:

> Call them by the names of their fathers: that is more just in the sight of God: but if you do not know their fathers' names, then they are your brothers in faith and your friends.
>
> (33:5)

> The Prophet is closer to the believers than their own selves; and his wives are their mothers. And blood relatives have closer relationships among themselves in the decree of God than have believers and the Muhajirun, except that you do good to your friends. That is written in the Book.
>
> (33:6)

The 'them' in 'Call them' of course refers to adopted sons. Perhaps the closeness of the relationship between the believers and the Prophet has been brought in to prevent the issue of the marriage becoming a wedge between the Prophet and his followers. The well-accepted tenet among the believers that gave the Prophet's wives the status of mothers to them is brought in here, presumably as further support to protect Zaynab against unholy speculations. Note that in order to emphasise blood relations, the cherished closeness of the relationship between the Muhājirūn and the Anṣar (called here 'believers'), so vital politically, is downplayed, even though, in practical terms, blood relationship almost always wins out. It is also unclear why 'believers' refers strictly to the Anṣar, when those who migrated from Mecca were *a fortiori* believers too. At least one translator added 'other' to 'believers', perhaps to make the necessary distinction.[258]

Most of the verses that follow – 33:9 through 33:27 – concern the Battle of the Trench. The narrative then turns to the wives of the Prophet, the reason for the juxtaposition of such disparate themes remaining unclear.

Verse 33:28 and the five subsequent verses are also extraordinary in a number of ways: the wives are presented as importuning Muḥammad for greater material comforts of life, an all-too-human foible. They are told that they can have a life of luxury if that is what they want, but the rewards of the hereafter are far greater; they are then directly castigated by God; and, finally, they are told that they not like any other women:

> O prophet! Say to your wives: if you prefer the life and adornments of this world, come I shall make provisions for you and set you free in a kind parting.
>
> (33:28)

> But if you seek God and His Messenger and the home in the Hereafter, verily God has prepared for the virtuous among you a great reward.
>
> (33:29)

The next verse is truly extraordinary, in that in it God addresses the wives of Muḥammad directly. Elsewhere, the Koran emphasises that God does not address any human beings directly, except his prophets.[259] No companion of the Prophet is so addressed. In fact, God's message to Muḥammad comes only through the intermediation of Gabriel. In this verse – as well as in verses such as 33:31, 33:32, 33:33, 66:4 or 66:5 – God is talking to Muḥammad's wives. Gabriel's role is also absent, because he

[258] Qur'ān/Muḥammad Ali.

[259] 'It is not fitting for a man that God Should speak to him except by inspiration, or from behind a veil, or by the sending of a Messenger…' (*Sūrā* 42:51)

too does not address an ordinary mortal. It is therefore difficult to see who the speaker is, unless of course it is Muḥammad himself, which makes immense sense; but this would also make the narratives non-divine.

The severity of punishment promised for mischief-making wives also stands out. Some of the verses sound like admonitions of a paterfamilias addressed to wayward wives of the sons of a big family. The circumstances that produced such threat of punishment for grave misconduct remain shrouded in mystery.

Thus, we read:

> O wives of the Prophet! If anyone among you is guilty of manifestly gross conduct, the punishment to her shall be doubled. And that is easy for God.
>
> (33:30)

In the next verse, the reward for goodness is also doubled:

> And whosoever of you that is obedient to God and His Messenger and does good, her reward will be doubled, and We shall give her a generous sustenance.
>
> (33:31)

A marked softening of tone follows. But there is also an extraordinary piece of advice to these women: they are asked to be not soft in their speech so that it does not produce in some hearts unholy desires. One translation puts it this way: 'If ye are god-fearing, be not abject in your speech, so that he in whose heart is sickness may be lustful … '.[260] It is not clear what led to such dire advice to women with no less a stature than that of the wives of the Prophet himself:

> O wives of the Prophet! You are not like any other women; if you fear God be not soft in your speech, so that he in whose heart is a disease should be moved with desire; but speak words of goodness.
>
> (33:32)

[260] Koran/Arberry.

The verse that follows puts the wives of the Prophet in their place. Once again, it is quite out of the ordinary to read a verse that sounds like reprimand as well as preaching to the members of the household of the Prophet himself, whose very mission was to preach. And once again, the emphasis is on setting the Prophet's wives right; in this case, by cleansing them of abomination. We will never know what kind of abomination existed in the household that warranted receipt of such sweeping censure. Available exegeses are singularly inadequate to explain the circumstances which led to such censure here and in the earlier verses. The admonition continues:

> And stay in your houses, and do not display your beauty as in the former time of ignorance; perform the prayer, give in charity, and obey God and His Apostle. O people of the household, God only wishes to cleanse you of all abomination and make you pure.
>
> (33:33)

The narrative then returns to Muḥammad's marriage to Zaynab. The next verse on the issue suggests that there must have been considerable talk among the populace about the matter and that many eyebrows must have been raised. The finality of divine approval of the marriage is brought to bear in order to quash public misgivings:

> It is not for a believing man or a believing woman, when a matter has been settled by God and His Messenger, to have a choice in their decision. And whoever disobeys God and His Messenger has strayed into manifest error.
>
> (33:36)

The next verse continues the theme. This time, it is addressed to the Prophet, but clearly meant to be heeded by everybody else:

> And remember you said to him, one whom God favoured and you favoured, 'Keep your wife and fear God;' and you concealed in your heart what God would reveal: you feared people. And God has a better right to be feared:

> and when Zaid had dissolved his marriage with her We gave her in marriage to you so that there would be no difficulty for the believers about the wives of their adopted sons, when they dissolve their marriage. And God's command must fulfilled.
>
> (33:37)

The person referred to as 'one whom God favoured ... ' is Zaid. The verse is significant for a number of reasons. First, it acknowledges Muḥammad's hidden love for Zaynab ('and you concealed in your heart what God would reveal'). Second, Muḥammad's marriage to Zaynab is sanctioned so that there will be no difficulty for others in marrying their adopted sons' wives. This raises the rather obvious question of why such a marriage is given so much importance, especially since it could not have been a widely desired act or a common practice. Third, the verse expressly mentions Zaid. No other person in Muḥammad's entourage is mentioned by name in the Koran, not even any of the four closest companions of Muḥammad or any of his wives.

In the next two verses, the case for Muḥammad marrying Zaynab is further fortified by presenting it as a prophetic duty. The marriage is also presented as having precedence in the historical past:

> There can be no difficulty to the Prophet in performing what God has ordained for him; that was the commandment of God for those who had gone before. And God's commandment is a decree absolute.
>
> (33:38)

In the next verse, the system of adoption is again condemned. It is noteworthy that the verse is widely used in *milad,*[261]invocations widely practised in many communities in the Indian subcontinent, with little regard to the context of the verse.

---

[261] A *milad* (*maulud*, in Arabic) is strictly a communal celebration of the birth of the Prophet of Islam, involving recitations from the Koran, hymns, and prayer. In some Islamic societies, *milad* can also be held at any of a host of other social, personal, or family events which also include invocation of the Prophet's name, even when the occasion is not the birthday of the Prophet.

> Muhammad is not the father of any of your men, but a messenger of God and the seal of the Prophets; and God has knowledge of everything.
>
> (33:40)

The theme of the marriage recedes in the next verses, but it comes back later in the narrative.

The following verse gives Muḥammad special dispensations regarding the taking of wives and the categories of women 'made lawful' to him. This verse and a few subsequent verses appear to sum up what was a relatively short episode in Muḥammad's life in Medina, which was crowded with a fairly large number of marriages:

> O Prophet! We have made lawful to you: your wives to whom you have given their dowers, and those whom your right hand possesses out of what God has given you as prisoners of war; (and has made lawful for you for marriage) daughters of your paternal uncles and aunts, and daughters of your maternal uncles and aunts who have migrated with you; and a believing woman if she gives herself up to the Prophet if he wished to marry her. This is for you only and not for the believers at large – We know what We have ordained for the believers about their wives and those their right hands possess – so that there should be no difficulty for you. And surely God is All-forgiving, All-merciful.
>
> (33:50)

This is a puzzling verse. It is quite unclear in which respect this is a special dispensation for the Prophet, alluded to in 'This is for you only,' and exegeses on it look unconvincing. Marrying daughters of uncles, etc. could not have been barred to ordinary Muslims, nor could marrying a woman who gave herself to the prospective husband be forbidden. Commentators have, rather unconvincingly, taken this verse to mean, among other things, that Muḥammad was entitled to marry more than four wives, something not permitted to his disciples.[262] Muḥammad,

---

[262] Qur-ān/Muhiuddin. I believe most readers will still find the meaning rather opaque.

however, already had many more than four wives at the time. Perhaps this very fact needed a special dispensation for the Prophet so that 'there should be no difficulty' for him.

Also note that in the Arabic text the parenthetic 'and has been made lawful for you for marriage' is entirely absent, which makes it look as if a sexual relationship with the women mentioned after 'God has given you as prisoners of war' was permitted outside the bond of marriage, just as it was permitted with those whom the Prophet's 'right hand possessed'. God could not have meant this. A majority of the translations I have used ignore the difficulty and assume the existence of the parenthetic expression. Only two translators felt that it was necessary.[263] The parenthetic proviso also makes it clear once again that marriage was not a precondition for cohabitation in cases of those whom the believers' right hands possessed.

Having more than one wife necessarily entails rather obvious problems to which Muḥammad's household was not immune. It is as a result of such difficulties that the following verse comes, giving the Prophet a wide choice from among his wives as to whom to spend his nights with:

> You may put off any one of them you please and you may receive anyone you desire; and there is no blame on you if you desire whom you had kept away. This it is more likely to cool their eyes, they will not grieve, and they will all be pleased with what you give them.
>
> (33:51)

In the Koran, many of the wishes of the Prophet are quickly granted by providence, and many read like self-fulfilling prophecy. Concerning the Prophet's discretion given in the verse above, one *ḥadith* reports that his wife, 'A'ishah, quipped:[264]

> ... when the verse: (O Muhammad) You can postpone (the turn of) whom you will of them (your wives)'(v.

[263] Qur'ān/Muhiuddin and Qur'ān/Islamic Academy.

[264] al-Bukhāri, vol. 7, 45.

> 33:51) was revealed, 'Aishah said, 'O Allah's Messenger! I do not see, but, that your Lord hurries in pleasing you.'

The matter of Zaynab would simply not be left behind, however, and it comes back once again, and abruptly, in the next verse. The Prophet is told that this marriage had to be his last, though women prisoners of war were still excepted from the proscription. The line was finally drawn:

> It is not lawful for thee to marry any more women after this, or to take wives in lieu of other wives, even though their beauty attracts you, except those whom your right hands possess. And God is on all things ever watchful.
> (33:52)

The following verse of the same *sūra* has an important lesson in etiquette, but its background is equally important to note, coming as it did in the wake of Muḥammad wedding Zaynab. *Sahih Al-Bukhāri* itself provides the background. There are several *ḥadiths* on the event. The following is chosen for its brevity:[265]

> Narrated by Anas bin Malik: I, of all the people know best this verse of *Al-Ḥijab*, When Allah's Messenger [...] married Zainab bint Jahsh [...], she was with him in the house and he prepared a meal and invited the people (to it). They sat down (after finishing their meal) and started chatting. So, the Prophet [...] went out and then returned several times while they were still sitting and talking. So Allah revealed the verse: 'O you who believe! Enter not the Prophet's house,' ...

The full verse follows below. 'A'ishah's remark about the Lord hurrying to fulfil Muḥammad's wish should cross our minds. Notice how well it reflects the mind of any ordinary human: irate, keen to join his bride, and yet diffident:

[265] Ibid. vol. 6, 270.

> O you who believe! Do not enter the Prophet's houses, until permission is given to you to come to a meal, but not so early that you have to wait for the food to be prepared; but when you are invited, enter, and when you have eaten, depart, and not engage in talk. Surely this hurts the Prophet, but he is ashamed before you; and God is not ashamed to tell the truth ...
>
> (33:53)

The theme of seclusion of the Prophet's wives, along with the much-discussed word *ḥijab,* comes in here, as we have noted before. For the sake of completeness, the rest of the verse is reproduced here:

> ... And when you ask (of the Prophet's wives) anything, ask from before a screen: that is purer for you hearts and purer for theirs ...
>
> (33:53)

'His ladies', of course refers to the Prophet's wives. A reader may wish to digress here and ask why the prohibition of visual contact between the ladies and the male companions of the Prophet should be conducive to purity of heart. A logical implication of the statement can be that mere visual contact could be polluting. That possibility would be extraordinary, particularly since the wives of the Prophet were considered to be Mothers of the Believers. On the other hand, such a situation was not inconceivable; it needed an edict, in the rest of the verse itself, to explicitly forbid a believer from ever marrying a wife of the Prophet:

> And it is not right for you to hurt the Messenger of God or to marry his wives after him ever. That will be in the sight of God a monstrosity.
>
> (33:53)

The Zaynab theme has not yet disappeared, however. It comes back in one of the last verses of the *sūra,* which recalls a story of Moses deemed relevant to the theme of Muḥammad marrying Zaynab, specifically in terms of how it was initially received in society. The verse follows:

> O ye who believe! Do not be like those who hurt Moses. But God cleared him of what they said. And he was in the sight of God worthy of respect.
>
> (33:69)

The other *sūra* in which Muḥammad's wives figure prominently is *Sūra* 66 (*Taḥrim*).The opening verse is crucial, but impossible to understand without its historical background:

> O Prophet! Why do you hold as forbidden what God has made lawful to you? You seek your wives' pleasure. And God is All-forgiving, All-merciful.
>
> (66:1)

Apparently, Muḥammad had vowed to refrain from something, or shun certain persons. What really happened? We will perhaps never know for sure, thanks to an array of confusing and unconvincing exegeses.

The favoured explanation among the traditional exegetes is the story of the honey. The Prophet, who was fond of honey, is said to have stayed with one of his wives, Zainab,[266] one afternoon, drinking a special variety of honey she had received as a present. Perhaps he overstayed, taking up the time allotted to some of the other wives. This reportedly kindled the envy of 'A'ishah, who plotted with Ḥafsah to hold their noses the next time their husband came into their presence, pretending that he smelled of unsavoury honey. The plot was activated, and a shocked Muḥammad was said to have vowed not to eat honey any more. He also asked them not to divulge the matter, least of all to Zainab. In the traditional exegeses, it is honey that God refers to in the above verse as the thing which He made lawful and which the Prophet vowed to shun. Also in the tradition, it is the plot of the two wives of the Prophet over honey that is alluded to in verse 66:3, below.

There is a second story about the vow, and one that is perhaps more credible. Pickthall, while also recounting the story of the honey, puts it thus:[267]

---

[266] This is not necessarily the Zaynab of *Sūra Aḥzab*.

[267] Koran/Pickthall.

> Ḥafsah found the Prophet in her room with Marya – the Coptic girl, presented to him by the ruler of Egypt, who became the mother of his only male child, Ibrahim –on a day which custom had assigned to Ayeshah. Moved by Hafsah's distress the Prophet vowed that he would have no more to do with Marya, and asked her not to tell Ayesha. But Hafsah's distress had been largely feigned. No sooner had the Prophet gone than she told Ayeshah with glee how easily she had got rid of Marya.

There is also a third version of the speculation on the vow. This concerns Muḥammad's temporary separation from his wives. Exegetes relate that he once vowed to have nothing to do with them, but there are great doubts about the reasons behind the decision. There are suggestions that he was extremely annoyed with 'A'ishah and Ḥafsah for divulging matters he had wished they would keep to themselves. There is also a hint that the wives had become disrespectful towards their husband and were perhaps even talking back to him.[268] In any event, the separation was brief, and Muḥammad returned to his normal conjugal state. Whichever version of the story we accept, it again reveals the all-too-human side of the Prophet of Islam and his household.

But there is still the matter of a vow. Muḥammad had vowed to forego something or shun some person. The Koran places great importance on the sanctity of oaths. But, as expected, expiation for breaking a vow was also readily available.[269] The following verse clears the Prophet to dissolve his vow:

> God has already granted you the absolution of your vows. And God is your protector. And He is All-knowing, Wise.
> (66:2)

This is closely followed by a narrative describing how the Prophet confided in one of his wives, and she then divulged the confidence:

---

[268] Ibid.

[269] This has been taken to refer to verse 5:89, which calls for expiation through freeing a slave or fasting.

> When the Prophet confided a matter to one of his wives, and she divulged it, and God revealed it to him (Muhammad), he confirmed one part of it and omitted the other. Then when he told her about it, she said, "Who told you of this?" He said, "He told me who is All-knowing, All-aware."
>
> (66:3)

Quite extraordinary are the following verses, addressed directly to the wives of the Prophet. They probably had something to do with a tension in the Prophet's household related to certain events hinted at in verse 66:1, above. A great show of divine support for Muḥammad is stacked against the women in his household – women who are supposed to be a notch above the rest in piety as well as in their devotion to their husband. They are even threatened with divorce. Note that the verse invokes the power of Gabriel to protect the Prophet, while the adversary is a group of mere female human beings:

> If you two turn to Him in repentance, then your hearts are inclined. And if you support each other against him, then know that God is is his friend, so is Gabriel and the righteous believers. And the angels, besides, are his helpers.
>
> (66:4)

The two wives addressed here are apparently 'A'ishah and Ḥafsah. Both are mentioned in the background of the verse given above. The tone hardens in the next verse, apparently addressed to all of the wives:

> It may be, if he divorced you all, God will give him in lieu wives better than you – those who are submissive, believing, obedient, penitent, devout, and who fasts, previously married or virgin.
>
> (66:5)

It is quite possible that verses 33:30, 33:31, 33:32, and 33:33, which we read above, are not unrelated to these two verses. Perhaps they should be read together, even though they appear in different *sūras*. Even then, traditional accounts of the circumstances underlying them would seem inadequate. There may be more to it than the mere matter of eating smelly honey, or even the Māriyah affair.

Here, underneath these narratives, we have a picture of a large household, which included perhaps just under a dozen women, presided over by a single male in the person of Muḥammad. None of the women bore Muḥammad any children. The number of women of childbearing age was large, including most certainly 'A'ishah, Ḥafsah, Juwayriah, and Safiyyah, and most probably also Umm Habibah, Umm Salama, and at least one of the two Zaynabs, perhaps both. And not all of them could have been incapable of bearing children. A household of so many women deprived of the glory of motherhood cannot be expected to be entirely normal, or happy. The human dimension of the circumstance is easy to comprehend. The threats of punishment for unseemly conduct (verse 33:30), cautioning against too-complaisant speech that could rouse desire (verse: 33:32), the possibility of Muḥammad divorcing all of his wives in retribution (verse 66:5), and the sweeping directive to the wives to stay within the confines of home and spend their lives in pious devotion to God (33:33), all can be seen to have at least partly arisen from the childless state of Muḥammad's household. None of the wives were mothers, and most of them might have been unhappy about it. The episode of Māriyah and her pregnancy might have only exacerbated the discontent. It is amazing that the Koran, so eloquent on the wives in the verses mentioned above, is so silent on the childless state of the same women.

And then there is the story of slander involving the favourite wife of the Prophet. It was important enough to call for Koranic directives.

It was Muḥammad's practice to take along a wife when he set out on an expedition. A lot was cast to choose the companion. So it was 'A'ishah who accompanied the Prophet at the battle against Banu al-Mustaliq, which was several days' march from Medina. With the battle over, the Muslim contingent was on its way back, bearing a large booty. The distance from Medina called for stops in the march, and during one of these breaks in the journey, a necklace 'A'ishah had been wearing slipped from her neck without her being aware of it. The necklace was precious to her. It was given to her by her mother as a wedding gift. She searched frantically for it once she realised it was missing. The Muslim contingent had still not broken camp, and 'A'ishah went some distance to look for the necklace, travelling to a place she had earlier been to satisfy the call of nature. She found the necklace, but it took some time. When she returned, Muḥammad and his men had gone. Also gone was the camel she had been riding, along with its drivers.

The account of what happened next was 'A'ishah's.[270] Despondent, but hoping that she would soon be missed and sent for, she wrapped herself in her robe and lay down. As she recounted later, while the Muslim troops were leaving, her camel was saddled and her litter was mounted. The men who lifted the litter onto the camel thought that the Prophet's wife was in it. In those days, 'A'ishah explained, women used to eat only enough to stay alive; they would not gorge themselves on meat, so as to avoid becoming heavy. 'A'ishah was also very young. Usually, as her camel was saddled, she sat in her litter, out of view from the saddlers, who came and lifted the litter and fastened it onto the camel's back. Because of her small body weight, she recounted, the men did not realise that the litter was empty, and so they led the camel to join the rest of the Muslim party.

To continue her account of the story, now she lay and waited. Presently, a man named Ṣafwan b. al-Mu'attal came along.[271] He was with the Muslim forces and had fallen behind because he needed to take care of some business of his own while the others were encamped. Ṣafwan recognised the sleeping woman, as he had seen her before. 'A'ishah woke up just as he approached her. She must have explained her situation to the man, but according to her account, she did not talk to him, which has awkward implications for communications between them. Ṣafwan made his camel kneel so that she could mount it, and soon they were on their way to Medina, he leading the camel on foot. The Muslim forces had still not reached Medina and had camped not far from it. 'A'ishah had not been missed till the morning, and it was midday when Safwan was seen leading his camel into the camp, with the Prophet's wife riding on it. 'A'ishah's absence during the night turned into a rich source of

[270] The story of the necklace is the same in Ibn Ishaq, al-Tabarī, and al-Bukhāri, with only minor variations.

[271] According to al-Bukhāri, she had fallen asleep, and it was dawn when Safwan stumbled on her. This is probably a more realistic account than other versions which have her waiting in the dark, as Safwan could recognise her only in the light of dawn.

gossip, though only a small number of people were directly involved in it. According to 'A'ishah, she knew nothing about the gossip.

'A'ishah's account continues. The next few weeks were very difficult for her, her parents, and the Prophet. It was difficult for 'A'ishah because, though she still did not know about the slander, she could not bear to see the sullen face of her husband and the pained demeanour of her parents. It was weeks before she learned what was happening, and then she was heartbroken. Muḥammad, for his part, had a very difficult time fending off the spreading rumour. He also did what any other proud human being who had been grievously hurt by a scandal would do: he refused to speak to 'A'ishah about it, and, instead, stubbornly shunned her. At the same time, he was desperately wishing for divine guidance. After weeks of shunning her, he finally asked 'A'ishah to tell him the truth, and of course she swore that she had not done anything wrong. As we would expect, soon enough, the inspiration the Prophet had been waiting for came: God confirmed her innocence.

Several people were connected with the slander. The main instigator was said to be the leader of the Hypocrites, 'Abdullah b. Ubayy, but there were others who openly spread the rumour. Among them was the poet Hassan bin Thābit; a poor but close relation of Abū Bakr called Mistah; and Hamnah, a sister of Zaynab, Muḥammad's wife. All were flogged, as prescribed in the Koran. The prescription must have been come with great swiftness after the divine confirmation of 'A'ishah's innocence.

The incident is said to have inspired a number of verses in the Koran. Most of these are in *Sūra* 24 (*Nūr*). The flogging is prescribed in verse 24:4, which we read earlier.[272] 'Abdullah bin Ubay, the chief instigator of the slander, went scot-free, if only in this world. Apparently, he was too powerful among the Prophet' antagonists to be punished, even under divine sanction.

The narrative continues. This is addressed to the entire community:

> When you heard about it, why did not the believing men
> and women, of their own account, think good thought,
> and say: This is a manifest lie?
>
> (24:12)

[272] See Chapter 12.

This is specifically for the slanderers:

> When you received it on your tongues, and spoke with your mouths, things of which you had no knowledge, and you considered it a trifling thing, and to God it was most serious.
>
> (24:15)

One of the footnotes to this incident, as supplied by history, is 'A'ishah's comment about Ṣafwan b. al-Mu'attal: 'Questions were asked about Ibnu'l-Mu'attal,' she said, 'and they found that he was impotent; he never touched women.'[273] This must have been a later reflection on her part. Even so, the gratuitous nature of the comment is hard to overlook.

Ibn Ishaq reports that, following the slander, Safwan was said to have confronted Hassan b. Thābit and smote him with his sword. The wounded Hassan and his assailant were brought before Muḥammad for adjudication in the dispute. In a puzzling gesture, the Prophet gave Hassan a piece of property, consisting of a castle in Medina, as compensation for his pain. He also gave him the Egyptian Coptic captive girl Sirin, sister of Māriyah, the Prophet's concubine. For his part, Hassan wrote a poem praising 'A'ishah for her integrity.[274]

While the slander was circulating, Muḥammad had been questioning people as to their opinion of 'A'ishah. Most spoke highly of her. Not 'Ali b. Abū Talib, the Prophet's cousin and son-in-law. Ibn Ishaq records this of 'Ali's reported response: 'Women are plentiful,' he told Muḥammad, 'And you can easily change one for another.'[275] *Sahih al-Bukhāri* broadly corroborates the story.[276]

'A'ishah never forgave 'Ali for this. The resentment it fostered in her came to the fore in her open hostility to 'Ali during the latter's rule as the last of the four 'rightly guided' caliphs after Muḥammad's death. This, however, takes us beyond the realm of the Koran and into history.

---

273 Ibn Ishaq, 499.

274 Ibid. 499.

275 Ibid. 496.

276 Al-Bukhāri vol. 5, 284.

Afterword

This book was intended primarily for those who might not feel that reading the Koran except as a means of strengthening their faith was necessarily impious. With them I wished to share my thoughts on the Holy Book of Islam. They can of course come up with ideas of their own, especially as they read with me the eight hundred plus verses from the pages of the Book I examined in this work, and the conclusion I draw from them. There will, inevitably, be those who disagree with me on many of the issues I take up. From them I expect not denunciation but reasoned rebuttals. These I welcome, even the most critical.

There are yet others who have irrevocably opted for reason and abandoned faith, or think they have, and see the Koran as a man-made text of dubious origin. Some of them will perhaps be unhappy with the low mileage of my sojourn beyond faith. I still expect them to read the book and, having read, go beyond. They may yet find some of the ideas here useful for their own exploration.

Bibliography

Translations of the Koran Used

Ali, A. Yusuf, *The Holy Qur'ān: Text, Translation and Commentary* (Brentwood, MD: Amana Corp., 1983).

Ali, Maulana Muḥammad, *The Holy Qur'ān with English Translation and Commentary* (Ohio: Ahmadiyya Anjuman Isha'at Islam Lahore Inc., 2002).

Arberry, A. J., *The Koran Interpreted* (New York: Simon & Schuster, 1996).

Islamic Foundation Bangladesh, *Al-Qur'ānul Karim* (in Bengali) (Dhaka, Bangladesh: Islamic Foundation, 2005). Translations from the Bengali used in the text are by the present author.

Khan, Maulana Muhiuddin, *Qur'ānul Karim, Bengali Translation and Brief Commentary* (originally *Tāfsir M'āriful Qur'ān* by Hazrat Maulana Mufti Muḥammad Shafi) (Medina, Saudi Arabia: King Fahd Qur'ān Printing Project, H 1413, 1992/93). Translations from the Bengali used in the text are by the present author.

Pickthall, Marmaduke, *The Meaning of the Glorious Koran: An Explanatory Translation* (New York and Toronto: Everyman's Library/Alfred A. Knopf, 1992).

Collection of *Ḥadiths* Used

Azmi, Maulana Nur Muhammad, *Meshqat Sharif: with Bengali Translation and Commentary*, Vol.1. (Dhaka, Bangladesh: Imdadia Library, 1978). Translation from the Bengali is by the present author.

al-Bukhāri, *Sahih Al-Bukhāri* (Arabic-English), tr. Dr Muḥammad Muhsin Khan (Riyadh, Saudi Arabia: Darussalam, 1997).

Maja, Ibn-e, *Sunan Ibn-e-Majah,* tr. Muḥammad Tufail Ansari, 3rd edn (New Delhi, India: Kitab Bhavan, 2005).

Other Works Cited

Fakhry, Majid, *Averroes (Ibn Rushd): His Life, Works and Influence* (Oxford: Oneworld, 2001).

Ishaq, Ibn, *The Life of Muḥammad,* tr. A. Guillaume (Karachi, Pakistan: Oxford University Press, 1995).

Kadri, Sadakat, *Heaven on Earth: A Journey Through Shari'a Law from the Deserts of Ancient Arabia to the Streets of the Modern Muslim World* (New York: Farrar, Straus and Giroux, 2012).

Lings, Martin, *Muḥammad: His Life Based on the Earliest Sources* (London: George Allen and & Unwin, 1983).

Pedersen, Johannes, *The Arabic Book,* tr. Geoffrey French (Princeton: Princeton University Press, 1984).

Rahman, Fazlur, *Islam*, 2nd edition, (Chicago: University of Chicago Press, 1979).

—— *Islam and Modernity* (Chicago: University of Chicago Press, 1982).

—— *Major Themes of the Qur'an* (Chicago: University of Chicago Press, 1980).

al-Suyūṭī, Imam Jalal-al-Dīn 'Abd al-Rahmān, *Al-Itqān fī-'Ulūm al Qur'ān, The Perfect Guide to the Sciences of the Qur'ān* (Reading, UK: Garnet Publishing, 2011).

al-Tabarī, *The History of al-Tabarī,* 38 volumes (Albany, NY: The State University of New York Press, 1989).

Thanvi, Maulana Ashraf Ali, *Ashraful Jawab, Part 2* (Bengali translation from the original Urdu by Muḥammad Abū Ashraf) (Dhaka, Bangladesh: Islamic Foundation Bangladesh, 1997). Tanslations from the Bengali used in the text are by the present author.

al-Wāhidī, Alī ibn Ahmad, *Asbāb al-Nazūl* ('Occasion of Revelation') (Amman, Jordan: The Royal Aal al-Bayt Institute for Islamic Thought, 2008).

Watt, W. Montgomery, *Muḥammad in Medina* (London: Oxford University Press, 1956).

Index

'Ikrimah b. Abi Jahl 113
Inspiration vii, 3, 5, 6, 7, 8, 9, 12, 13, 18, 19, 23, 57, 69, 77, 120, 131, 132, 140, 173, 249, 252, 265. *See also* Revelation
Islam, Islamic vii, viii, ix, xi, xii, xiii, xiv, xv, xvi, 2, 3, 5, 6, 7, 8, 14, 16, 17, 18, 19, 20, 22, 24, 25, 26, 27, 28, 31, 33, 42, 46, 49, 52, 53, 57, 62, 63, 64, 65, 67, 69, 72, 73, 77, 79, 86, 88, 89, 91, 98, 100, 101, 102, 105, 108, 109, 112, 113, 114, 115, 117, 119, 121, 123, 129, 130, 132, 134, 135, 141, 142, 145, 147, 148, 150, 151, 153, 156, 158, 160, 162, 163, 166, 167, 169, 170, 173, 181, 186, 191, 192, 196, 197, 198, 204, 217, 218, 219, 220, 221, 224, 232, 233, 236, 238, 243, 244, 247, 255, 257, 261, 267, 269, 270
Islamism xv

J

Jesus 58, 136
Jews 2, 29, 76, 77, 83, 84, 86, 89, 96, 97, 124, 125, 137, 142, 143, 248
Jihad 24, 52, 54, 58, 61, 71, 73, 123, 129, 130, 131, 134, 136, 137, 140, 142, 143, 218
jinn x, 46, 54, 57, 195, 200
Jizya 105, 142, 143
Justice 54, 58, 60, 213, 218, 224
Juwayriyah 93
Juxtaposition (of disparate themes of the Koran) ix, xiii, 10, 51, 52, 57, 59, 61, 62, 152, 195, 248, 252

K

Ka'ba 28, 107, 109, 113, 156
Khaybar 23, 24, 66, 76, 86, 87, 95, 96, 97, 101, 107, 113, 143
Koran *passim*

L

Lapsarian 187
Lauḥ Maḥfūz 152

M

Man
- biological development of 176, 178
- creation of 62, 165, 166, 168, 169, 170, 174, 177
- humiliation of 45, 209
- insignificance of 181

Martyrs 30, 61, 70, 79, 129, 196
Mashaf 18
Mecca, Meccan 2, 5, 8, 11, 13, 18, 20, 22, 23, 24, 27, 49, 66, 67, 68, 70, 76, 78, 79, 86, 98, 99, 101, 103, 105, 106, 109, 110, 111, 112, 113, 116, 120, 121, 122, 123, 124, 129, 131, 132, 137, 140, 141, 145, 148, 153, 155, 156, 157, 173, 196, 199, 219, 252
Medina, Medinan x, 3, 8, 18, 19, 20, 21, 22, 23, 24, 46, 64, 68, 69, 70, 74, 76, 77, 79, 83, 86, 87, 89, 90, 91, 93, 94, 95, 96, 100, 101, 102, 103, 104, 105, 109, 110, 112, 113, 122, 125, 131, 134, 140, 143, 256, 263, 264, 266, 269, 270
Messenger of God xvi, 6, 28, 69, 76, 88, 91, 98, 108, 256, 259
Michael 29, 78
milad 255
Moses 2, 56, 58, 137, 259, 260
Mother of Cities 2, 116
Muḥammad (the Prophet) *passim*
Muharram 67
Mulaykah 113
Mumtaḥana 111

CPSIA information can be obtained at www.ICGtesting.com
Printed in the USA
LVOW08*2319290916

506806LV00001B/7/P

9 781491 782781